RENEWALS 458-4574

WITHDRAWN
UTSA LIBRARIES

South African textual cultures

Manchester University Press

South African textual cultures

White, black, read all over

Andrew van der Vlies

Manchester University Press
Manchester and New York

distributed exclusively in the USA by Palgrave

Copyright © Andrew van der Vlies 2007

The right of Andrew van der Vlies to be identified as the author of this work has been asserted by him in accordance with the Copyright, Designs and Patents Act 1988.

Published by Manchester University Press
Oxford Road, Manchester M13 9NR, UK
and Room 400, 175 Fifth Avenue, New York, NY 10010, USA
www.manchesteruniversitypress.co.uk

Distributed exclusively in the USA by
Palgrave, 175 Fifth Avenue, New York,
NY 10010, USA

Distributed exclusively in Canada by
UBC Press, University of British Columbia, 2029 West Mall,
Vancouver, BC, Canada V6T 1Z2

British Library Cataloguing-in-Publication Data
A catalogue record for this book is available from the British Library

Library of Congress Cataloging-in-Publication Data applied for

ISBN 978 0 7190 7614 5 *hardback*

First published 2007

16 15 14 13 12 11 10 09 08 07   10 9 8 7 6 5 4 3 2 1

Library
University of Texas
at San Antonio

Typeset
by Action Publishing Technology Ltd, Gloucester
Printed in Great Britain
by The Cromwell Press Ltd, Trowbridge

For my parents
and for Patrick

Contents

Illustrations

Figures

Plates

Acknowledgements

Lincoln College's warm collegiality was a great source of intellectual and material support during the gestation of part of this work as a doctoral thesis; thanks to the Rector and the Fellows, especially Stephen Gill and Peter McCullough. I am grateful to my colleagues in the School of English Literature, Language and Linguistics at the University of Sheffield for helping to make my first years of full-time employment pleasantly productive – in particular: Neil Roberts, Dominic Shellard and Richard Steadman-Jones. Financial and institutional support from the following is gratefully acknowledged: the Commonwealth Scholarship Secretariat, Association of Commonwealth Universities; the South African National Research Foundation; the Board of Graduate Studies, Faculty of English Language and Literature, Oxford University; Lincoln College, Oxford; the University of Sheffield Learned Societies Fund; and the University of Sheffield Arts and Humanities Devolved Fund, which graciously provided support for colour plates.

I owe a great deal to friends and family for intellectual and emotional support over the years. For homes from home, long phone calls, food, music and encouragement, inadequate words though they are, 'Thank You' Pascale Aebischer, Camel, Natasha Distiller, Michele Gemelos, Joanna Gill, Somdatta Ghosh, Lucy Graham, John Holmes, Karen Junod, Thomas Knollys, Hamish Mathison, Peter McCullough, Lisia Moala, Paige Newmark, Grant Olwage, Lisa Retief, Adrianne Rubin, Deborah Seddon, Timothy van Niekerk, Undine Weber, Sandra Willows and Angela Wright. Special thanks to my Scottish family: Marti, Alasdair, Kirsty, Catriona and Annabel MacLeod, and Casper. Gail L. Flanery and James A. Flanery have become family: I am very lucky. Thanks, too, to my early teachers and mentors at Rhodes University in Grahamstown, particularly Wendy Jacobson and John Gouws, whom I now count as friends. Valued support and advice has been received from, among others, David Attwell, Rita Barnard, Laura Chrisman and Stephanie Newell, who did me the honour of reading part or all of the manuscript; Elleke Boehmer and Hermione Lee, who examined my thesis; and Paul Eggert and Isabel Hofmeyr. Particular credit is due to Peter D. McDonald, an exemplary thesis supervisor who continues to be a wise, enthusiastic and generous mentor. Manchester University Press's anonymous readers made very useful observations, and I am grateful to the press's staff for their professionalism and good humour in seeing this book into print.

Participants and audiences at conferences and seminars – in St Andrews ('Re-Ma(r)king the Text'), Grahamstown ('Colonial and Postcolonial Cultures of the Book'), York ('Texts, Ma(r)kers, Markets'), Cardiff (CEIR), Cape Town (SAHS), Stirling ('Textual Cultures'), Edinburgh ('Material Cultures'), London ('Colonial and Postcolonial Lives of the Book'), and Kolkata/Calcutta ('New Word Orders') – have provided timely comments during the course of this project.

A great many people have facilitated research for this book: Mrs Blanche La Guma honoured me with her willingness to recall details of her and her late husband's extraordinary lives; Mr Justice Albie Sachs gave generously of his time to reminisce about his friendship with Alex La Guma; James Currey and Keith Sambrook spoke with me about their pioneering work at Heinemann Educational Books; Ulli Beier corresponded with me from Australia; Mark Spencer Ellis discussed his school edition of *Cry, the Beloved Country*; Hugh Macmillan lent me Lewis Nkosi's copy of *A Walk in the Night*; Mike Kirkwood recalled publishing Coetzee at Ravan Press; Zakes Mda spoke to me by telephone from Ohio; Isobel Dixon met with me in London. Numerous others – in Britain, South Africa, the United States and Germany – responded to telephone, e-mail and written enquiries, and I am grateful to them all.

I acknowledge the following with thanks for research assistance, access to, and permission to quote, archival material: the National English Literary Museum, Grahamstown (especially Paulette Coetzee, Malcolm Hacksley, Anne Torlesse, Crystal Warren and the late Elaine Pearson); the National Library of South Africa, Cape Town; the Alan Paton Centre, University of KwaZulu-Natal, Pietermaritzburg (Jewel Koopman), and Mrs Anne Paton; the Robben Island Mayibuye Archive, University of the Western Cape, Belville, Cape Town; the Harry Ransom Humanities Research Center, University of Texas at Austin; the Poetry Collection of the University Libraries, State University of New York at Buffalo; Special Collections, the University of Reading Library (especially Michael Bott); the Stefan Heym Archive, University Library, Cambridge (David Lowe); the British Library (Rare Books and Music Reading Room, the Sound Archives, and Newspaper House at Colindale); Macmillan Publishers Ltd and the Macmillan Archive at the British Library; Random House (especially Jo Watt); Harcourt Education; J. Murray Wilson and Michael Friher, the Owl Club, Cape Town; Theresa Campbell; Mrs Alison Mégroz Lord; Duff Hart-Davis and the William Plomer Trust. Thank you to Peter McDonald and Faith Binckes for making available material from the Publications Control Board Archive, Cape Town, and to Nicole Leistikow for permission to cite her unpublished thesis on Bessie Head. I wish to record my particular appreciation to library staff in Oxford – at the

Bodleian Library of Commonwealth and African Studies at Rhodes House, the Vere Harmsworth Library and the Bodleian Old Library (especially David Busby, Sally Matthews, Helen Rogers and Vera Ryhajlo in the Upper Reserve) – for their efficiency and helpfulness.

I acknowledge permission to reprint, in revised form, material previously published, as follows:

- 'The Editorial Empire: The Fiction of "Greater Britain" and the Early Readers of Olive Schreiner's *The Story of an African Farm*'. *TEXT: An Inter-Disciplinary Annual of Textual Studies* 15 (2002), 237–60.
- '"Your Passage Leaves its Track of ... Change": Textual Variation in Roy Campbell's "Tristan da Cunha", 1926–1945'. *English Studies in Africa* 46.1 (2003), 47–61.
- 'Introduction: The Institutions of South African Literature'. *English Studies in Africa* 47.1 (2004), 1–15.
- '"Hurled By What Aim to What Tremendous Range!' Roy Campbell and the Politics of Anthologies, 1927–1945'. *English Studies in Africa* 48.1 (2005), 63–85.
- '"Local" Writing, "Global" Reading and the Demands of the "Canon": The Case of Alan Paton's *Cry, the Beloved Country*'. *South African Historical Journal* 55 (2006), 20–32.

Like a number of the authors discussed in this book, I have crossed borders and negotiated complicated relationships with national identity and 'home'. I thank my parents, Nan and Eddie van der Vlies, for their love and example, and dedicate this book to them, with profound gratitude. It and a great deal else would have been impossible without the support of Patrick Denman Flanery, whose sharp eye and patient presence has been, and remains, a source of calm and constant wonder.

Andrew van der Vlies
Sheffield and Oxford

Abbreviations

APC	Alan Paton Centre, University of KwaZulu-Natal, Pietermaritzburg
AWS	Heinemann African Writers Series
BL	British Library, London
Cry (C)	*Cry, the Beloved Country*. London: Jonathan Cape, 1948.
Cry (S)	*Cry, the Beloved Country*. New York: Scribner's, 1948.
Heart (H)	*From the Heart of the Country*. New York: Harper & Row, 1977.
Heart (R)	*In the Heart of the Country*. Johannesburg: Ravan, 1978.
Heart (S)	*In the Heart of the Country*. London: Secker & Warburg, 1977.
HEB	Heinemann Educational Books Archive, University of Reading
HRHRC	Harry Ransom Humanities Research Center, University of Texas at Austin
MABL	Macmillan Archive, British Library, London
NELM	National English Literary Museum, Grahamstown
NLSA	National Library of South Africa, Cape Town
PCB	Publications Control Board Archive, National Archives of South Africa, Cape Town
Mayibuye	Robben Island Mayibuye Archive, University of the Western Cape, Belville
RUL	Special Collections, University of Reading Library, Reading
RUL Cape	Jonathan Cape Archive, University of Reading Library, Reading
RUL Hogarth	Hogarth Press Archive, University of Reading Library, Reading
SAF	*The Story of an African Farm*
SUNY	Poetry Collection, University Libraries, State University of New York at Buffalo

1

Introduction: South African textual cultures

Books and the nation

The cover of *South Africa*, a weekly British journal established in 1889 as a guide to Southern African financial and mining news but promoted as being 'for all interested in South African affairs', carried a banner representing the processes of exchange which supported the British Empire and on which it modelled itself in the late Victorian age.[1] Ships transport various commodities from the South African colonies, represented by Cape Town's idyllically conceived Table Bay, to Britain, represented by the City of London's spires and the dome of St Paul's Cathedral. No reciprocal commerce is figured: the outer edges of Empire provide rugged natural iconography and raw materials, and their recompense is membership of a virtual body politic over which the sun of Empire never sets (we see it here, shining on the royal coat of arms) and, most importantly, a model: history, religion, civilisation.[2]

The cover of the *South African Book Buyer*, a 'co-operative catalogue' and journal of 'literary articles' published in 1906 for British publishers wishing to advertise to South African readers and booksellers, offers a version of similar imperial–colonial traffic: a ribbon, tied around a single

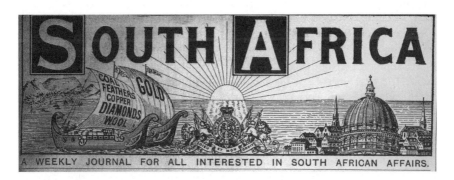

1.1 *South Africa*, 14 January 1911

1.2 *The South African Book Buyer*, September 1906

book, binds colony and metropolis, represented – as in *South Africa*'s banner – by Table Mountain and the dome of St Paul's, but here reversed so that if any narrative is to be constructed it should start with London.[3] While the colonies might be said to sustain the imperial centre by providing raw materials, in terms of cultural production, the relationship is emphatically one of dependence.

This banner is nonetheless richly and usefully suggestive in its placement of a physical book at the centre of its representation of cultural commerce. Many scholars have explored the role of books and writers in the construction of postcolonial national identities, and there is by now a large body of work in the field. Timothy Brennan, for instance, observes that nations are 'imaginary constructs' whose existence depends on 'an apparatus of cultural fictions in which imaginative literature plays a decisive role'; Homi Bhabha suggests that the 'repetitious, recursive strategy of the performative' informs the 'conceptual ambivalence' of national identity – that it is literally a case of '*writing the nation*'.[4] The book arguably has been central to processes by which South Africa has always defined itself in relation to an elsewhere (the geographic designation itself bespeaks the urgency of being other than *Africa*). It is this elsewhere which has interpreted South African literary production as *South African*, validating, contesting, consuming it, adducing it as proof in political arguments, using it to calm its own displaced anxieties. Leon de Kock observes: 'Just as South Africans have, over the past three centuries, fashioned themselves in response to projections of a bigger world out there, so their collective struggles have come to assume a certain allegorical significance for that world.'[5] This is often a *textual* process, and it is exactly these processes of exchange, identification and anxiety in relation to writing from the country which form the subject of this book.

Almost no book written and none produced in Southern Africa was advertised in the *South African Book Buyer*; that the journal lasted for just three issues hints at the relatively small market in the region, either for books in general or for books in English. Printing came late to Southern Africa, the first press arriving only in 1784, and for much of the nineteenth century almanacs, newspapers for the growing white and small, black, educated classes, and religious and educational material (including in indigenous vernacular languages) published by missionaries accounted for most of its printed material.[6] Manfred Nathan's seminal 1925 survey of literary production in the region, *South African Literature*, noted that books produced in Britain 'have always had a large and authoritative circulation in South Africa', while 'the indigenous author has had to struggle in the teeth of a constant prejudice against "the local article"'.[7] The majority of intended and likely readers of colonial novels in the late nineteenth and early twentieth centuries were British, inhabitants of Great – as opposed to Greater – Britain, and metropolitan critical opinion, or sales, sealed the success and set the tone for the reception of work written in the colonies and published in Britain. This early reliance on overseas markets for writing from South Africa, and the country's consumption of material produced abroad, persist to the present day, with only a very recent suggestion that the situation is changing. Michael Chapman notes that, in the last decade of the twentieth century, publishers of literary novels could usually hope to sell only 1,000 copies in South Africa.[8] In 1999, local publisher Annari van der Merwe suggested that local publishers, while hampered by the greater margins possible for metropolitan publishers, were faced too with the fact that 'writers themselves' still 'opt to have their books published in the United Kingdom rather than in South Africa', '[b]ecause English is an international language; because there are historically such strong ties with Britain, and because the South African market for fiction is so small'.[9] As a consequence, many *South African* novels continue to be edited and published abroad, and re-imported into South Africa, despite an increase in new local imprints.

This was not initially only a matter of savvy economics, of course: many English-speaking, white South Africans regarded themselves as largely British and looked to the home country for models *and* markets. That they would naturally do so was taken for granted in metropolitan British critical circles. In 1891, Theodore Watts-Dunton argued in the *Fortnightly Review* that there was an unbroken line of descent from *Piers Plowman* to the work of 'certain English, American, Canadian, Australian and South African bards', that all writing in English was 'the birthright of every English-speaking man wheresoever he may have been born'; as such, it was 'to be judged by the canons of criticism of the mother-land'.[10] Gail Low remarks that this 'tropic emphasis on English Literature's origin, parent or root status' persisted well into the 1950s, as a way of 'containing centrifugal forces in anglophone writing'.[11] John Lehmann's *London Magazine*, for example, expressly endorsed a metropolitan standard, Lehmann believing that one should judge South African writing 'more as if South Africa were part of Britain as the South [*sic*] States of America are part of the USA, than a separate country of colonists from Europe who have grown from nationhood'.[12]

Dominion critics largely echoed this opinion for much of the early twentieth century. In 1926, the New Zealand journalist Hector Bolitho, working briefly in South Africa, declared that the country could 'not expect to have culture' because 'as long as England [was] England, she [would] be the pulse of English culture and her dominions must be suburbs. Standards are set here and the South African who writes must achieve English standards: he must have his books published in England.'[13] In describing South Africa as a suburb of metropolitan England, Bolitho invoked British and European intellectuals' widespread distaste for the mass market, the public of the sprawling suburbs (a dismissive appellation freighted particularly at this time), but while he recognised the restrictions on literary production in colonial societies, Bolitho nonetheless acted as a kind of impresario for their writers.[14] He edited *The New Countries: A Collection of Stories and Poems by South African, Australian, Canadian and New Zealand Writers* (1929), introducing it with the assertion that the time had come to believe that something more important than agricultural products could be produced in these 'young countries': their writing.[15] Writers had to appear in London, but this did not mean they should efface their origins.

A deference to standards set in Britain – or Europe more broadly, and later in North America – has produced what J. M. Coetzee calls 'white writing', writing which is 'white only insofar as it is generated by the concerns of people no longer European, not yet African'.[16] This 'Eurocentrism', suggests Daniel Herwitz, is best understood as a result of a refusal by twentieth-century, white South African society to remake its cultures 'in a way that reflects essentially new conditions of existence which are neither European nor "native"'.[17] Because so many South African writers in English have sought to publish abroad, the 'character and identity of South African literature', veteran South African critic and writer Lewis Nkosi noted in 1994, has been largely 'determined somewhere else, by people outside of the community in whose name the writer claims to be speaking'.[18] Stanley Ridge argues that no history of South African literature can pretend to any degree of comprehensive treatment without considering 'the literary and political role of the metropolitan standard in some detail', accounting for the 'exigencies of publishing in enforcing the standard, and making the colonial writer address a metropolitan (imperial) public'.[19]

Contested categories: 'South African', 'South African literature'

Naturally, any attempt to write about 'South African literature' begs a number of questions which I have not been blithely ignoring. For a start, what is 'South African'? The *Oxford English Dictionary* dates its first use, as a noun for a 'native or inhabitant of South Africa' (defined as the 'area of southernmost Africa' now constituting the Republic of South Africa), to the beginning of the second British occupation of the Cape in 1806, when, according to G. M. Theal's *Records of the Cape Colony* (1899), the outgoing Batavian Governor, J. W. Janssens, referred to 'Dutch South Africans'.[20] The adjective 'South African' had entered common usage by the 1820s: the South African Public Library was founded in 1822, the South African College (a forerunner of the University of Cape Town) in 1829 and the region's first weekly newspaper in English, the *South African Commercial Advertiser*, edited by John Fairbairn and Thomas Pringle, began publishing in 1824. By the late 1840s, 'South Africa' had begun to refer to the region encompassing its British colonies, independent Boer republics and black African chieftaincies, as an entity within Britain's sphere of influence if not wholly under its sovereignty. Sir Henry Pottinger became the first High Commissioner for South Africa in January 1847; Sir George Grey, Governor of the Cape Colony and High Commissioner for South Africa (the positions were ordinarily linked until 1900), actively promoted a South African federation during the 1850s.[21] He was unsuccessful, and a distinct regional identity was slow to emerge, along with the disentanglement of a proto-postcolonial South African polity from the Empire. Many English-speaking writers from South Africa's British colonies (the Cape after 1806, Natal after 1843, the Orange Free State and Transvaal after 1902) and, later, from the Union of South Africa (formed in 1910 from those territories) had long considered themselves British.[22] As subjects of the British Empire they were, strictly speaking, British – although a distinct but co-existent (with imperial) South African citizenship was established in 1928.[23] Black South Africans arguably developed a national(ist) consciousness in response to their exclusion from this racial and geographical identity, after 1910.

As Rosemary Jolly notes, different linguistic and ethnic communities have experienced different kinds and structures of colonialism, and political and cultural liberation, in different degrees, and at different times. With such a fraught history of staggered, partial and racially overdetermined national identity formation, there has naturally long been fierce debate about when – and indeed if – South Africa became a post-colonial state.[24] Was it with the Union of the Cape and Natal colonies and the defeated Boer republics in 1910 or the Statute of Westminster which granted relative autonomy to the Commonwealth's Dominions, in 1931? For many Afrikaans-speaking whites, the watershed was undoubtedly the election of an Afrikaner nationalist Government in 1948, or the Union becoming a white-ruled Republic, outside of the Commonwealth, in 1961. It was only in 1994, however, that the first fully multiracial democratic elections heralded a *new* South African nation state.

The complexities of these changing polities demonstrate, Dennis Walder suggests, 'the limitations of thinking of "colonial" and "post-colonial" as distinct, rather than intermingled conditions which vary according to the historical and cultural specifics of the place'.[25] Stephen Slemon suggests that 'settler' literatures inhabit a '"Second World" of discursive polemics', a 'space of dynamic *relation* between ... binaries such as colonizer and colonized, foreign and native, home and away', and while this is certainly the case for much white writing from South Africa (as for Australia or New Zealand), some would argue that the situation is even more complex.[26] David Attwell offers the phrase 'textured postcoloniality' to describe the peculiarly inflected temporal space of South Africa's multiple partial transitions, its history combining those of settler–colonial and autochthonous, indigenous societies.[27]

Given the contested identity of the nation, and the peculiar conditions of much of the writing produced there in any language, attempts to offer generalised accounts of literary production have been bedevilled by ideological pitfalls. The category of a South African literature has always necessitated ingenious elaboration, or wilful exclusion. Manfred Nathan's *South African Literature* defined its subject as writing in numerous genres '*in or of South Africa*'.[28] It went without saying that the literature in question was by white writers, in English or Dutch; 'Black writing in English or indigenous tongues was ignored, even as a possibility', comments Walder.[29] Francis Carey Slater needed a footnote on the opening page of his Preface to the *New Centenary Book of South African Poetry* (1945) to describe the work selected for the anthology. Intended as clarification, it does little but obfuscate:

> NOTE.—For the purposes of this preface (1) English Poetry = the poetry of the British Isles; (2) Afrikaans Poetry = poetry of South Africa, written in Afrikaans [and] (3) South African Poetry = poetry of South Africa, written in English.[30]

Contemporary scholars, recognising that writing in English is but one of a number of literatures which might be called 'South African', are necessarily similarly cautious. Many are sceptical, too, of any project which fails to interrogate its own assumptions about the existence of a national literary identity. Michael Chapman's admirably ambitious 500-page volume in the Longman Literature in English series, *Southern African Literatures* (1996, republished 2003), attempted to chart a multilingual, regional, literary heritage, but subjectively evaluated all 'identities, practices and aesthetic possibilities in the context of a just idea', that of a progressive, humanitarian, multiracial nation.[31] His Introduction dismissed 'the cause-and-effect mode of explanation associated with traditional historiography', readily admitting that his study sought to intervene 'in the construction of a literary and moral narrative'.[32] Stephen Gray, who had himself produced an earlier survey history, had reservations about Chapman's dogmatism, but praised the volume as a whole for offering an 'argument about pertinent issues' which 'open[ed]' the field.[33] As if in response, however, David Medalie suggested that genuinely opening the field of South African literature(s) should entail 'resisting the ideological pressures of the present', exactly what he and others judged Chapman not to have done.[34] Denis Walder called Chapman's 'a progressive, historicist approach' which dismissed 'anything which doesn't contribute towards the forward march of the shared national culture', and Leon de Kock accused it of constructing 'an evaluative and openly teleological' national literary narrative which was exclusionary and, hence, undesirable.[35]

This scepticism about metanarrative projects – narrating 'nation', or defining the 'literary' – in the language of Chapman's critics, reveals the influence in the South African English academy in the 1990s of a post-structuralist-informed critical practice, wary of the Marxist materialism which dominated much of the 1980s. Chapman himself made an attempt to gesture towards the insights of both of these 'not entirely complementary interests', recognising in his Introduction that while 'deconstructive textual analysis' views all writing as texts (indeterminate, contingent on context and intertext), 'politically conscious criticism' suggests 'that we know the society not only by interrogating texts but by experiencing its determinative effects on our lives'.[36] Chapman's critics accused him of betraying the insights of the former, establishing – and even validating – the tyranny of his historical moment's concern with nation-building as the ruling context. In an implicit critique of Chapman's method, Michael Green suggested that 'even a national literary history understood as contingent construct should be careful of the insidious ways in which, almost by definition', it could 'become an agent in the present's imperialisation of the past'.[37] Many others have attempted survey histories, and most have attracted criticism of one kind or another, often for oversights, for privileging canonical authors, for ignoring indigenous languages or, more seriously (as with Christopher Heywood's 2004 *South African Literature*), perpetrating eccentric and even ignorant misreadings.[38]

The field of South African literary production

Because many writers looked elsewhere for publication, for ideological or economic reasons, or because their publication in apartheid-era South Africa was actively prevented, either they or their work, or both, crossed borders marking the actual and imaginary spaces of the country (the colony, the dominion, the republic, the multiracial nation). Most writers from the region, and certainly all of those considered in this study, have consequently, as Ian Glenn writes of Daphne Rooke, had 'to play out [their careers] not on one literary field (to evoke Pierre Bourdieu's notion of the *champ litteraire*), but on several simultaneously'.[39] Glenn's reference to Bourdieu is useful; perhaps the leading French sociologist of the past thirty years, Bourdieu's notions of the literary field and of symbolic capital have had a significant impact on the way scholars conceive of the operation of literary texts in the multiple spheres in which they are produced and circulated. Bourdieu describes the field of literary production as the 'site of struggles in which what is at stake is the power to impose the dominant definition of the writer'.[40] It might be imagined as a series of interconnected cultural and social systems, with their own hierarchies and structures of authority and prestige, implicating authors and their books in various struggles to construct, appropriate, contest and validate cultural production as a kind of capital with symbolic value. 'To take as one's subject of study the literary or artistic field of a given period and society', Bourdieu suggests, is to undertake to re-construct 'the space of positions and the space of the position-takings ... in which they are expressed'.[41]

The 'space of position-takings' for South African writers working or publishing abroad, or writing in South Africa and aiming (even partially) at a foreign audience, has necessarily been varied and heterogeneous, and inadequately historicised or accounted for in survey histories of the country's literary production. Both 'nation' and 'book' are deeply unstable categories. Both refer, as Robert Gross observes, 'to processes and relationships, not to states of being', and the complicated processes by which national identities are imagined and counter-imagined, appropriated and subverted form 'a central theme in the history of books'.[42] In other words, it is not only the symbolic constructs *in* texts, but also *of* texts, the lives of books, that inform national literary mythologies. This formulation suggests a fruitful means of imagining new and nuanced approaches to the study of colonial and postcolonial literatures, which consider their implication in the traffic of symbolic capital across boundaries of metropole and colony, revealed to be more permeable and contingent than conventionally figured. How, then, might such processes and relationships be approached?

Nicholas Visser suggested in 'Postcoloniality of a Special Type' (1997), an assessment of the reception and propagation of theories of the postcolonial in South African academia, that, while postcolonial theory as embraced by certain elements in the South African academy had been eloquent on 'discursive practices and conditions', it was 'largely silent' about 'material and social conditions and political praxis'.[43] Visser, working with a hostile Marxist reading of poststructuralism, echoed other voices with similar investments in critiquing the silences in works by poststructuralist-informed postcolonial critics which focus on uncovering self-alienating hybridity within colonial discourse itself, but which risk retreating from specificities of place and time into what Stephen Slemon and Helen Tiffin call 'a domain of pure "textuality"'.[44] Attuned to the productive interplay between materialism and poststructuralism, Robert Young suggests that those who perceive 'a certain textualism and idealism in colonial-discourse analysis' occurring 'at the expense of materialist historical enquiry' are guilty of 'a form of category mistake'; he argues that investigations of the 'discursive construction of colonialism' need not 'exclude other forms of analysis'.[45] Nonetheless, the near orthodoxies created by postcolonial discourse analysis in the 1980s and early 1990s do often elide less glamorous, but no less important, detailed examinations of what Bruce King calls the 'actual social contexts, cultural networking, and literary careers of writers', the kind of study I have suggested the predicaments of South African writing demand.[46]

Jerome McGann argued three decades ago that we ought to consider not only a work's historical contexts, but the history of its embodiment in successive texts (its 'textualisations') and its circulation and reception (its 'socialisations').[47] Over the past two decades, a new field of study, *book history*, drawing on these and related concerns, has developed, framing questions like: Which 'intervenient institutions' have enabled or impeded authors?[48] How has each instance of publication affected the text and its status or the author's reputation? Book history, a series of cognate fields of related study, draws on previous disciplines like social and intellectual history, Anglo-American bibliography and textual criticism, its 'relative distinctiveness', David Finkelstein and Alistair McCleery suggest, deriving from a new 'emphasis upon print culture and the role of the book as material object within that culture'.[49] Limited and inadequate term that it is, book history has thus become a convenient way to refer to social histories of the 'creation, diffusion, and reception of the written' and, more particularly, the printed, word.[50] Its reconstruction and analysis of both historical and contemporary sites and strategies of reading push cultural materialism beyond 'its accustomed concern with historicizing the words on the page' to consider 'the economics of literature' in its broadest possible sense, the influences of historical, material and economic variables on the making of books as physical artefacts, and the processes by which the meanings of the texts they define are made and circulated.[51] Seminal studies and methodological interventions by Roger Chartier, D. F. McKenzie, Robert Darnton, George Bornstein, and Jerome J. McGann (among others), the establishment or renovation of journals like *Book History* and *Textual Culture* (formerly *TEXT*) and of print culture and book history monograph series by prominent academic presses, and several international conferences and colloquia, have raised the profile of a field whose methodological energy is striking.[52]

Scholars in the field are sometimes criticised, however, for concerning themselves with the materiality of text to the exclusion of a work's narrative strategies (for example), with the space of position-taking *by* texts, rather than position-taking *in* texts. They are accused of being obsessed with the material circumstances of publication, or with discussing the opinions of critics and reviewers without offering their own 'readings'. One response to these ignorant but inevitable criticisms is to suggest, as Jonathan Rose does, that while book history is concerned with general literary–theoretical issues like authorship, the canon and reading, 'many theorists disdain' as 'brute empiricism' what 'book historians prefer to call "research"'.[53] A less confrontational and more intellectually challenging response is to argue that, while literary criticism has always been concerned with the meanings of texts, book history explores how those meanings are influenced by factors often beyond the control of authors themselves, how they are constructed and change, and how these process-es are intimately connected with, for example, publishing pressures, the ruling discourses of reviewing, censorship, abridgement, educational insti-tutionalisation and the valorising economics of literary-prize cultures.

If what is at issue in such studies is an imperative to chart and trace texts' 'various material and social predicaments, and the history of [their] uses and meanings', Peter McDonald suggests, rather than asking what book history may contribute to literary criticism, one might turn the ques-tion on its head and ask: 'what is the relevance of literary interpretation to book history?'[54] Book history, studies in print or textual cultures, studies of the institutions of literature – whichever label one prefers – might consequently be seen to offer the prospect of historically responsible, subtle, imaginative and invigorating accounts of the vagaries of meaning and the contingencies of *literariness* itself. Such a field of study, McDonald argues, 'refuses to accept the assurances of traditional histori-cism, or to define itself against reading, criticism, and "theory"', but offers a way of drawing on the insights of both critical orientations.[55] Both *theory* and book history (or whatever else one might seek to call it) in effect focus on the changes in a text's meaning enacted by different contexts; both, that is, share a concern with 'the problematics of dissemi-nation and its implications for classical ideas of close reading'.[56] 'The point', McDonald concludes, 'is not to celebrate the document at the expense of writing – in Derrida's sense of the term – but to study its attempts to contain the disruptive forces of dissemination, and, in so doing, to make publishing history the foundation of a larger history of reading', and of meaning-making in general.[57]

South African textual cultures

Colonial and postcolonial book-historical scholarship has been compara-tively slow to develop, but the early twenty-first century saw several 'book history' conferences outside of metropolitan Europe and North America, with particularly vibrant communities of Australasian, South Asian and Canadian scholars working in the field.[58] South African literary scholar-ship, long and 'badly served', in Sarah Nuttall's words, by a 'mixture of belles-lettristic and New Critical formative pedagogical influences' which have 'paid little attention to the materiality and context of texts', has generally been even slower to respond to those imperatives, although a number of scholars are beginning to attend to what might very loosely be called book-historical, or textual–cultural, concerns.[59] Until recently, the concern has understandably been with current economic and political challenges to the local publishing industry (educational publishing, indigenous language publishing, the influence of multinationals), and with charting what is actually being published and purchased in the country.[60] However, there are also studies of reading formations in Southern Africa, illuminating, as Isabel Hofmeyr puts it, 'how print culture has been "baptised" in African intellectual and spiritual traditions', and how racial and ethnic identities have been interpellated by and variously implicated in projects of national identification, or consumer cultures.[61]

Three special issues of local academic journals have spoken to book-historical concerns. Hofmeyr, long an eloquent champion of the field in the region, collaborated with Sarah Nuttall on an issue of *Current Writing* (2001) broadly concerned with 'The Book in Africa', and with Lize Kriel on an issue of the *South African Historical Journal* (2006) making a case for the development of lively interdisciplinary areas of research in South Africa.[62] My special issue of *English Studies in Africa*, 'Histories of the Book in Southern Africa' (2004), collected a series of essays exploring the textual conditions and transnational institutions of literariness influencing the lives of books from the country.[63] There is, however, still relatively little work that is rigorously historical or determinedly transnational in its focus. This book attempts to be both of those things.

The debate about literary historiography focused on Chapman's *Southern African Literatures* serves to caution any scholar foolhardy enough to attempt a grand narrative of the field, with whatever methodology. 'Our histories need to give up their pretensions to comprehensive cover', Leon de Kock suggests: '[i]nstead of the canopy, the wedge'.[64] My study responds to the challenge. Each of the six chapters which follow is a wedge, part of a provisional, punctuated, diachronic account of *some* South African writing in English. These 'biographies' track the movement of a specific text or texts through different cultural matrices, attending to the social, economic and cultural commerce which structured every stage of their lives and afterlives, generating multiple meanings from their changing material manifestations and ideological appropriations. I consider how they were constructed or contested as 'South African', and as 'literature', asking what special categories, criteria, institutions and protocols of reading affected their reception. Each chapter offers a snapshot of the material and socio-political predicaments of particular works in different local and global circumstances; together, the chapters cover a period of roughly 120 years.

The range of work discussed has had significant purchase in discourses in and through which a provisional 'national' literary identity has been contested in South Africa, and through which it has been constructed by and for readers elsewhere. Historians of postcolonialism note the necessity of attending to what Bart Moore-Gilbert and Elleke Boehmer call the '"thick" empirical sense of post-coloniality as an interactive horizontal "web"', a 'global network of transverse interactions' among various anti-colonial movements, writers and activists.[65] This observation is useful on two counts, methodological and thematic, by gesturing to Geertsian 'thick empirical' investigation, and by foregrounding the significance of transnational transactions.[66] Clifford Geertz calls the discrete anthropological studies collected as *The Interpretation of Cultures* (1973) 'a treatise in cultural theory as developed through a series of concrete analyses', and describes his method using a notion borrowed from Gilbert Ryle: 'thick description'.[67] In anthropological terms, this offers an interpretative description of an observed fact, action or practice, setting it in what Geertz calls a 'stratified hierarchy of meaningful structures'.[68] Each of my case-study chapters is usefully viewed as an instance of empirical 'thick description': each considers a moment in which particular writers and their works are implicated in a complex network – and hierarchy – of transnational and international institutional operations.[69] My focus is on writing in English because I am concerned most, in this study, with writing which has been read – and written *to be read* – by a global anglophone community.

From Schreiner to Mda, 1883–2005

Olive Schreiner negotiated a complicated transnational career: she regarded Britain as an intellectual home, but struggled to balance a desire for metropolitan validation of her work with a deeply felt commitment to South Africa – then a loosely geographical term rather than the name of a unitary state – as an idea, if not always as a place. Chapter 2 offers the most comprehensive account to date of the publication and reception history of Schreiner's first published and most famous novel, *The Story of an African Farm* (1883), often considered the first significant work of a 'South African' literature. The expectations of publishers' readers and the manner in which they prevented or facilitated publication, the mediation of Schreiner's text by its changing material manifestations and the manner in which multiple interest groups interpreted Schreiner's own perceived national and geographic origins and affiliations provide evidence to challenge and extend work on colonial writing in general, and so-called 'South African' writing in particular, providing a salutary lesson in the conditional, ideological and provisional nature of any attempt to claim a work of literature for any strictly circumscribed category or tradition, including that of a national literature.

Chapter 3 considers the contrasting reputations of two South African-born writers who came to prominence in the 1920s and 1930s, Roy Campbell and William Plomer, as they negotiated complex identities in a period of great definitional turbulence. The historical moment is significant: writers in the Union of South Africa were engaged in hotly contested debates about national identity, imperial affiliation, language policy, and racial segregation during the period, especially after the rise of a nationalist government coalition in 1924 (Afrikaans became an official language and South Africa acquired its own flag during the ensuing years) and the recognition of the equal status of British Dominions in the Commonwealth in 1931. For some editors and commentators, Campbell was primarily a 'colonial', for others he was 'British', while he often called himself 'South African'. Plomer described himself as 'doubly displaced', simultaneously a South African writer and English reader, and an English writer and South African reader, highlighting his position of and between two sites of cultural production and identification. By the 1930s, both writers were well-known in South Africa and Britain, where the two then lived; they were assimilated, too, to very different poles in an increasingly politically polarised field, Campbell on the *right*, Plomer on the *left*. This chapter explores the instability of many of these categories, demonstrating that literary cultures are constructed in relation to public and political cultures in volatile ways.

In March 1948, a reviewer in the American *New Republic* suggested that not '[s]ince Olive Schreiner's *The Story of an African Farm*' had 'colonial literature' produced something like Alan Paton's *Cry, the Beloved Country* (1948).[70] Other reviews of the novel noted Paton's apparent contribution to a specifically 'South African' literature; he had 'taken his place in the history of South Africa beside Olive Schreiner', one argued, and encouraged reconsideration of an impression, gained from the examples of Campbell and Plomer, that South Africa 'was a good place for a writer to have come from, but a bad place for him to live'.[71] Paton's novel and its reception (rapturous in the USA and Britain) appeared to evidence 'the production of a native literature' for the first time.[72] However, *Cry, the Beloved Country* was not so rapturously received in South Africa, contrary to the status it continues to enjoy as perhaps the most famous single book written about the country. Chapter 4 argues that *Cry, the Beloved Country* provides an exemplary case of a work having been made into a cultural icon – having become 'hypercanonical' – almost entirely outside of South Africa, by reading communities and institutions driven by their own particular imperatives. Rather than asking whether Paton's novel has deserved its reputation, one might more fruitfully ask: who has validated and endorsed the novel, how and why? Uncovering the implications of these judgements allows us, in the words of David Hall, to expand 'our understanding of authority – social, cultural, and political'.[73]

Schreiner shuttled between the Cape Colony, South African Republic (Transvaal) and Britain. Campbell and Plomer left South Africa of their own accord. Paton remained in the country. Some writers, however, were forced to leave. By the end of 1966, many black writers, in particular, were in exile: Peter Abrahams (for example) was in Jamaica, Alfred Hutchinson in Ghana, Es'kia Mphahlele in Kenya, Can Themba in Swaziland, and Bloke Modisane, Todd Matshikiza and Lewis Nkosi all in London.[74] Their work became what Coetzee has called 'a kind of émigré literature written by outcasts for foreigners'.[75] Among them, one of the most politically active, and thought by many to be one of the finest writers, was Alex La Guma. As a banned person and, after September 1966, an exile, his work was barred from publication or dissemination in apartheid-era South Africa. That he would have been a significant, highly regarded writer in South Africa, had it been possible for his novels to be published there, is accepted by many observers, and he is now, rightly, widely read and taught in South Africa, and his oeuvre considered one of the most complex and challenging within what might be called the '"protest" canon'.[76] Chapter 5 employs a wealth of new evidence to reconsider the histories of the publication, marketing and reading of La Guma's work, focused through *A Walk in the Night* (1962), and its implications for the idea of 'South African' literature – and *literariness* – in the terminal years of the apartheid State. His critical reception and the attitude of different publishing institutions to his work speak to an ongoing debate about literary value within which all of the authors and works considered in my study are involved.

In 1981, on the occasion of accepting one of South Africa's most prestigious literary awards, the CNA Prize, for *Waiting for the Barbarians* (1980), Coetzee wondered whether it was a 'good idea, a just idea', to regard South African literature in English as a 'national literature, or even an incipient national literature'.[77] South African writing's relation to Western Europe and North America, the 'centres of the dominant world civilization', was that of 'province to metropolis', he suggested, and South African writers were not 'building a new national literature', but instead adding to 'an established provincial literature' – although 'rehabilitating the notion of the provincial' was not to admit defeat.[78] More than two decades later, Coetzee is one of South Africa's most recognisable literary names, his status confirmed by the award of the Nobel Prize for Literature in 2003, but much of his writing, both critical and creative, militates against its being read as necessarily 'South African' at all (besides which, he now lives in Australia).[79] Chapter 6 focuses on the material predicaments of the first of his works to be published in South Africa, Britain and the USA, *In the Heart of the Country* (1977, 1978), and asks what the fact of the novel's multi-textual history contributes to an understanding of Coetzee's oeuvre, and what its material history suggests about his engagement with the idea of a national literature.

If, in the words of the African National Congress journal *Sechaba*, it was 'necessary for cultural workers, writers, artists and educationists to identify themselves and their works with the struggle for the liberation of South Africa from the racist yoke', what would happen once that yoke had, at least officially, been lifted?[80] Many commentators, in South Africa and abroad, expected a new kind of writing from the country, and most particularly from black writers, after 1994. For many, the leading contemporary black writer to have come closest to filling this brief is Zakes Mda. Already a prolific playwright and poet by the time he returned to South

Africa from thirty years in exile (in Lesotho and the USA) in 1995, Mda
has published five novels since then. At first, they appeared only in South
Africa, but are now published by large British and American trade firms –
although they are always, on his insistence, published in South Africa
first. Significantly, too, he has a comparatively large readership inside
South Africa, and maintains that he writes 'primarily for the South
African audience'.[81] Chapter 7 considers the circumstances of the publication of Mda's fiction, particularly *The Heart of Redness* (2000), asking
how his work has been presented to and received by local and international reading communities, and how it engages issues of cultural production
and identification in local and global contexts. Mda's work speaks explicitly to anxieties about national identity, the aesthetics of *South African*
'literature' and the globalisation of postcolonial identities, recurring
concerns of this book as a whole.

The chapters which follow present themselves, then, as tentative instalments in a history of reading in and of *South Africa*. Collectively, they
consider the constitutive influence of different institutions in the fields of
cultural and literary production – including publishing practices, reviewing, anthologies, literary coteries, the educational system, libraries,
magazines, book clubs, censorship, prizes and awards. Each case study
also evidences the contingency of the category of *the nation*: for each
writer, there were (and are) always other identifications in play, be they
subnational, supranational or transnational. And, as important for my
study as the forms of labelling imposed on writers are the forms and
degrees of resistance they and their work offered, and continue to offer, to
the ways they were and are read; the literary, after all, is an inherently
unstable category, liable to complicity with, and resistance to, the designs
of other ideological and discursive formations. Each of the authors is both
exemplary and exceptional, and while they are, for the most part, well-
known figures, there are many major writers who are not discussed here.
Such omissions, which will doubtless seem significant to some (and the
gaps suggested differently to individual readers will hopefully be a spur to
further necessary work in this field), highlight that this book is *not* a
representative survey of 'South African literature'. It is, rather, a study of
significant transactions in a history which puts that category under
erasure, a history so variegated that it renders the adjectival description
'South African' one of the least definite, or definable, one might apply. It
would be foolhardy to attempt to generalise further on the basis of the
studies the limited pages of this study will allow.[82]

Notes

1 See fig. 1.1.
2 See Note in *South Africa* (14 January 1911), 71. It claimed the 'largest circu-

lation of any South African newspaper': *South Africa* (21 January 1911), 137.

3 Anon., Editorial Note, *South African Book Buyer*; see fig. 1.2.

4 Brennan, 'The National Longing for Form', 49; Bhabha, 'DissemiNation', 297; see also Anderson, *Imagined Communities*; Jameson, 'Third-World Literature'; Lazarus, *Nationalism and Cultural Practice*.

5 De Kock, 'South Africa in the Global Imaginary', 21.

6 Bickford-Smith, 'Words, Wars and World Views', 9; see also Bradlow, *Printing for Africa*; Harries, 'Missionaries, Marxists and Magic'; Comaroff and Comaroff, *Christianity, Colonialism, and Consciousness* and *The Dialectics of Modernity*; De Kock, *Civilising Barbarians*.

7 Nathan, *South African Literature*, 15.

8 Chapman, *Southern African Literatures*, 129. London-based South African author and agent Sarah Penny says in 'A Literary Vox Pop' it might be between 2,000 and 5,000.

9 Van der Merwe, 'Did the First Democratic Elections' (online).

10 Watts-Dunton, 'The Future of American Literature', 917.

11 Low, 'Finding the Centre?', 26.

12 *Ibid.*, 27, quoting John Lehmann's Foreword from *The London Magazine*, 4.1 (1957), 9–11.

13 Bolitho, 'Culture and South Africa', 12; see also Bolitho, *My Restless Years*, 107–15.

14 See Carey, *The Intellectuals and the Masses*.

15 Bolitho (ed.), *The New Countries*, 13–20.

16 Coetzee, *White Writing*, 11. For a different use of a similar analogy, see Guy Butler's suggestion, in 1950, that 'fragments of systems and broken emotional patterns which originated in Europe' did not, 'like so many shrubs and flowers, readily take root in African soil': Butler, *Essays and Lectures*, 39.

17 Herwitz, 'Modernism at the Margins', 407.

18 Nkosi, 'Constructing the "Cross-Border" Reader', 48.

19 Ridge, 'The Meaning of the Map', 90.

20 *Oxford English Dictionary*, OED Online, 'South African, *n.* and *a.*'. The Theal reference is to vol. 5, 298. The Dutch settlement at the Cape, ruled by the Dutch East India Company from 1652 (and, by the end of the eighteenth century, an ever-expanding region), was occupied by Britain in 1798 during the Napoleonic Wars, handed back to the Batavian Republic in 1802, and reoccupied permanently by Britain in 1806.

21 Walker (ed.), *Cambridge History*, vol. 8, 885–7; see Davenport and Saunders, *South Africa*, 104–6, 139, 196, 199–202, 706.

22 Lambert, 'South African British?'.

23 The Union Nationality and Flags Act (Act 40 of 1927) came into effect on 31 May 1928. Its first chapter made provision for a distinct 'Union Nationality': see *Statutes of the Union*, vol. 2, 2–6. By comparison, a distinct Australian citizenship was only established in 1949. See Hassam, *Through Australian Eyes*, 16.

24 Jolly, 'Rehearsals of Liberation', 21–2; see Ashcroft, Griffiths, and Tiffin, *The Empire Writes Back*, 25–7.

25 Walder, *Post-Colonial Literatures*, 156; see also Elleke Boehmer's suggestion, applicable to South African literatures, that 'definitions of the postcolonial tend to assume that this category of writing is diametrically opposed to colo-

nial literature', rather than existing in a more ambiguous, overlapping contin-
uum: Boehmer, *Colonial and Postcolonial Literature*, 4.

26 Slemon, 'Unsettling the Empire', 38.

27 Attwell, *Rewriting Modernity*, 1.

28 Nathan, *South African Literature*, 13.

29 Walder, *Post-Colonial Literatures*, 157.

30 Slater, Preface, *New Centenary Book*, v.

31 Chapman, *Southern African Literatures*, 430.

32 *Ibid.*, 4.

33 Gray, 'Opening Southern African Studies', 210, 211; see Stephen Gray, *Southern African Literature*.

34 Medalie, 'Keeping History Open', 305; Medalie's review, while not of Chapman's book, speaks to the same debate.

35 Walder, *Post-Colonial Literatures*, 157; De Kock, 'An Impossible History', 105, see 103.

36 Chapman, *Southern African Literatures*, 5.

37 Green, 'Resisting a National Literary History', 234; Green's paper was delivered at a colloquium in 1995 at which Chapman delivered a version of the Introduction to *Southern African Literatures*.

38 Gray, *Southern African Literature*; Smith, *Grounds of Contest*; Heywood, *A History*. For a critique of Heywood, see Van der Vlies, Review. See Ricard, *Languages and Literatures of Africa*, 98–118, on African-language literatures in South Africa.

39 Glenn, 'The Production and Prevention of the Colonial Author', 85.

40 Bourdieu, *The Field of Cultural Production*, 42; see 29–73, 176–91; see English, *Economy of Prestige*, 9–10.

41 Bourdieu, *The Field of Cultural Production*, 29, 30; see McDonald, *British Literary Culture*, 10–11; Huggan, *The Postcolonial Exotic*, 5.

42 Gross, 'Books, Nationalism, and History', 119, 110.

43 Visser, 'Postcoloniality of a Special Type', 89.

44 Slemon and Tiffin, Introduction, x. Bhabha's description of the 'third space' through which any 'act of communication' is mobilised – as both 'the general conditions of language' and 'the specific implication of the utterance in a performative and institutional strategy of which it cannot "in itself" be conscious' – seems open to a reading which demands that the material institutions of literature be considered: Bhabha, *Location of Culture*, 36.

45 Young, *Colonial Desire*, 163.

46 King (ed.), 'New Centres of Consciousness', 18. Ashcroft, Griffiths and Tiffin call for similar 'assessments of the material conditions of cultural production and consumption in post-colonial societies': *Post-Colonial Studies Reader*, 463. Griffiths has himself incorporated this kind of analysis in a survey history very productively, in his *African Literatures in English*.

47 McGann, *The Beauty of Inflections*, 9.

48 Rainey, *The Institutions of Modernism*, 4.

49 Finkelstein and McCleery (eds), 'Introduction', 1.

50 Rose, 'How to Do Things', 462.

51 Clery, Franklin, and Garside (eds), Introduction, 2.

52 See McKenzie, *The Panizzi Lectures*; Darnton, 'What Is the History of Books?', in *The Kiss of Lamourette*; Bornstein, *Material Modernism*;

McGann, *The Beauty of Inflections*, and *The Textual Condition*; see also Greetham, *Textual Scholarship*; Grigely, *Textualterity*; Hall, *Cultures of Print*; Johns, *The Nature of the Book*; Jordan and Patten (eds), *Literature in the Marketplace*. For an exemplary survey of the field see Hofmeyr and Kriel (eds), 'Book History in Southern Africa', 5–10.

53 Rose, 'How to Do Things', 462.
54 McDonald, 'Implicit Structures', 120–1.
55 McDonald, 'Modernist Publishing', 241.
56 *Ibid.*, 231.
57 *Ibid.*, 232.
58 See, for example: Gupta and Chakravorty (eds), *Print Areas*; Joshi, *In Another Country*. There are numerous national 'history of the book' projects.
59 Nuttall, 'Literature and the Archive', 283.
60 See Seeber and Evans (eds), *The Politics of Publishing*; Land, 'The State of Book Development'; Galloway, 'Statistical Trends'; Galloway and Venter, 'Book History, Publishing Research and Production Figures'.
61 Hofmeyr and Kriel (eds), 'Book History in Southern Africa', 12, 13, 15; see Harries, 'Missionaries, Marxists and Magic'; Hofmeyr, *We Spend Our Years*, and 'Metaphorical Books'; Nuttall, 'Reading in the Lives and Writing'; Kruger and Shariff, 'Shoo – This Book Makes Me to Think!'; Laden, 'Making the Paper Speak Well'; Dick, 'Building a Nation of Readers?'; Nuttall, 'Stylizing the Self'.
62 Hofmeyr and Nuttall, with Michael (eds), 'The Book in Africa'.
63 Hofmeyr has repeatedly stressed the need for transnational studies: Hofmeyr, 'From Book Development', 4; Hofmeyr, 'Spread Far and Wide', 17.
64 De Kock, 'Impossible History', 114; see also De Kock's 'A Central South African Story' and 'The Pursuit of Smaller Stories'; Crehan, 'Broken History'.
65 Boehmer and Moore-Gilbert, Introduction, 12.
66 Although I am not concerned here with the kind of relations among colonial elites which is the subject of Boehmer's *Empire, the National and the Postcolonial*.
67 Geertz, *Interpretation of Cultures*, viii, 6.
68 *Ibid.*, 7. For example, a wink might be a contraction of the eyelid, but might also be faked, or a parody, or a ploy to deceive someone into inferring a conspiracy.
69 Claire Colebrook suggests that '[d]escriptions of texts would be "thick"', in a Geertsian sense, 'if they referred to the social and cultural forms in which the text operated': Colebrook, *New Literary Histories*, 75.
70 Stern, 'Out of Africa', 28.
71 Calder-Marshall, 'In the Soil', 6.
72 Young, 'Out of Africa', 3.
73 Hall, 'History of the Book', 28.
74 Lindfors, 'Post-War Literature', 59. Many of these exiles, and many others still in South Africa, were 'banned', including Dennis Brutus, Masizi Kunene, Alex La Guma, Todd Matshikiza, Bloke Modisane, Es'kia Mphahlele, Lewis Nkosi and Can Themba.
75 Coetzee, *Doubling the Point*, 344. On the detention, banning, and 'listing' of writers, see Merrett, *A Culture of Censorship*, 47–54; Chapman, *Southern African Literatures*, 246; De Lange, *The Muzzled Muse*, 13–14.

76 Both Sipho Sepamla and Miriam Tlali, for example, recorded their regret at not being able to obtain copies of La Guma's work easily, or at all: Sepamla, 'The Black Writer', 116; Tlali, 'In Search of Books', 45.

77 Coetzee, 'SA Authors Must Learn Modesty', 16.

78 *Ibid*.

79 During the inaugural international Cape Town Book Fair, in June 2006, the *Weekender*'s 'Weekend Review' ran a survey of 20 prominent writers and journalists to find the nation's 'best book', and while Coetzee was the most cited author (12 respondents listed at least one book in their selection of 5 titles; 2 listed 2 titles), the paper observed that, now that he had emigrated, 'we should probably no longer call him exclusively our own': Cohen and Rossouw, 'Search for SA's best book', 1.

80 Anon., 'Censorship in South Africa', 62.

81 Wark, Interview.

82 I echo, consciously, the defence offered by David Attwell for his coverage in *Rewriting Modernity*, 26.

2

Farming stories (I): Olive Schreiner's fates

In late 1882, the London publishing firm Chapman & Hall decided, on the advice of its reader, the novelist George Meredith, to publish a daring and unconventional novel set in the distant Cape Colony. Neither a tale of polite society nor an exotic imperial adventure, its characters instead inhabited an isolated farm on an arid Southern African plain, suffered crises of faith, and tested the limits of the period's accepted gender roles: the agnostic heroine, Lyndall, refuses to marry the father of her child, and her frustrated suitor dresses as a woman to nurse her on her deathbed. Although its author's name was given as 'Ralph Iron', this masculine pseudonym did not long conceal the identity of a young colonial woman, Olive Schreiner, who soon became widely known. In the 125 years since its publication, *The Story of an African Farm*, her most famous novel, has been accorded a pre-eminent position in the history of proto-feminist fiction, and in the development of a putative South African literary canon.[1]

The physical presentation and promotion of recent editions of the novel suggest its multiple identities, with two predominant clusters of images having provided the cover decoration for most of its late twentieth-century editions. Images of a girl or young woman emphasise Lyndall's experience and the novel's advancement of the so-called 'woman ques-tion', while images of the landscape of the novel focus attention on its colonial provenance and presciently suggestive proto-postcolonial chal-lenge. An example of the first class of images is provided, for example, by Virago's 1989 'Modern Classics' edition, which advertises the publisher's aim to rediscover and reprint women's writing, promoting the idea of a 'female tradition in fiction'.[2] The volume's prefatory material and its posi-tion in the context of Virago's list conspire to present Schreiner as pre-eminently a 'Free-Thinker, pacifist, feminist and socialist'.[3] The cover reinforces this construction by inviting a connection between Dante Gabriel Rossetti's *Head of a Girl* and Schreiner's (anti-)heroine, casting Lyndall as a (not uncompromised) challenger of Victorian gender stereo-types. Somewhat differently, the cover of the 1995 Penguin Classics edition – Frans Oerder's painting of a young girl reading – emphasises Lyndall's childhood introspection and intellectual development rather than her later challenges to social conventions.[4]

South African editions have tended to favour the second class of images. The dust-jacket of Ad Donker's 1975 edition features a photograph of the cottage on the farm where Schreiner wrote much of the novel, while its 1986 paperback uses a painting of a dilapidated farmhouse in a Karoo-like landscape.[5] The cover of Hutchinson's special 1987 illustrated hardcover edition – not a South African publication, but introduced by Doris Lessing, who had written about another African farm in *The Grass Is Singing* – has an iconic Cape Dutch farmhouse, surrounded by stylised Bushman rock art figures, staging a fascinating confrontation between a representation of white South African settlement and the inscription of an aboriginal presence on the land itself; the attentive reader is reminded of Waldo in Schreiner's novel, encouraging Lyndall and Em to consider the traces of the farm's previous inhabitants – Bushman paintings on the 'kopje'.[6]

The cover of the 1992 Oxford World's Classics edition conflates these tropes, reproducing Henry Stratford Caldecott's 1926 neo-impressionist painting of a female figure, perhaps an artist, before a mountain and a painting of the mountain, in an expressly South African landscape (*Early Morning, Worcester*, in the Western Cape).[7] To a reader aware of attempts to represent *The Story of an African Farm*'s narrative method as anticipating modernist techniques, Caldecott's painting might invite thoughts of Lily Briscoe in Woolf's *To the Lighthouse* (1927). As such, the image engages with the edition's editor's privileging of Schreiner's relation to Western intellectual traditions alongside her status as a South African writer – Joseph Bristow emphasises the influence on Schreiner's work of Mill's political economy, Spencer's social Darwinism and Emerson's transcendentalism, foregrounding the novel's status as the 'first distinctly "feminist" fiction in English'.[8]

In 1987, feminist press Pandora published a collection of extracts from Schreiner's autobiographical fragments, journalism, dream allegories and fiction, as *An Olive Schreiner Reader: Writings of Women and South Africa*, expressly to give British readers access to work justifying Schreiner's reputation as a feminist *and* a South African. Its cover includes a dark photograph of the author on a background of green and gold, clearly suggesting the black, green and gold of the African National Congress, banned in South Africa at the time of the collection's publication. Furthermore, the editor, Carol Barash, dedicated the volume to Winnie Mandela, and reprinted, as an Afterword, staunchly anti-apartheid novelist Nadine Gordimer's appreciative review of Ann Scott and Ruth First's biography of Schreiner. A chronology of Schreiner's life is extended to include a history of the black liberation struggle and emphasise the severely repressive conditions in South Africa under the state of emergency in the late 1980s.[9] While not an edition of *The Story of an African Farm*, this collection suggests how Schreiner's reputation, solidly based on the success of her first novel, continued to be reinvented, her oeuvre presented to an international audience as speaking directly to the crisis in late-apartheid South Africa.

Pandora's promotion of Barash's collection and the 1989 Women's Press paperback reprint of First and Scott's biography both instance what Laura Chrisman describes as a 'flurry of metropolitan interest' in South Africa in the late 1980s. This involved a complicated commodification of the country's women's writing for (mostly) white British readers who, while concerned about the injustices of apartheid South Africa, were, given British sensitivities about black political emancipation in the wake of UK race riots in the early 1980s, considered more likely to respond to marketing tactics which depoliticised black writers and cast 'white women as the most significant agents of anti-racist movement'.[10] The blurb on the rear cover of Barash's collection explicitly positions Schreiner, a white woman, as 'both coloniser and colonised'.

If that is how the reputations of *The Story of an African Farm* (and of Schreiner) are continually repositioned in critical discourse and through material re-presentations of the novel, what was the case in the decades after its first publication? Gerald Monsman argues that it was deemed geographically, 'scenically' and 'structurally marginal' in 1880s Britain because of its colonial origins and setting, and its deviation from reigning ideals 'of mimetic representation'.[11] Revisiting the language with which the novel was first described and reviewed, however, complicates these assertions. Readers interpreted the novel differently, the marginality of its setting was not always noticed, and to suggest that a universal ideal of mimetic representation applied as a critical standard in the 1880s and 1890s is to oversimplify a complex field.

Literary works, Jerome McGann suggests, are 'particular forms of transmissive interaction', the socio-historical conditions under which each text enters the world establishing the 'horizon' within which its life-history is played out. Each reader's reception of a work involves a comparison of his or her conception of its aesthetic value with that of previously read texts, a test which redefines the horizon of that reader's expectations.[12] For Hans Robert Jauss, any study of reading requires attention to 'the objectifiable system of expectations that arises for each work in the historical moment of its appearance, from a pre-understanding of the genre, from the form and themes of already familiar works'.[13] Considering how *The Story of an African Farm* was packaged for its initial audiences and how, as far as can be ascertained or inferred, it was received recognises that readings of new editions make possible new works in each act of interpretation. In a subtly changing field, they become symbolic capital whose exchange value is altered by new circumstances, and whose changing investments highlight the artificiality of any fixed idea of a national literature.

Policing the text: metropolitan institutions of the novel

Between 1880 and 1882, when it was accepted by Chapman & Hall, the manuscript of what became *The Story of an African Farm* was rejected by five publishers, several of them established and influential firms. Because the manuscript itself has not survived, there is no way of reconstructing the actual text encountered by the publishers' readers, and also little evidence of their responses. It is possible, however, to reconstruct the most likely series of judgements which led to publication, illuminating the conventions against which Schreiner's novel initially struggled.[14] Samuel Cronwright-Schreiner's 1924 biography of his wife, *The Life of Olive Schreiner*, claims that Schreiner sent a manuscript version of the novel, entitled 'Lyndall', to Dr and Mrs Brown, English friends from the Cape Colony who had since returned to live in Lancashire, sometime in early 1880. The Browns sent the manuscript to a friend in Edinburgh, Dr J. Taylor Brown, who in turn passed it to his friend David Douglas, a publisher. Douglas thought it promising but in need of editing, and the manuscript was returned to Schreiner at Lelie Kloof, near Cradock, where she was a governess, later that year. The manuscripts of what became *The Story of an African Farm* and the posthumously published *From Man to Man* almost certainly accompanied Schreiner when she left the Cape in March 1881.[15]

A 1909 account of George Meredith's role as reader for Chapman & Hall, based on archival material which has subsequently been lost, suggests that he rejected an early version of *From Man to Man* – entitled 'Saints and Sinners' – during 1881.[16] The Macmillan Archive records that Schreiner, as 'Ralph Iron', subsequently submitted this manuscript there, but its reader, almost certainly John Morley (who will be referred to as such hereafter), rejected it in November 1881, calling it 'irrational' and 'senseless', 'morbid and sinister', with a 'violent and fantastic and even revolting plot'.[17] Macmillan endeavoured to maintain 'an intellectual cast' to its list, and had taken to fiction comparatively slowly, remaining always a 'high minded religious and educational concern'.[18] A glance at the list reveals that Schreiner's proto-feminist work would certainly not have suited the publisher's profile. Morley had been Macmillan's reader since the mid-1860s. He entered the House of Commons in 1883 (later serving as Secretary of State for both Ireland and India), and as an avowed liberal – and Liberal – was a proponent of a doctrine of *gradualism*, believing that progress required both *social energy* and *social patience*. It is not surprising that he found Schreiner's advocacy of radical views anti-thetical to his ideas of progressive moderation.[19] George Macmillan returned the manuscript to 'Ralph Iron' – care of Olive Schreiner, addressed ostensibly as a friend of the author – at an address in the Strand on 1 November, with a letter quoting liberally from the reader's report, and sparing none of its criticism of the unevenness of the writing or the manuscript's 'morbid and sinister' plot. 'We have given this opinion in detail', Macmillan wrote, 'as Mr Iron may be glad to see on what grounds his book is rejected', but he added that the firm would gladly receive any material 'Iron' may care to submit in the future.[20]

Schreiner appears to have taken him at his word: her diary (according to Cronwright-Schreiner) records that she was reading the manuscript of 'Story of an African Farm' at Ventnor, on the Isle of Wight, in the winter of 1881, and it seems she sent it to Macmillan at the end of December 1881. On 19 January 1882 she recorded in her diary that she had sent her 'poor MS.' to Bentley & Sons. On 11 March she wrote that 'Bentley won't take the book' and that she was 'sending it to Smith Elder', but without much hope. An entry for 18 April records her going to 'Remington's' (Remington & Co.), who published on share-profits terms, with authors financing at least some of the publication costs in advance.[21] She later told her friend and mentor Philip Kent, who reviewed *The Story of an African Farm* in *Life* in February 1883, that this firm had 'offered to publish', but only if she ran 'a small share of the risk'; because she felt unable to lose money she 'drew back', taking the manuscript instead to Chapman & Hall.[22] Following the manuscript on its journey from Macmillan to Chapman reveals much about the manner in which the novel was being read by these, its earliest readers.

Morley's report on 'The Story of an African Farm' appreciated Iron's 'description of scenery, of light and colour', and remarked favourably on characterisation ('one feel[s] that the writer is often drawing from life'), but objected strongly that Lyndall ('the young woman who is in place of heroine') was 'so unreal in every respect, and her action is so unrealizable, that the whole effect is marred, the last third or more is horribly mawkish and morbid, as well as fantastically improbable. There is something of originality and interest in the book – but as a whole it is a failure, and a disagreeable one, into the bargain.'[23] Interesting assumptions about realism abound in this passage: Morley commends the author for 'drawing from life', but dismisses the plot as unreal, relying on a requirement for verisimilitude to particular standards of propriety and probability, based on assumptions about femininity, to police the content.

Reports on other manuscripts deemed unsuitable for the Macmillan list in the same period grant further insight into Morley's perceptions of publishable and saleable literature. For one, non-English subject matter was often regarded warily. He declined George Ranken's 'Windabyne: A Lifetime in Australia' in December 1880, describing it as a 'story of colonial life – & really a story of colonial life, not a European story', the Australian '"local colour" … almost too strong'. The report concludes with a damning dismissal: 'It will have a considerable interest for colonists (if colonists buy books). But as literature it is decidedly second rate.' It took Ranken another fifteen years to find a publisher.[24] In May 1881, Morley described Henry Johnston's 'Chronicles of Glenbuckie', containing as it did 'long pages of dialogue in Scotch vernacular', as a 'very real-istically conceived picture of Scottish life', but hence 'on the whole not likely ... to suit the English palate'; its characters, being Scots, were 'people who are in no sense interesting & whom we cannot care about'. Johnston's novel found a publisher only in 1889 – in David Douglas, the Edinburgh firm which had read and rejected the early draft of *The Story of an African Farm* – and soon became constructed as minor, quaintly regional Scottish fiction.[25]

While Schreiner's novel is set far from the fringes of metropolitan England, and its marginal setting thus likely contributed to Morley's judgement, it would undoubtedly have been read, too, with an eye to its suitability for an audience of women readers. Morley had little patience with the 'young lady's romance' – a description he used in refusing Mrs Blathwayt's 'Damaris' in April 1881. Numerous other manuscripts were likewise dismissed for plots judged 'intrinsically unreal & flimsy', 'wild and too sentimental', or 'morbid, unreal & not very agreeable'.[26] Those opinions might all be thought to bear witness to the necessity felt by most mainstream publishers' readers to keep in mind their lists' likely appeal to circulating libraries. Both Mudie's Select Library and W. H. Smith's, the railway stationers, exercised a powerful influence on the methods of production of the mid- and late-Victorian novel and if, as frequently happened, either withdrew from circulation a novel thought likely to corrupt the hypothetical young woman reader, the career of its author could be jeopardised and the reputation – and finances – of its publisher harmed.[27] It was usually sensational fiction and not the romance, the adventure or their increasingly popular amalgam in the imperial romance, though, which most attracted circulating library censure. However, in an indication of the complex structure of the field of publishing, Morley actively sought to avoid association with the circulating library romance, which he thought frivolous and for young ladies alone, declining several manuscripts precisely on the grounds that they were 'full of the conven-tionalities and artificialness of the circulating library romance'.[28] There is, of course, no indication that Morley (or any of the other firms' readers) knew that 'Ralph Iron' was a woman, as she consistently submitted her manuscripts under her male pseudonym. Nonetheless, Morley's report suggests that he guessed the author's gender, and thought the novel unsuit-able on the basis of similar criteria used to dismiss other work, much of it by women (although this is not to suggest that Macmillan did not publish women).[29] The novel was, it seems, doubly condemned, by the standards of the circulating library romance and by those of a publishing house apparently eschewing such romances.

Macmillan returned the manuscript to 'Ralph Iron', and Schreiner appears to have responded under her pseudonym, querying the rejection of a second manuscript, because, on 19 January 1882, the publisher sent another letter to 'Iron' at Ventnor with the following very frank advice:

'We have today seen our adviser on the subject of your letter of the 16th, and in spite of certain qualities in your writing that attracted him he cannot honestly recommend your adopting literature as a profession.'[30] In particular, the letter continued, 'what struck him, and would certainly strike other people, as unpleasant was the action of the heroine in each case, action which was not only not defensible but not even intelligible'.[31] Morley clearly thought that, judged by the conservative consensus about gender roles, both of Schreiner's manuscripts contained highly reprehensible actions. He described 'The Story of an African Farm' as 'mawkish and morbid', the latter a powerful term of aesthetic legislation used, according to Oscar Wilde, in addition to 'immoral' and 'unhealthy', to dismiss challenging new kinds of art.[32] This description recurs in some newspaper appraisals of *The Story of an African Farm*. Arabella Shore, for example, wrote in the *Westminster Review*, in August 1890, that it had 'a soul in it', despite being 'vague, often morbid'.[33] That assessment is marginally more positive than Morley's, yet still bears the full weight of the mainstream popular judgement of material regarded as unpleasant, if not subversive. It was brave indeed of Meredith to recommend Chapman & Hall's publication of a work which he considered might elicit such a response.

Readers' reports have not survived for this period either for Richard Bentley & Sons, or for Smith, Elder, and the only remaining record of the reactions of those publishers to Schreiner's manuscript is a series of letters she wrote to Philip Kent between 8 February and 11 December 1883.[34] Schreiner's account of Michael Bentley's response, in this correspondence, is illuminating: he

> kept the MS. a long time, & then wrote that he would like to see me. I went. He said that three of his readers had read the book and that he had read it through twice himself. That he had never felt such a reluctance in letting a book pass from his hands, but that Lyndall's conduct was highly reprehensible. Of course I couldn't change that ... [35]

While the firm might well have been interested in a novel with a South African setting (they had, after all, published Louisa Hutchinson's *In Tents in the Transvaal* in 1879), Schreiner's manuscript was no travel narrative, and the tenor of novelist Geraldine Jewsbury's nearly contemporaneous reports for the firm indicate the likely reception for subject matter like Schreiner's.[36] Bentley's made a profit by publishing work which appealed to the circulating libraries, so Jewsbury was less likely to reject novels for their appeal to that market but *was* likely to reject those which would offend Mudie's sense of propriety.[37] Schreiner told Kent that she had tried Smith, Elder first, before Macmillan or Bentley, but her husband's report of her diary (although not necessarily correct), and the evidence of the Macmillan Archive, would seem to contradict this.[38] It is clear from several of her letters to Kent that Schreiner was eager to try other work on Smith, Elder, evidently holding the firm (publisher of

Blackmore, Hardy, Gissing, Collins, Rhoda Broughton and Marie Corelli) in high esteem.[39] It routinely sent letters of advice with returned manuscripts, and while its letter to Schreiner does not survive she told Kent that it was 'a long and very kind letter about talent & pathos & originality and all that sort of thing', but 'they couldn't take the book because it was depressing', and the 'English public do not like to be depressed'.[40]

So, having been rejected for publication by Macmillan, Richard Bentley & Sons, and Smith, Elder, the manuscript reached Meredith at Chapman & Hall, his records indicating that he sent the manuscript back to 'Ralph Iron' for revisions on 2 May 1882. Schreiner met Meredith at Chapman & Hall's offices on 1 June, and wrote afterwards that she felt sure the firm would publish the novel.[41] Meredith saw the revisions on 10 August, accepted the manuscript and wrote to Frederic Chapman on 16 August that it was better than others he was reading at the time and that he felt 'compelled to retain it'.[42] He did wonder, however, whether its publication would 'pay' because, while 'the picture is good', 'strong interest seems wanting'.[43] Meredith was as likely to have advised the rejection of a manuscript featuring a shockingly daring female protagonist as of one which appeared old-fashioned – evidenced by his rejecting work by Ouida and by Mrs Lynn Linton, respectively – but he seems to have supported Schreiner's determination not to compromise.[44] She later rejected inferences in the press that she had revised the manuscript in line with his suggestions, and told Havelock Ellis in 1909 that it was Frederic Chapman who had urged her to add 'a few sentences saying that Lyndall was really secretly married' to her lover, because, if she was unmarried, 'the British public would think it wicked, and [W. H.] Smiths, the railway booksellers, would not put it on their stalls'. [45] She explained that Chapman had suggested he spoke 'only out of consideration' for her: 'I was young, and people would think I was not respectable if I wrote such a book, but of course if I insisted on saying she was not married to him it must be so.' She was adamant in her refusal to believe that Meredith, 'who *was* an artist, would ever have made the suggestion to Chapman'.[46]

In January 1883, Chapman sent Schreiner advance copies of the novel, which was published in two volumes at the end of that month, and advertised at 21s in the *Publishers' Circular* in mid-February.[47] Chapman offered Schreiner £10 for the copyright, exerting considerable pressure on her to accept; he argued that he doubted his profit would amount to that much.[48] Chapman also warned her off other publishers, she told Kent: 'he is so sorry [for] me; he knows they will cheat me if they can'. Schreiner later considered that she had been unwise in making 'no arrangement in black and white before the printing of the book'. She stood up to the firm, and Chapman offered £30 for a planned 1,000 copies of a second edition, demanding right of first refusal on Schreiner's next manuscript. This irked Schreiner, who claimed the publisher had reneged on his agreement to pay her five shillings for each copy over 200 sold. She also chafed at the idea of being obliged to return to Chapman, hoping she could play the field more effectively the next time around.[49] The first edition sold out by early May, and on the strength of that success Chapman paid Schreiner £18 2s 11d. She offered to accept £30 for the second edition on condition it would be a 1,000 copies and that the rights would revert to her on its being sold out.[50] The single-volume second edition, the first of many from Chapman (and later from Hutchinson) before the end of the century, was duly advertised for sale at five shillings in the *Publishers' Circular* in mid July 1883.[51]

This single-volume second edition bore a dedication to Schreiner's friend Mary Brown ('my friend Mrs. John Brown of Burnley') and a 'Preface' which sought to direct the reading of the novel and indicate its distance from certain conventions. This sketches 'two methods' by which '[h]uman life may be painted': the 'stage method' (predictable, satisfying and unrealistic), and another, truer to life, in which 'nothing can be prophesied'.[52] Schreiner addresses metropolitan expectations of colonial fiction directly. A kind critic suggested, she writes, that her novel should have been 'a history of wild adventure; of cattle driven into inaccessible "krantzes" by Bushmen; "of encounters with ravening lions, and hair-breadth escapes"'. Such literature was 'best written in Piccadilly or in the Strand', she counters, describing her task as that of the artist who must paint 'what lies before him'.[53] The reality of colonial experience was very different, she suggests, from contemporary generic, and specifically metropolitan, expectations.

Contested spaces: disaggregating the metropolis

On a green cloth binding, the two volumes of the January 1883 first edition feature the title and author's pseudonym in gold lettering on the spine, along with a black ostrich and a palm frond-like ostrich plume. The cover illustration depicts an arid, mountainous landscape, framed by a palm tree which, while slightly out of place on the fictional Karoo farm of the novel, evokes an exotic landscape doubtless calculated to appeal to British readers of colonial romance or travel writing. Some of Schreiner's most sympathetic critics, however, complained that the expectations created by the title and cover were not of high romance, but of colonial agricultural economics. As early as 1883, Edward Aveling expressed the hope that the 'cumbersome title of this very remarkable work' would not 'frighten away readers', suggesting that 'Mr. – or is it Miss? – Ralph Iron would have done more wisely in this helter-skelter age of helter-skelter reading had she invented a name for her book more likely to arrest popular attention'.[54] Canon McColl's long review in the *Spectator* in 1887 apologised to its readers for the late notice given to the novel, excusing the oversight by explaining that 'the title of the book misled us. It seems to promise information about the rearing and management of

bullocks and ostriches.'[55] W. J. Dawson remarked in 1891: 'People imagined it had something to do with ostrich-farming, possibly with
gold-discoveries or diamond-mining, and the average novel-reader let the
book severely alone'; most readers were 'not careful to inform themselves
on matters which relate to the distant dependencies of the empire', he
wrote, 'and the title of this book suggested colonial statistics rather than
romance'.[56]

Schreiner's was one of two novels published in London in 1883
purporting to be stories of a farm in the Karoo. The cover iconography of
Mrs Carey-Hobson's *The Farm in the Karoo; or, What Charley Vyvyan
and His Friends Saw in South Africa* bears a striking resemblance to that
of Schreiner's novel, although its differences are highly significant.[57] A
single volume in green-cloth binding, Carey-Hobson's novel also features
an illustration, in black, of a palm tree snaking up the left side of the front
cover. This palm, however, bears coconuts or dates, and spreads an
improbably long frond over the top of the cover, against which the short
title is emblazoned in gold lettering. Bushes on the horizon approximate
the shape of the mountains on the cover of *The Story of an African Farm*,
but the latter's mysterious emptiness contrasts with this cartoonish illustration of a mounted hunter shooting an elephant. The spine repeats the
short title and the author's name above an illustration of a black man, in
Western dress, carrying a rifle.[58] Unlike Schreiner's, Carey-Hobson's cover
suggests a peopled landscape, although one even less Karoo-like than that
depicted on the cover of *The Story of an African Farm*, and one which has
no apparent value apart from being a staging ground for imperial adventure.

Mary Ann Carey-Hobson (1832–1911) was born in Britain and taken
to the Cape aged 12. She returned to Britain on the death of her second
husband, in 1873, settling in London and becoming known as a writer,
editor and promoter of South African colonial life.[59] Coincidentally, her
manuscript had been rejected by Macmillan at approximately the same
time as Schreiner's. Dismissing it as merely a lacklustre account of young
men going out to the South African colonies to take up ostrich farming
(the original title was 'Ostrich Farming'), its reader (again, probably
Morley) criticised its 'gushing style', noted that its subject was 'not really
very new', and suggested that it was unlikely 'to add to the reputation of
the firm'.[60]

Both Schreiner's setting and that suggested by Carey-Hobson's title
would not have been wholly unfamiliar to the English reader. Ostrich
farming featured in travel narratives like Anthony Trollope's *South Africa*
(published by Chapman & Hall in 1876); Schreiner's allegorical 'A Dream
of Wild Bees' would be published in *Woman's World*, in 1888, in the same
issue as Miss Bessie Wood's heavily illustrated account of 'A Visit to a
South African Ostrich Farm'.[61] The contrast between these two 'Karoo'
novels is as striking as the manner in which the covers are constructed to

2.1 Mrs Carey-Hobson's *The Farm in the Karoo*, 1883

exploit different aspects – and their titles arguably the same aspect – of an almost uniformly conceived exoticism. Schreiner's depiction of Waldo's crises of faith, Gregory Rose's 'womanhood' and Lyndall's passionate rejection of girls' education, marriage and patriarchy in all its forms is in stark contrast to Carey-Hobson's discourse of masculine adventure. The latter's Africa is one of wild animals, noble savages and vigorous, honest settlers. Schreiner's farm is tentatively inhabited by introspective characters struggling with much larger issues. It features brutalised and hence understandably ignoble native servants, ruthless opportunists like Blenkins and effete cynics like Waldo's stranger. And, ironically, the novel of masculine adventure was expressly presented as a female production, while Schreiner presented her novel under a male pseudonym, and one calculated to suggest a firm, masculine disposition, one which would allow her to escape the expectations of a young ladies' or circulating library romance, and to write the kind of serious account of 'what lies before him' for which she argued in her Preface. 'Ralph Iron', of course, and the names 'Waldo' and 'Em', also echo Ralph Waldo Emerson, a strong influence on Schreiner.

Four years after the first two 1883 editions, a 'new edition' included Schreiner's name in parentheses after her pseudonym on the title page, for the first time. All Chapman & Hall editions between 1887 and the 1892 shilling edition included the title and both Schreiner's pseudonym and name, in that order, on the covers. Hutchinson used only 'Olive Schreiner' on the spine, but, like Chapman & Hall after 1887, retained both name and pseudonym on the title page. In its 1896 edition, Hutchinson included a photograph of Schreiner, printed above her signature, between the half-title and title pages (facing the title page), emphasising her gendered identity.[62] While one might consider the retention of the pseudonym unnecessary, the novel had arguably acquired a reputation – or notoriety – which required it to be marketed as it had first appeared and become known, and the name 'Ralph Iron' appears at this point still to have been as much a part of the work's identity as its title.

It is a critical commonplace that nineteenth-century women writers adopted male pseudonyms to overcome prejudices in the publishing and literary circles of the day. However, as Alexis Easley suggests, women writers' 'manipulation of authorial gender' participated in a wider controversy about the nature of authorship in Victorian culture: most Victorian women writers did *not* use pseudonyms, while many of those who *did* used *female* pseudonyms, or published anonymously.[63] Quite how Schreiner conceived of her pseudonym, particularly after her identity became widely known, is open to speculation. It is certainly clear that Chapman & Hall knew she was a woman before publishing her novel, although Chapman appeared to think that using her real name would have its advantages. In December 1883, Schreiner had written to Kent: 'I shall certainly stick to my nom de plume. Mr. C[hapman]'s idea is that if it were known as the work of a girl from the Cape it would be more read and more gently reviewed. That is just what I don't want. It must stand on its own merits, and fall by its own faults.'[64] She repeated those sentiments, in May 1884, to Henry Norman, who had reviewed her novel in the *Fortnightly Review* in December 1883: 'the more a book is left to stand alone, without any kind of external help, the better', she argued; 'I always think that if I were a great writer I should like each book to be brought out under a new name so that it got no help from its forerunners, and stood or fell alone.'[65] This appears slightly naive; it remains unclear whether the continued use of the pseudonym, even alongside Schreiner's real name (once her identity became known), was on the author's or her publishers' insistence. The woman writer was conventionally portrayed either as engaged in commercial writing, captivated by the promise of economic reward, or as a genius embodying a claim to intellectual equality with men – a claim, however, which set her apart from other women because she became expressly *not* like them. A male pseudonym could protect a woman writer's female identity 'from the tarnish of the marketplace' and preserve her claim to possess a 'disinterested, universal voice marked with the stamp of Romantic genius', Judd suggests.[66] It is possible that Schreiner cannily exploited this potential.

Professional writers like Charlotte Brontë and Mary Ann Evans (or Marianne Evans Lewes, as she sometimes styled herself) did not expect their pseudonyms – Currer Bell and George Eliot – to disguise their identities, but saw them as masks assumed for specific reasons.[67] Easley suggests that Evans employed her pseudonym early 'as a means of capitalizing on the public's desire to know and to gender authorial identity'; in place of revealing details about her private life, she gave the public 'the unknowable "George Eliot", who expressed a cultured rather than essentially gendered perspective on moral questions'.[68] It is remarkable how often during the period Schreiner was contrasted with George Eliot, and, as a corollary, compared with Charlotte Brontë. In the February 1891 issue of the *Young Man*, W. J. Dawson, one of the magazine's editors, wrote of *The Story of an African Farm* that a 'stronger note of passion had not been struck since Charlotte Brontë died'. Whereas George Eliot was supremely an artist, Dawson argued, both Brontë and Schreiner wrote novels which were really 'autobiographies and their creations the mouths through which their own souls find utterance'.[69] Brontë was often, as here, figured as a woman of excessive passions and Eliot, of excessive intellect. Schreiner herself participated in this performance of difference from Eliot, writing to Havelock Ellis in April 1889 that no one's 'feelings could possibly be further removed with regard to artistic work' than hers and Eliot's. While Eliot's 'great desire was to teach', Schreiner's, she claimed, was 'to express [her]self' for herself 'alone'.[70]

Willing her work to stand or fall independently of the author's proper name, and suggesting (by distancing herself from Eliot) that she wrote for herself alone (in the nature of a passionate genius like Brontë), Schreiner's use of a pseudonym, at least initially, may also evidence a deep anxiety about the public consumption of deeply personal work. She wrote to Havelock Ellis in 1889:

> The thought that hundreds of thousands will read my work does offend me and hinder me, not because I wish to teach them, but because terrible as it is to show them my work at all, the thought of throwing it to them to be trodden underfoot is double desecration of it ... It was like a knife in my heart to-day when I

saw *An African Farm* stuck up in a window. I get to loathe it when I think of how many people have read it.[71]

However, Schreiner also seems almost contradictorily to have desired the widest possible circulation. In 1890, Chapman & Hall issued the novel in its Shilling Select Library, its first promotion in a series in Britain, and it was reprinted in that series in 1891 and 1892. Schreiner was delighted at reductions in price, and claimed in 1892 that she had 'insisted' on the novel being published at a shilling because she intended it 'for working men', and 'wanted to feel sure boys like Waldo could buy a copy, and feel they were not alone'.[72] During the previous year, and at Chapman's request, she allowed an edition of the novel to be printed at 3s 6d, she explained to Unwin, publisher of her 1890 *Dreams*, because she 'felt sure most poor lads would have it within reach' at that price. [73] Schreiner's views on pricing were reiterated that year in a letter to Edward Carpenter about 'a cheap [2s] edition' of the novel: 'I'm glad because the only people I really care to read it are people struggling with *material* want and the narrowness and iron pressure of their surroundings who won't be so likely to get a more expensive book.'[74] She had previously demonstrated a concern for the affordability of literature she felt might contribute to uplifting the disadvantaged in a review of Karl Pearson's *The Ethic of Freethought* in the *Pall Mall Gazette* in January 1889, arguing that its price (12s) was 'prohibitive', especially for women.[75] How to account for these apparent contradictions is unclear. Was Schreiner a naïve idealist at sea in the stormy world of Victorian publishing and public opinion or a canny player of the field, performing apparently wildly fluctuating roles, each calculated to appeal to different constituencies' constructions of writer, woman writer, colonial writer?

Schreiner was certainly aware of the role of reviewers in the process of effecting literary reputation and legislating literariness and meaning: she wrote to Pearson in 1886 that the press was 'manifestly becoming the governing and ruling power'.[76] Joseph Bristow credits Henry Norman's December 1883 review of *The Story of an African Farm* with producing early 'a huge amount of interest in Schreiner's exceptionally innovative novel' in Britain, but while Norman's was the first review to appear in a comparatively widely read publication, the novel received two earlier notices which situated it in radical political contexts.[77] A lengthy extract from Lyndall's discussion of the subjection of women, along with an appreciative review, appeared in August 1883 in the radical *Englishwoman's Review* (its very title disavowing the genteel associations of 'lady' for 'woman', much as Wilde had done in changing the *Lady's* to the *Woman's World*). If Ralph Iron's portrayal of the narrowness of women's education in the Cape was accurate, the reviewer remarked, it demonstrated that 'the Colony has quite as necessary lessons to learn as the mother country'.[78] The second was Edward Aveling's review in *Progress, a Monthly Magazine of Advanced Thought*, where it appeared

in the second issue, in September 1883, alongside articles critical of capitalism and the Church of England, and an article by Eleanor Marx (Karl's
daughter, Aveling's lover and Schreiner's friend) on the political underground in Russia.[79] This was the kind of journal whose readers would
most definitely have empathised with Lyndall and Waldo. Aveling down-
played the novel's setting on the colonial periphery, arguing that, despite
'not a little local colouring' and passages and words that were uniquely
South African, 'the events and the thoughts recorded in the two volumes
might, with but slight modification, be recorded of an Indian bungalow or
an English homestead'.[80] Gesturing towards a Marxist view of religion as
false consciousness, Aveling commended those who wrote 'from that
entirely irreligious standpoint that is to be the foundation of all thought-
ful men and women of the coming generations'; it was in its engagement
with religion, he felt, that *The Story of an African Farm* would interest
most readers of *Progress*.[81] The novel's geographical setting, in other
words, was not as important as its potential for being enlisted in an
overtly political argument.

   Norman's praise for *The Story of an African Farm* came in his essay
'Theories and Practices of Modern Fiction' in the *Fortnightly Review* on 1
December 1883, some ten months after the publication of Schreiner's
novel. Norman attempted to assess the status of contemporary critical
theories of the novel, glossing over 'foreign theories' with passing references to Zola, Howells and James, before claiming that the most
memorable setting he had ever encountered was 'that *African Farm*': 'a
weary flat plain of red sand, broken only by a solitary hillock and a clump
or two of prickly pear-trees' with herdboy, sheep and ostriches in the
distance.[82] Norman praised the novel for engaging widely with a host of
contested issues, from religion to women's suffrage, and for offering the
'unspeakable relief' of an 'escape from the domains of the ordinary novelist – from Hamburg and the Highlands, from yachts, clubs, hansoms, and
Piccadilly'. It was what might be called 'the *Romance of the New Ethics*',
he suggested, figuring the novel both as a new – an ethical – kind of
romance and as a kind of *anti*-romance, breaking with what he portrays
as the 'ordinary' novelist's obsession with frivolity and escapism.[83] The
cover of the 1887 (third) edition of the novel both declared itself '*A
Romance*' and retained the original subtitle, *A Novel*, on its title page.[84]
These acts of labelling clearly implicated Schreiner's work in a highly
contested field, one in which the novel's setting and Schreiner's status as a
colonial writer were either ignored or used as excuses to cite the novel in
support of various positions. There were, for the readers of Schreiner's
novel in the 1880s and the 1890s, multiple systems of expectation, the
definitions of which were, themselves, contested. The manner in which the
meanings of *The Story of an African Farm* were repeatedly renegotiated
by different reading strategies and institutions of reading evidences a
multipolar metropolis, less unified and coherent than conventionally

represented, which 'needs to be disaggregated' (Laura Chrisman urges), 'seen not as a homogeneous unit, but ... composed of different and competing interest groups, institutions, and classes, whose ideological relationship to imperialism' – and anything else, for that matter – was extremely varied.[85]

A woman's novel? Schreiner's readers

Judging from the frequency with which *The Story of an African Farm* was reviewed in the late nineteenth century, it is clear that it maintained a sustained presence in the public mind. It is nonetheless difficult to ascertain who exactly was reading it. A short review of Schreiner's *Trooper Peter Halket of Mashonaland* (an allegorical 'novel' attacking Cecil Rhodes and his British South Africa Company), in the *Saturday Review* in April 1897, recalled that *The Story of an African Farm* had 'created a considerable amount of interest in literary circles' and enjoyed both 'a bookstall and public library success'.[86] Records show that the novel was added to the lending section of the public libraries of Newcastle-upon-Tyne, between 1887 and 1889, and of Battersea, in 1890, while Fulham Public Libraries' 1899 catalogue lists the 1890 shilling edition.[87] Needless to say, it was not considered appropriate for – or, at least, actively encouraged by – parish lending libraries. Minister's wife Caroline Hallett included a list of suitable books in a volume entitled *Parish Lending Libraries: How to Manage and Keep Them Up*. Beecher Stowe's *Uncle Tom's Cabin*, Haggard's *King Solomon's Mines*, numerous Dickens titles, Gaskell's *Life of Charlotte Brontë* (but no novels by the Brontës themselves) are included, but Schreiner's novel is not.[88] No early editions remain in the Grahamstown Public Library's collection, which was one of the Cape Colony's largest, Grahamstown having been the second city after Cape Town prior to Kimberley's rapid expansion after the diamond rush in the 1870s.[89]

In addition to lists of other books on the publisher's list, the 1891 Chapman & Hall Shilling Library edition, housed in the Bodleian Library, contains advertisements for settlers for an irrigation scheme on Australia's Murray River, Aspinall's enamel and Eno's Fruit Salts. Not only had this volume entered into processes of exchange between publisher and reader but had become a vehicle for other commercial exchanges. The advertisements are explained by an embossed stamp declaring the book the property of 'WH SMITH & SON / LONDON'. This, along with entries for the first edition in Mudie's annual catalogues between 1888 and 1893, confirms that *The Story of an African Farm* had clearly made its way into the stock of the circulating libraries, despite Chapman's concerns.[90] Havelock Ellis recalled encountering Schreiner's novel as a circulating-library volume, and playwright and pamphleteer Laurence Housman remembered having 'appalled' his Worcestershire community by ordering it through the local circulating library.[91] It seems probable that Schreiner's novel, despite its agnosticism, unmarried mother and indictment of the treatment of women, was regarded by Mudie's readers as sufficiently exotic, picturesque or contemplative to qualify as a romance of the lending-library species. These varying interpretations illustrate how contrary interests and differently nuanced reading strategies constructed texts in very different ways, producing readings which both determined and were complicated by the critical language with which the text would be encountered by its early readers – critics, library patrons, ordinary readers purchasing any of a number of differently packaged editions, and readers of newspapers and magazines in which extracts from the novel were published.

One of the most significant constructions, of course, despite Schreiner's attempts to disguise her gender, was that of the developing genre of the novel of the 'new woman'. In his *Review of Reviews* in July 1894, W. T. Stead featured not the usual single book of the month, but an essay on a new genre, 'The Novel of the Modern Woman', under a large photograph of Olive Schreiner and her husband tending sheep on their farm in the Karoo. Stead called Schreiner a 'Modern Woman, *par excellence*, the founder and high priestess of the school', and declared *The Story of an African Farm* 'the forerunner of all the novels of the Modern Woman'. These were not merely by women about women, Stead explained, but also written 'from the standpoint of Woman'; many women's novels had 'hitherto considered women either from the general standpoint of society or from the man's standpoint, which comes, in the long run, to pretty much the same thing', he suggested.[92]

Initially a staunch supporter of British policy in Southern Africa and defender of Rhodes, but later an opponent of the Anglo-Boer War, Stead had been a friend of Schreiner's since her first residence in Britain.[93] He wrote in July 1891, in a review of her article 'Stray Thoughts on South Africa', that just as there was 'only one Rhodes in South Africa', there was 'only one Olive Schreiner' and that the Cape Colony had been 'fortunate indeed in producing a statesman to make history and a writer of genius to record it'.[94] His 1894 announcement of the 'new woman' novel reiterated this opinion, claiming that the Cape was a 'pivot of the Empire' which had 'done yeoman's service to the English-speaking world' in producing its 'most pronounced type of Imperial Man and of the Emancipated Woman': Rhodes and Schreiner.[95] Stead's claim was ambitious, but indicates the extent to which Schreiner's contribution to the idea of a Greater Britain was being constructed in some quarters, negating the radical nature of the critique of imperialism and patriarchy in *The Story of an African Farm*. It was doubly remarkable, Stead suggested, that what was 'in many respects the most distinctive note of the literature of the last decade of the nineteenth century' had come from the pen of a young woman 'reared in the solemn stillness of the Karoo, in the solitude of the African bush'.[96] It is

THE BOOK OF THE MONTH.

THE NOVEL OF THE MODERN WOMAN.*

"It is a subject," murmured Strange, with a slight movement of the shoulders, "which I must admit I find painful to discuss with young ladies."
"Ah," said Alison, in her quiet, serious voice, "but then I am not a 'young lady.' I am only a woman taking a great deal of interest in others of my own sex."—"*The Story of a Modern Woman.*" Page 205.

THE Novel of the Modern Woman is one of the most notable and significant features of the fiction of the day. The Modern Woman novel is not merely a novel written by a woman, or a novel written about women, but it is a novel written by a woman about women from the standpoint of Woman. Many women have written novels about their own sex, but they have tributed to the perfecting or the marring of the said heroes' domestic peace and conjugal felicity. The woman in fiction, especially when the novelist was a woman, has been the ancillary of the man, important only from her position of appendage or complement to the "predominant partner." But in the last year or two the Modern Woman has changed all that. Woman at last

OLIVE SCHREINER AND HER HUSBAND COUNTING THE AFRICANDER SHEEP OUT IN THE EARLY MORNING AT KRANTZ PLAATS.

hitherto considered women either from the general standpoint of society or from the man's standpoint, which comes, in the long run, to pretty much the same thing. For in fiction there has not been, until comparatively recently, any such thing as a distinctively woman's standpoint. The heroines in women's novels, until comparatively recently, were almost invariably mere addenda to the heroes, and important only so far as they con-

has found Woman interesting to herself, and she has studied her, painted her, and analysed her as if she had an independent existence, and even, strange to say, a soul of her own. This astonishing phase of the evolution of the race demands attention and will reward study. It bewilders some, angers others, and interests all. In place, therefore, of describing any one book of the month I propose to devote this article to a rapid glance at some of the more prominent of the novels of the Modern Woman, illustrating it with their portraits, and giving, wherever it is possible, their own statement in their own words of the message which in their novels they sought to deliver to the British public.

The Modern Woman, *par excellence*, the founder and high priestess of the school, is Olive Schreiner. Her "Story of an African Farm" has been the forerunner of all the novels of the Modern Woman. What a

* "The Story of an African Farm," by Olive Schreiner. (Hutchinson.) 3s. 6d.
"The Daughters of Danaus," by Mona Caird.
"Dr. Janet of Harley Street," by Arabella Kenealy. (Digby.) 2s.
"The Heavenly Twins," by Sarah Grand. (Heinemann.) 6s.
"The Superfluous Woman." (Heinemann.) 6s.
"Keynotes," by George Egerton. (Mathews.) 6s.
"The Yellow Aster," by Iota. (Hutchinson.) 6s.
"The Story of a Modern Woman," by Ella Hepworth Dixon. (Heinemann.) 6s.
"Joanna Traill, Spinster," by Annie E. Holdsworth. (Heinemann.) 3s. net.
"A Sunless Heart." Two volumes. Ward and Lock. 21s.

2.2 'The Book of the Month: The Novel of the Modern Woman', July 1894

ironic, of course, that Schreiner had published it under a man's name, although, as noted, her name appeared on all copies printed after 1887.

Schreiner prepared the way for other writers of 'new woman' novels, like Mona Caird, Sarah Grand and George Egerton, all active in the later 1880s and the 1890s. Her influence on later generations of suffragettes and feminists was also profound, *Woman and Labour* (1911), her proto-feminist treatise, enjoying widespread influence.[97] Research into canon formation does not adequately explain why novels such as Schreiner's enjoyed consistent popularity in Britain at and after the turn of the century; exclusive focus on institutional evaluative processes like formal reviews, works of literary criticism or school curricula, obscures the role of what Ann Ardis calls the 'semi-underground economy that kept books such as *The Story of an African Farm* passing from hand to hand in the early years of the twentieth century'.[98] It is almost impossible to reconstruct networks of friendships and reading groups, operating by word of mouth, by which the novel's reputation was sustained in Britain, and the extent to which it made as great an impression on South African women is even more difficult to ascertain. Constance Barnicoat attempted to canvas the reading habits of the 'colonial girl' in an article published in the journal *The Nineteenth Century and After* in late 1906. She suggests that '*The Story of a South African Farm*' – the misquotation suggests the extent to which the novel was for British readers allied with the country – was 'rarely, if ever, cited' by South Africans.[99] The expectation that it would have been reveals the extent to which its reputation in Britain, as a proto-feminist text, may have been higher than in South Africa.

On 'purport[ing] to portray South African life': novels and nations

Just how 'South African', then, was Schreiner's work considered to be *in* South Africa? Manfred Nathan, in his seminal survey of the fledgling Union of South Africa's literary heritage, *The South African Commonwealth* (1919), lamented that there was 'no South African Thomas Hardy to describe … life as it is lived on the lone steadings and mysterious farms of the vast Karroo [*sic*]' despite 'a host of women writers' having 'purported to portray South African life' and the country having been 'the scene of many a novel "best written in Piccadilly or in the Strand"'.[100] While judging literary work produced in or about the Union and its predecessor colonies and territories with a specific British exemplar in mind, it is noteworthy that Nathan quotes from Schreiner's Preface to *The Story of an African Farm* without acknowledging his source, and that he does so in order to dismiss the same kinds of novels she dismisses. Nathan assumes that to write about the Karoo – as Schreiner did – is the test of the nation's (or region's) literature, but it is unclear whether the apparent lack he detects indicates a dismissal of Schreiner's attempt to write about this landscape and whether she is included among the 'host of women writers' who have merely 'purported' to capture the country in fiction. When Nathan does mention Schreiner elsewhere, it is in a deeply ambivalent manner: noting that she was 'described by the late W. T. Stead as "the only woman of genius South Africa has ever produced"', he refuses himself to say if he thinks 'she answers to these descriptions'.[101]

Schreiner died in 1921, and Nathan's 1925 *South African Literature* was more generous. In its 'earnest discussion of the deepest problems of life ... bold treatment of psychological and sex-relationships, and in the keen delineation of character', he claimed, *The Story of an African Farm* had 'not been surpassed by any South African writer, not even by the gifted authoress herself'.[102] By qualifying his praise in the final clause, Nathan both avoids praising the novel (it has merely not been surpassed) and echoes an impression of Schreiner which had become commonplace since her death, that she was endlessly frustrated in her efforts to write a worthy successor to her most famous novel. It thus becomes something of a freak, a one-off 'South African' novel, the product of hysterical genius. Schreiner's widower, Samuel Cronwright-Schreiner, was primarily to blame for this characterisation. His strangely qualified hagiographic biography of his late wife and his Introduction to a new Fisher Unwin edition of *The Story of an African Farm*, published in 1924, and his edition of her *Letters* (1925), represented Schreiner as frail, selfish and naïve, and exercised a decisive influence on her subsequent reputation. Cronwright-Schreiner also destroyed many of Schreiner's letters and diaries after publishing his *Life* and *Letters*; her friends called the former Cronwright-Schreiner's novel about his wife.[103] Incidentally, just as he seeks in his *Life* to form and inform Schreiner's reputation, so his 1924 Introduction encroaches on the text of her novel: the Fisher Unwin edition's contents page inexplicably lists it under the heading for the first part of the novel, an order (and introduction) which became standard for the next thirty years.[104]

By the late 1920s, it had become a critical commonplace – abroad – that *The Story of an African Farm* was, despite its flaws, distinctively 'South African'. Schreiner's name, too, had become inextricably linked to the South African landscape. In 1925, an article in *Vogue* extolled the wonders of the country in the language of adventure, promise and wide open space so often used in connection with southern-hemisphere dominions. Schreiner's name came early in a revealing list of associations:

> Orange-farms, kopjes, Olive Schreiner, outspanning, Hottentots, illicit diamond-buying, sjamboks, stoeps, Oom Paul, Table Mountain, kraals, General Smuts, Groote Schuur, ostriches, Bulawayo, and the Taungs skull – some such confused sequence of images is likely to flit across the brains of most people in England at the mention of South Africa.[105]

In 1929, Winifred Holtby declared, in an article in the London *Bookman* entitled 'Writers of South Africa' which carried on its first page a photograph of Schreiner reading, that Schreiner was the 'first and greatest of South African writers'.[106] Francs Brett Young wrote in the same year in the *London Mercury* that while 'the earliest stages' of 'the literary evolution of what condescending Europeans are pleased to call "new countries"' were 'usually barren', Schreiner's most famous novel had made a beginning which, while '[p]erhaps, after all ... not very great', was, 'at least, South African'.[107] Frank Harris, man of letters and one-time editor of the *Fortnightly Review*, writing in the same year, but reminiscing about meeting Schreiner in Chapman & Hall's offices in 1883, recalls being entranced by the novel, his language emphasising exoticism (the 'witchery of the high veldt', 'the strange barbaric land', 'the entrancing climate', 'intoxicating air', 'fairy sunsets and magic sunrisings'),[108] his recollection encoding multiple responses to Schreiner's African setting and her apparently representative characters – romantic and modern, alien and strangely, disconcertingly familiar – evident in many early reviews which used Schreiner's gender alongside her novel's African setting in qualifying their praise, or to offer condescending excuses for the novel's supposed failure to meet metropolitan expectations.

Introducing a new catalogue of books from and for sale to the colonies in September 1887, Edward Augustus Petherick made clear that his *Colonial Book Circular and Bibliographical Record* was intended to illuminate readers at home and abroad, offering a guide to the thousands of titles published annually. For this endeavour he chose an epigraph from Sir Richard Steele, likening 'knowledge of books' to 'a torch in the hand', showing to the 'bewildered the way which leads to their prosperity and welfare'.[109] The epigraph appeared on the cover of the second number, flanking an engraving which had appeared alone on the front of the first: Mercury, bearing a pouch, flying from right to left, from a seascape with a ship in full sail making for port, into a library. It is tempting to invent a narrative for the engraving, featuring the transmission of knowledge as a

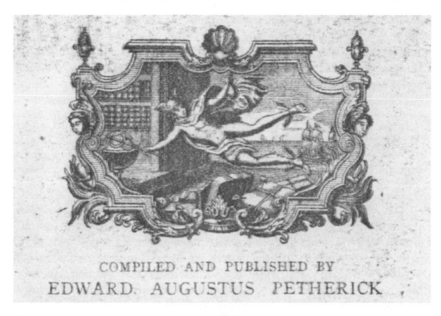

2.3   *Colonial Book Circular and Bibliographical Record* illustration,
September 1887

valuable commercial commodity across borders, from colonies – zones of trade and exploration – to the book-lined studies of London. The magazine was entitled the *Torch and Colonial Book Circular* for its second number, in which Petherick explained that his chief field of business was the foreign market.[110] Petherick was attempting to acquire a share of a new market, one in which several publishers issued series of cheap editions of books for sale to the colonies.[111] Chapman & Hall's Shilling Library edition of *The Story of an African Farm*, while never, it seems, issued expressly in a colonial edition, was listed in Petherick's catalogue in an advertisement displayed prominently on the rear cover of the edition dated 31 December 1888 and appears again in the catalogue on 30 March 1889.[112] Apart from hinting briefly at the network through which Schreiner's novel was distributed, the symbolic function of Petherick's publication is useful here in suggesting Schreiner's implication in the process of the dissemination of literature to the furthest reaches of the English-speaking world. It was part of the cargo of light exported (back) to the world's darker places, just as its author and her work had travelled in the other direction.

Schreiner's identity is complicated by her status as radical thinker, proto-feminist and suffragette, pacifist and advocate of native rights, by her ambivalent relations both to the Cape Colony (and subsequently to the Union of South Africa) and to Britain. Moreover, her writing's experimental formal aspects deconstruct metropolitan descriptions of the colonial periphery and rework tropes of the imperial romance.[113] Carolyn Burdett argues, citing Schreiner's oeuvre as evidence, that 'the so-called "margins" were often more central than the "centre" in articulating and enacting what might loosely be called issues of modernity'.[114] Schreiner was concerned to negotiate sexual identity, hybrid national affiliations and post-religious ethics, and to find forms of articulation adequate to the task of representing those urgent explorations in South Africa and in Britain. Like its characters, the novel itself crossed boundaries and asserted hybrid identities; in Judith Raiskin's words, Schreiner was a 'Creole' writer, the term proving useful for its suggestion of contact between cultures and for problematising 'the surrounding colonial vocabulary of nationality and racial identity'.[115]

Nations emerging out of empires have sought to write their identities in literature, finding a voice and making their own those genres apparently conceived, validated and authored in the former imperial centre(s). Nevertheless, the capacity of the novel in particular to represent *nations* has made it (Deidre Lynch and William Warner suggest) 'a relay for transnational exchange, in a way that challenges the monopolies on representation sometimes claimed at the metropolitan centre'.[116] The South African colonies were only a few faltering steps along what would prove to be an uncommonly rocky path to legitimate nationhood when Schreiner's novel came to enjoy early success. *The Story of an African*

Farm has subsequently been cast as among the most important early texts in a putative Anglophone 'South African' literary canon. Insofar as it has been constructed as a founding text of a notional national literary tradition, its reputation, like that of its author, has undergone endless mutation 'for new phases of South African life', in Cherry Clayton's words. By 1968, for example, in his Introduction to a selection from Schreiner's writing published in South Africa, Afrikaans writer Uys Krige could call her 'both poet and prophet, and a truly great South African' with little fear of contradiction.[117]

Notes

1 For biographical details see: First and Scott, *Schreiner*; Schoeman, *Schreiner* and *Only an Anguish*; Stanley, *Imperialism*; Van der Vlies, 'Olive Schreiner'.

2 Schreiner, *The Story of an African Farm* (1989), 309; multiple editions of the novel are referred to as *SAF* (date) hereafter.

3 *Ibid.*, 7; see Genette, *Paratexts*.

4 Schreiner, *SAF* (1995). Oerder (1867–1944), a Dutch artist, was based in the South African Republic (Transvaal) between 1890 and 1908: Alexander and Cohen, *150 South African Paintings*, 38–9.

5 Schreiner, *SAF* (1975 and 1986).

6 Schreiner, *SAF* (1987); for Waldo's reference to Bushman paintings, see *SAF* (January 1883), vol. 1, 39, or (1992), 16.

7 Schreiner, *SAF* (1992).

8 Bristow, Introduction, viii; see Green, 'Stability and Flux', 160.

9 Barash (ed.), cover, iv (dedication), 229–33 (chronology); see Gordimer, 'The Prison-House of Colonialism'. First was also an anti-apartheid lawyer and activist, spouse of the South African Communist Party's Joe Slovo, and had only recently been assassinated, in exile, by South African government agents.

10 Chrisman, 'Transnational Productions', 4–6.

11 Monsman, *Olive Schreiner's Fiction*, 48.

12 McGann, *The Textual Condition*, 11, 9.

13 Jauss, *Toward an Aesthetic*, 22.

14 Tuchman mentions the reader's report in a short note: *Edging Women Out*, 216.

15 Cronwright-Schreiner, *Life*, 146–7; see also Voss, 'Revisions of Early Editions', 3–4.

16 Matz, 'George Meredith', 288; see Ravilious, 'Saints and Sinners', 1, 10.

17 Macmillan Archive, British Library, London (MABL), MS Add. 55935, Anon. (Morley), 'Saints and Sinners'.

18 Sutherland, *Victorian Novelists*, 119; see Morgan, *House of Macmillan*.

19 Gross, *Rise and Fall*, 120, quoting Morley's *On Compromise* (1874); see also 120–6, and Tuchman, *Edging Women Out*, 69–72.

20 MABL, MS Add. 55413, Macmillan & Co., 1 November 1881.

21 Cronwright-Schreiner, *Life*, 153; on Remington, see Eggert, '*Robbery Under Arms*', 129.

22 Cronwright-Schreiner, *Life*, 152, 153; Harry Ransom Humanities Research Center, University of Texas at Austin (HRHRC), Schreiner to Kent, 19 April

1883. All HRHRC material quoted with permission, Harry Ransom Humanities Research Center, University of Texas at Austin. See Anon. (Kent), 'The Story of an African Farm'.

23 MABL, MS Add. 55935, Anon. (Morley), 'Story of an African Farm'.

24 *Ibid.*, 'Windabyne', 30, 31; Ranken, *Windabyne*.

25 MABL, MS Add. 55935, Anon. (Morley), 'Chronicles of Glenbuckie', 59. Johnston published at least four novels set in Scotland.

26 MABL, MS Add. 55935, Anon. (Morley), 'Damaris', 'Wild Birds of Kileevy', 'Princess Eithne'.

27 See Flint, 'Victorian Novel', 27; Flint, *Woman Reader*, 149; Griest, *Mudie's*, 120, 137, 257.

28 MABL, MS Add. 55935, Anon. (Morley), 'A Woman's Love'.

29 Male authors submitted more novels than female authors, but women were equally likely to be published: Tuchman, *Edging Women Out*, 57–8.

30 MABL, MS Add. 55413, Macmillan & Co., 19 January 1882.

31 *Ibid.*

32 Wilde, *Soul of Man*, 36.

33 Shore, 'Modern English Novels', 149.

34 Bentley's readers' reports in the British Library cease in 1876; the Smith, Elder Archive at the National Library of Scotland holds no readers' reports.

35 First and Scott, *Schreiner*, 120–1; HRHRC, Schreiner to Kent, 19 April 1883.

36 First and Scott note, for example, that Jewsbury regarded a novel about a secret marriage in Sicily as clever, but unpleasant: *Schreiner*, 117–18.

37 Tuchman, *Edging Women Out*, 81; see also 80.

38 HRHRC, Schreiner to Kent, 19 April 1883.

39 See Huxley, *Smith Elder*, 230; Sutherland, *Victorian Novelists*, 3.

40 HRHRC, Schreiner to Kent, 19 April 1883.

41 Cronwright-Schreiner, *Life*, 153.

42 Meredith, *Letters*, 669.

43 *Ibid.*, 669–70; see Matz, 'George Meredith', 288; Voss, 'Revisions', 2.

44 Vann, 'Chapman and Hall', 95–109, 102–3.

45 Cronwright-Schreiner, *Life*, 156.

46 *Ibid.*, and see 153–6. Despite Schreiner's protestations, it continued to be reported that Meredith had taken 'infinite pains' to 'ripen the young and immature talent of Miss Olive Schreiner', making *The Story of an African Farm* 'so far more interesting and moving than anything its author achieved later on': Waugh, *Hundred Years*, 148.

47 Chapman & Hall, Advertisement, February 1883.

48 HRHRC, Schreiner to Kent, 30 March 1883, 19 April 1883. See Cronwright-Schreiner, *Life*, 158.

49 HRHRC, Schreiner to Kent, 1 May 1883, 30 May 1883.

50 HRHRC, Schreiner to Kent, 26 May 1883; see Cronwright-Schreiner, Introduction, 4, and *Life*, 158.

51 Chapman & Hall, Advertisement, July 1883.

52 See Schreiner, Preface, *SAF* (July 1883), vii–viii; compare *SAF* (1992), xxxix.

53 *Ibid.* (July 1883), viii–ix; (1992), xxxix–xl.

54 Aveling, 'Notable Book', 156.

55 Anon. (McColl), 'Agnostic Novel', 1091.

56 Dawson, 'Books that Have Moved Me', 42.

57 See fig. 2.1. Compare plate 1.

58 Carey-Hobson, *Farm in the Karoo*.

59 She appears to have been friendly with or to have hosted, in London, both Schreiner and Francis Bancroft, among other 'South African' writers; she was also friendly with Rider Haggard: Anon., 'Death of Mrs Carey Hobson', 167.

60 MABL, MS Add. 55935, Anon. (Morley), 'Ostrich Farming'.

61 Trollope, *South Africa*, 169–76; Schreiner, 'Dream'; Wood, 'A Visit'.

62 Schreiner, *SAF* (1896), ii–iii.

63 Easley, *First-Person*, 185; see Judd, 'Male Pseudonyms', 250.

64 HRHRC, Schreiner to Kent, 11 December 1883.

65 Schreiner, *Olive Schreiner Letters*, 41.

66 Judd, 'Male Pseudonyms', 261; see Boumelha, 'Woman of Genius'.

67 Judd, 'Male Pseudonyms', 255, 250.

68 Easley, *First-Person*, 117.

69 Dawson, 'Books that Have Moved Me', 42.

70 Schreiner, *Olive Schreiner Letters*, 54.

71 National English Literary Museum, Grahamstown (NELM), MS Havelock Ellis Letters, Schreiner to Ellis. This letter appears in Rive and Martin's edition of Schreiner's letters (*Olive Schreiner Letters*, 54), but Rive relied for the text on Cronwright-Schreiner's edition (*Letters of Olive Schreiner*, 160–1), which has 'affect' and 'kindle' for 'offend' and 'hinder'; this does not agree with the tone of the rest of the sentence, and implies a wholly different attitude. The original letter, missing when Rive edited his collection, was rediscovered in the mid-1990s and gifted to NELM, where I transcribed it.

72 Schreiner, *Olive Schreiner Letters*, 209.

73 *Ibid.*

74 *Ibid.*, 210.

75 Schreiner, 'Professor Pearson', 3.

76 Schreiner, *Olive Schreiner Letters*, 109.

77 Bristow, Introduction, vii.

78 Anon., '*The Story of an African Farm*, by Ralph Iron', 362.

79 See Marx, 'Underground Russia'. Schreiner's friendship with Marx did not go unnoticed in apartheid-era South Africa, a Christian publisher's 1985 *History of Communism in South Africa* claiming that 'South African communists' had traded on Schreiner's 'name and fame to enhance their godless cause': Pike, *History of Communism*, 14.

80 Aveling, 'Notable Book', 156.

81 *Ibid.*, 162.

82 Norman, 'Theories and Practices', 882.

83 *Ibid.*

84 See Schreiner, *SAF* (1887). On Schreiner's complicated relation to the category of 'Romance', see Haggard, 'About Fiction'; Hannigan, 'Artificiality'; Chrisman, *Rereading*, 25; Van der Vlies, 'Editorial Empire', 256–7.

85 Chrisman, *Rereading*, 7–8; see Chrisman, *Postcolonial Contraventions*, 6, 10.

86 Danby, 'Case', 388.

87 Haggerston, *Newcastle-upon-Tyne*, 34; Barrett, *Catalogue*, 211, 359, 385; Inkster, *Battersea*, 93, 153, 164.

88 Hallett, *Parish Lending Libraries*.

89 First and Scott, *Schreiner*, 123; Hartzenberg to Van der Vlies, email correspondence.
90 Mudie's Select Library, *Catalogue* (1888), 306, and for 1889–93: 338, 356, 360, 352, 376, respectively.
91 Ellis, *My Life*, 181; First and Scott, *Schreiner*, 122.
92 Stead, 'Book of the Month', 64; see fig. 2.2.
93 See Krebs, *Gender*, 83.
94 Stead, 'Fascination', 36.
95 Stead, 'Book of the Month', 65.
96 *Ibid.*
97 See Bristow, Introduction, viii–ix; Flint, *Woman Reader*, 242, note 207.
98 Ardis, 'Organizing Women', 192.
99 Barnicoat, 'Reading', 944; see Flint, *Woman Reader*, 160.
100 Nathan, *South African Commonwealth*, 447.
101 *Ibid.*, 119.
102 Nathan, *South African Literature*, 204.
103 Stanley, *Feminism and Friendship*, 1.
104 See Schreiner, *SAF* (1924), and Cronwright-Schreiner, Introduction.
105 Anon., 'She Was Our South Africa', 76.
106 Holtby, 'Writers of South Africa', 280.
107 Young, 'South African Literature', 507, 509.
108 Harris, *Contemporary Portraits*, 290.
109 Petherick, *Colonial Book Circular*, 1.
110 With vol. 1.3 (March 1888), the qualifying subtitle had offered '*Classified Lists of New Publications, English, American, and Colonial, in All Departments of Literature*', which it remained.
111 By the turn of the century, about fifteen publishers had colonial editions: Nowell-Smith, *International Copyright Law*, 96.
112 Chapman & Hall, Advertisements, December 1888 and March 1889.
113 Raiskin, *Snow*, 23.
114 Burdett, *Olive Schreiner*, 6–7.
115 See Raiskin, *Snow*, 3.
116 Lynch and Warner, Introduction, 5.
117 Clayton, *Olive Schreiner*, 114; Krige, Introduction, 1.

3

'Hurled by what aim to what tremendous range!': Roy Campbell, William Plomer and the politics of reputation

In 1925, poet and anthologist Francis Carey Slater, introducing *The Centenary Book of South African Verse*, his choice of poetry written in English in or about Southern Africa, reminded readers of the 'adverse conditions' on the margins of Empire which explained the failure of colonial 'verse' to meet high metropolitan expectations of 'poetry'. Colonists, already too busy 'warring with savages, quarrelling with each another, reclaiming the desert, and wresting treasure from the unwilling earth', had the added disadvantage of living in an 'unhappy country' – the fledgling Union of South Africa – 'not dowered with the wealth of historical association and romantic tradition', which was 'inseparable from older civilisations', and a prerequisite for a national literature.[1] This 'colonial cringe', to borrow a term from Australian cultural criticism, overshadowed literary production in the region and, as in comparable dominions with *invader–settler* societies (Canada, Australia, New Zealand), a sense of colonial inferiority was only gradually displaced as settler and creole writers negotiated distinctly regional subjectivities and provisional proto-national identities.

The centenary commemorated in Slater's title was that of the settlement of 4,000 British immigrants along the eastern frontier of the Cape Colony in 1820, the first major influx since the Cape had come under permanent British control in 1806. Despite a deferral to metropolitan sensibilities, then, the *Centenary Book* was also a tentative statement of a desired (if not yet achieved) cultural coming-of-age, and Slater expressed the hope that it would stimulate the interest of a South African reading public in addition to reaching a sympathetic audience overseas. There were economic reasons for addressing two audiences: the South African reading public was small; and the production of books was prohibitively expensive.[2] Nonetheless, a cheap cloth-bound edition of the 1925 volume was popular in South Africa, and by the time Slater published a revised *New Centenary Book of South African Verse*, in 1945, he could assume a larger local readership. The new volume's biographical notes consequently stressed poets' connections to the region, and a chronological ordering of poets suggested a developing indigenous tradition which had made 'remarkable progress' in the preceding two decades.[3] This was attested to most markedly by the reputations of the two poets whose work took pride of place in the collection: Roy Campbell and William Plomer. In 1925, Slater had few of Campbell's and none of Plomer's poems from which to choose, and included only three of the former's. In 1945, he included 18 poems by Campbell and 4 by Plomer. Later anthologies of South African poetry in English confirmed their status: by 1959, Guy Butler's *Book of South African Verse* included twelve poems by each.

Roy(ston Dunnachie) Campbell was born in Durban in 1901. He travelled to Britain in 1919, and tried unsuccessfully to enter Oxford University, before moving to bohemian London, where he married artist Mary Garman in 1922. The couple lived briefly in Wales, where Campbell wrote a long narrative poem, *The Flaming Terrapin*, published by Jonathan Cape in May 1924 to immediate critical acclaim. He returned to South Africa in March 1924, and while living on the south coast of Natal, in 1926, ran a short-lived, avant-garde, literary magazine, *Voorslag* (Whiplash), with Plomer. The Campbells returned to Britain in early 1927 and later lived in France, Spain, and Portugal, where Campbell died after a car accident in 1957.[4] Campbell published several volumes of poetry, memoirs and translations from Spanish and Portuguese, and his work was widely anthologised in Britain and the USA. Still regarded as the pre-eminent English-language 'South African' poet of the first half of the twentieth century, he continues to enjoy a limited reputation in Anglo-American literary academia; his decision, as a recent and devout convert to Roman Catholicism in Toledo in 1936, to back Franco and his pro-Church nationalists during the Spanish Civil War, blackened his reputation among many left-leaning British writers and critics. Despite undergoing a measure of rehabilitation after serving in the British Army during the Second World War, he is nonetheless often still represented, as in Valentine Cunningham's survey of writers of the 1930s, as a right-wing fantasist with a 'loosened ... hold on reality'.[5]

William (Charles Franklyn) Plomer (1903–73) was born of English parents in Pietersburg (present-day Polokwane) in the northern Transvaal (now Limpopo), educated in England and South Africa, and lived in Natal until mid-1926, then in Japan and, after 1929, in Britain. He visited South Africa again only once, in 1956. Author of numerous novels and short stories, he is remembered in Britain chiefly for his ballads, as editor of Francis Kilvert's diaries and as one of Benjamin Britten's regular librettists. His South African reputation rests on his contributions to *Voorlsag* and especially on his first novel, the technically adventurous and bravely anti-racist *Turbott Wolfe* (1926). Plomer's relationship to South Africa was always ambivalent: while a resident, he railed against its bourgeois philistinism, and for most of his professional life in England sought to downplay his early life there.[6] South African critics tend to characterise his denials as defensive and misleading (Peter Wilhelm, for example, says 'Plomer was an African, of Africa, always'), pointing out that he consistently took an interest in South African writers abroad and acted as a kind of literary godfather to many – not least in his role as a reader for Jonathan Cape.[7] He did become increasingly nostalgic about the country and, in the year before his death, remarked to a South African friend that he thought of himself as being 'in a miniature way, a "regional" writer of the Stormberg' (although, significantly, not a 'South African' writer).[8]

Both Campbell and Plomer have featured prominently in descriptions, by South African critics, of the development of an indigenous Anglophone literature, but, with increasing interrogation of the commitment of 'liberal' writing during the late apartheid era, the definition of this category was increasingly contested. Malvern van Wyk Smith argues that the bulk of their work is not South African, although Plomer's *Turbott Wolfe* and Campbell's *Flaming Terrapin* and *Adamastor* (1930) are of lasting significance because they mark the beginning of modernist literature in the country.[9] Michael Chapman has offered a similar, if changing, analysis, including their work in his 1981 anthology *A Century of South African Poetry*, but suggesting in 1984 that while Campbell could be seen as 'the first "modern" South African poet' he may also be regarded as 'the last of the "stubborn colonials"'.[10] Similar claims were made with increasing frequency during the height of white, left-wing, intellectual self-interrogation by, among others, Nadine Gordimer and Jeremy Cronin.[11] In 1986, Chapman offered an impassioned defence of Campbell against those criticisms, but by 1996 was calling Campbell a 'sad case of the dislocated colonial whose romantic–symbolist imagination needs to be held warily to social account in a democratic South African response'.[12] Plomer, consistently outspoken in his opposition to racial segregation, was less susceptible to political criticism, his work having increasingly come to be seen as self-reflexive about the inevitable inadequacy of European responses to Africa. Poems like 'Devil-Dancers' (in *Visiting the Caves*, 1936) conveyed this analysis satirically but with great psychological subtlety.[13] By 1996, however, Chapman, too, viewed Plomer's work more ambivalently, describing his poetry as enacting challenges to the poet's own 'colonial hankerings after landscapes empty of the indigenous people, his own colonial fears about Africa as savage and atavistic'.[14]

These judgements illustrate the extent to which the work of *colonial* writers has been rendered increasingly marginal by postcolonial critics for its perceived failure to contribute to the development of a shared, multiracial, multilingual, national culture. The highly fraught field in which South Africa's identities were being negotiated and counter-imagined in the 1990s is uncannily like the cultural landscape of the white Union of South Africa in the mid-1920s, when Campbell and Plomer first came to local and metropolitan attention. Campbell was in Britain between 1919 and 1924, establishing connections in London's literary avant-garde.

During the same period, Plomer was writing in Johannesburg, the Stormberg and Zululand, but keeping an eye on literary developments in London. Both left South Africa permanently in 1926, but before then had already positioned themselves, by statement or action, in relation to literary movements in *English* poetry in the early 1920s in ways which implicated them in specific conceptions of readership, market and literary aesthetics. These positions, influenced too by the sites in which their early published work appeared, affected how they attempted to present themselves both in a South Africa experiencing growing nationalism and racial segregation and in a Britain in which both hoped to make a reputation.

Campbell's poetry, in particular, entered into complicated lives in print, his intentions inevitably and unavoidably altered or even effaced by different material conditions of publication; this chapter focuses on some of these contexts by way of a suggestive case study. It also offers, by way of comparison, discussion of Plomer's struggle to establish his metropolitan career. In 1931, Campbell declared dismissively, in a letter to Percy Wyndham Lewis, that Plomer had 'become a proper Bloomsbury'.[15] The remark, intended as a slur, illustrates the extent to which these former friends and collaborators became members of very different literary groups, assimilated to divergent positions in the world of writing in English – and *English* letters – by the early 1930s. How did this happen, and what are the implications for understanding the ways in which literary identities are constructed in relation to specific conceptions of literariness and national identity? The idea of a South African identity – particularly a cultural one – was highly contentious and tentative during the early decades of the last century; this chapter exposes the instability of those categories for writers like Campbell and Plomer, variously and sometimes simultaneously (or at least not contradictorily) regarded as South African, colonial *and* British, demonstrating that literary cultures are constructed in ways which are only precariously related to public or political culture.

Roy Campbell: dominion modernity

Campbell himself saw his work as part of a consciously modern literary movement. In the early 1920s, writing to his father from Britain about his aesthetic position, he declared that poetry had 'passed the ages of Romanticism, Parnassianism and Symbolism', and, in response to 'the faintness, the morbid wistfulness of the symbolists', needed to pull 'itself together for another tremendous fight against annihilation'.[16] *The Flaming Terrapin* (1924), Campbell's early sustained attempt at enacting this new poetic aesthetic, narrates the journey of Noah's ark, dragged south by a fiery terrapin, a self-engendering machine whose arteries flow with currents of electric sap, to its landfall in a recognisably South African landscape. The poem's celebration of physical energy employs descriptions of a vortex as the centre of a creatively destructive energy, zig-zag montages, word-patterning and kinetic imagery all suggesting debts to vorticism and futurism, and demonstrating affinities with the work of Wyndham Lewis, Campbell's early ideological mentor.[17] *The Flaming Terrapin* appealed to fears of degeneration after the catastrophe of war – the ark's crew is 'Purged by their agonies of all the dross/ Of fear and sloth', while 'their spirits shed their gross/ Rags of despair' – and an intellectual climate in which analyses and pseudo-scientific prognostications on mass society had great currency.[18] Its final affirmation echoes both Nietzsche and Whitman in its presentation of the soul's 'silent chanting': 'Pass, world: I am the dreamer that remains,/ The Man, clear-cut against the last horizon!'[19]

A. E. Coppard, writing in the *Saturday Review*, called Campbell's poem a 'dream of a renascence of the human spirit after a universal debacle', and Henry Newbolt, extracting from the poem in his anthology *New Paths on Helicon* (1927), drew attention to Campbell's apparent 'virile disgust at the weariness, the fever, and the fret of this old world'.[20] As Robert Young notes, late nineteenth-century social Darwinism, and its frequent invocation in the wake of the First World War, assigned to 'the "primitive" animal vitality and emotionalism of the lower races' a 'value to be retrieved for the benefit of the regeneration of a tired, degenerate, vulgarized, mechanical European civilization'.[21] This vitality became increasingly associated with the 'white' dominions, an association Campbell was keen to exploit. His poem's speaker is in search of a poetic idiom suited to his homeland: his new Helicon is a peak from which the ghost of the Zulu King 'Tchaka' can be heard, and in the final section Campbell suggests that the Ararat on which his Noah stands is Cathedral Peak in the Drakensberg Mountains of the colony (by 1924, province) of his birth: Natal.[22] Jonathan Cape advertised *The Flaming Terrapin* as by a 'young South African', indirectly inviting it to be read in terms of those references to the poet's origins, with all of their romantic associations.[23]

The image of South Africa as a site of adventure, and physical and spiritual rejuvenation, was commonplace in British media in the early 1920s. 'Few countries' could 'boast of such a romantic history as South Africa', an article in *Vogue* in late February 1924 claimed, praising the 'virile [white] race' which had 'sprung from the early British adventurers and from the Dutch and French Huguenot settlers'.[24] In June 1924, *Vogue* included two fascinating instances of the representation of a particular kind of 'South African-ness' – vigorous, white, strangely familiar but refreshingly other – in the British imagination. The first was Raymond Mortimer's short appreciative review of *The Flaming Terrapin*.[25] The second was an article by Osbert Sitwell on the British Empire Exhibition at the purpose-built Wembley Stadium. Open between late April and the end of October 1924, and again from May to November 1925, the Exhibition attracted more than 26 million visitors, and helped to

1 Vol. 2 of the 1883 Chapman & Hall edition of *The Story of an African Farm*

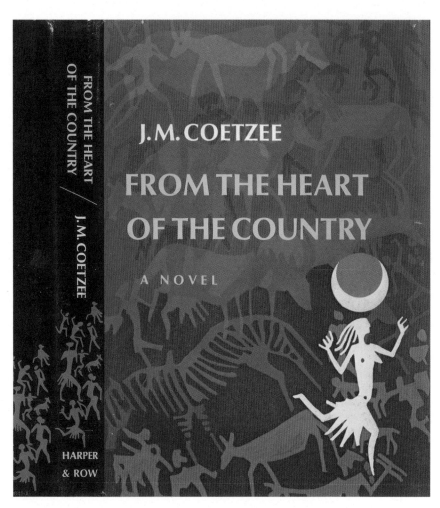

2 Jacket, Harper & Row's edition of *From the Heart of the Country*, 1977

construct representative stereotypes of colonial and dominion identities in the British psyche, both celebrating imperial products for a British market and encouraging white British emigration to the dominions.[26] Sitwell's feature carried a photograph of South Africa's Pavilion, modelled on Groot Constantia, the archetypal Cape Dutch estate built by Governor Simon van der Stel in the 1680s. It contrasted strongly with a photograph of displays in the Gold Coast Pavilion – a series of carvings with 'the great attraction of being strange to European eyes' – in a manner testifying to this early self-conscious (white) South African representation of its exemplarity and exceptionalism, its emphatic European heritage.[27] Nonetheless, as Dipti Bhagat suggests, South Africa's display at Wembley also presented an unsettling challenge to the grand narrative offered by the Exhibition's setting, a park-like interpretation of rural Englishness, and to its *imperial* context, by emphasising the frontier spirit of its white citizens, and highlighting incipient Afrikaner nationalist identity and iconography.[28]

A feature in *Vogue*'s late April 1925 issue concluded with the suggestion that, on the basis of *The Flaming Terrapin*, Campbell might finally be the longed-for poet which the 'natural splendours of the South African scene … deserve[d]'.[29] Campbell's dedication to traditional rhyme and metre led many to separate him from what they regarded as self-promoting English literary interest groups. His 'modern though not untraditional technique of expression', the *Liverpool Daily Post and Mercury* claimed, was 'no product of literary coteries – South Africa being its birthplace and the background of its inspiration'.[30] The connection of 'not untraditional technique(s)' with the 'white' dominions was also made by Francis Carey Slater, who suggested in the Preface to his *Centenary Book of South African Verse* that what might once have been regarded as derivative and romantic colonial verse was actually representative of a creative reinvigoration of old forms. According to this argument, it was the poets of the dominions who were in the best position to offer an antidote to a supposed contemporary 'formlessness' in English verse, one which betokened 'weakness and a lack of true originality'.[31]

Others, however, thought that the traditional form of Campbell's work belonged to the past rather than to a brave new future. For the *Dial*'s reviewer, *The Flaming Terrapin* evidenced 'the full-throated mode of twenty, thirty years ago'.[32] Harold Monro offered another criticism in the *Criterion*, in October, suggesting that the poem's imagery and vocabulary had 'a colonial flavour' and suffered from 'excessive elaboration'.[33] Monro's use of the adjective 'colonial' is non-specific: he might as easily have applied the term to work by an Australian or New Zealand poet. As we shall see, his review of Campbell's 1930 collection *Adamastor* is equally general. For Monro, then, as for other cultural commentators, Campbell, like any writer from the dominions, was *British* because a subject of the Empire. Simultaneously, however, his writing's exotic setting and conservatism of form, functions of distance from the latest literary fashions and metropolitan formal experimentalism, seemed not quite English, or inadequately literary. Such colonial writers were regarded in the metropolis as provincial, even if, like Campbell, they sought to distance themselves from the perceived provincialism of the dominions.

On his return to Natal in 1924, Campbell faced those tensions, magnified as never before. Between April 1925 and the end of 1926, he lived with his wife and daughters at Sezela, south of Durban, subsisting on the largesse of a wealthy patron. William Plomer's *Turbott Wolfe* was published by the Hogarth Press in London in March 1926 (though dated 1925), and he joined the Campbells in May, collaborating on the first issues of *Voorslag*, a journal styling itself *A Monthly Magazine of South African Life and Art*, first published in June. Campbell edited and, with Plomer, wrote much of the first two issues, but after conflicts with his wealthy patrons, Campbell resigned in July, and Plomer left for Japan shortly thereafter.[34] *Voorslag* precipitated a clash between Campbell and Plomer's internationalism and the prevailing cultural climate in the Union, a proto-nationalism which appeared to them redundant provincialism. Sarah Gertrude Millin, self-appointed grande dame of an emergent national literary elite, wrote in Johannesburg's *Rand Daily Mail* that *Voorslag* succeeded if judged against British or American standards, but that, 'for all its South African flavour', it was not sufficiently South African, but rather 'a branch of a well-defined overseas group'.[35] Other commentators echoed those sentiments, comparing *Voorslag* with, for example, the avant-garde American *Dial* or the British *Adelphi*: it was unable to evoke 'a countryman's sympathy'.[36] Understandably, given this climate, whether the Union possessed anything approaching a national literature was a topic of fierce debate in the mid 1920s. Novelist Ethelreda Lewis, in a series of survey essays in the *South African Nation* in 1926 and early 1927, commended the richness of local material to the native-born writer, and, ironically, cited Campbell's *Flaming Terrapin* as evidence of a new energy in the country's literature.[37] Debates about national literary identity and avant-garde internationalism were increasingly at loggerheads – and Campbell's work claimed for both formations.

Islanded: Campbell's 'Tristan da Cunha'

Evelyn Waugh commented in 1934 on the ubiquity of colonies and dominions in everyday public and private life in the period:

> One is always meeting Canadians and Australians; everyone has cousins in Kenya and Nigeria and Rhodesia, South Africans seem to have controlled English life twenty-five years ago; people are constantly going and coming to and from the Malay States and India; one way or another most of the Empire (and particularly Tristan da Cunha) comes to one's notice at some time ... [38]

We can only speculate about the South Africans to whom Waugh refers: he may have had in mind the many Britons with strong connections to South Africa (Milner, Kipling, Haggard, Buchan), colonial magnates and politicians (Rhodes, Jameson, Beit) or even writers like Schreiner, in the period between the Treaty of Vereeniging (ending the second Anglo-Boer War) in 1902 and Union in 1910. His glance at Tristan da Cunha, however, allows the introduction of an only superficially unlikely poem through which to focus attention on the construction of Campbell's reputation. While many of Campbell's better-known *African* poems in his 1930 collection, *Adamastor*, including 'The Zulu Girl', 'The Zebras', 'The Serf', and 'Rounding the Cape', have enjoyed a longer afterlife and remain those by which Campbell remains chiefly known today, a longer poem written in the same period, 'Tristan da Cunha', was the most reprinted and collected of his poems during the later 1920s and the 1930s.

A poem about an isolated island, in which Campbell doubtless saw a fit image for his own feelings of alienation from the parochialism of white Natal society, provides a remarkably apposite opportunity to consider the stormily contested constructions of Campbell's own poetic and *national* identity in the period. The poem's speaker addresses the island directly: 'Exiled like you and severed from my race/ By the cold ocean of my own disdain'. He muses on the power and place of the aesthetic in the face of metaphysical and aesthetic insecurity: 'You fish with nets of seaweed in the deep/ As fruitlessly as I with nets of rhyme –'.[39] There is, in the final lines of the poem, a suggestion that the poet understands that it is only through an audience that his work achieves a life, or lives, of its own; as the island battles in its sea, so the poet's readers are his disdainful ocean, and their feet his poem's:

> Yet what of these dark crowds amid whose flow
> I battle like a rock, aloof and friendless,
> Are not their generations vague and endless
> The waves, the strides, the feet on which I go?[40]

Written in Natal in early August 1926, the poem entered its public printed life in the 1926 issue of *The Waste Paper Basket of the Owl Club* (published early in 1927), a periodic annual of a Cape Town civil servants' and businessmen's club, after Campbell sent the manuscript to his patron, C. J. Sibbett, a member.[41] Campbell's appearance in this journal had more to do with his indebtedness to Sibbett for continued moral and financial support than it had with a particular desire to be published in the pages of what was no more than a miscellany for very limited circulation.[42] It suited the *Waste Paper Basket* to publish work by a celebrated if sometimes controversial young writer, but it is unlikely that Campbell would have regarded the magazine as having a more liberal or enlightened audience in the Cape than that which he vilified, before his departure to Britain with his family in December 1926, as the narrow-minded and parochial English-speaking community in Natal.

'Tristan da Cunha' first appeared in print in Britain in the *New Statesman* on 15 October 1927; the paper's literary editor, Desmond MacCarthy, had long held a high opinion of Campbell's work.[43] While still in Natal, Campbell had sent 'The Serf' and 'The Zulu Girl' to Leonard Woolf, who appears to have arranged their publication in the *Nation and Athenaeum* (of which he was literary editor) and the *New Statesman*, respectively, in late 1926.[44] 'The Making of a Poet', 'The Sisters', and 'African Moonrise' had appeared in the paper before 'Tristan da Cunha', and while the first contained reference to 'the slinking leopard', only the third had been expressly *African*.[45] Readers would nonetheless have been aware of Campbell's reputation as the precocious South African bard of *The Flaming Terrapin*, and also of his self-appointed role, as editor of *Voorslag*, as colonial *enfant terrible*. In fact, almost exactly two months before it carried 'Tristan da Cunha', the *New Statesman* published an intriguing piece which suggests that *Voorslag* had been noticed in Britain, 'The Voorloper Group', by Winifred Holtby, a regular reviewer of books on Africa and frequent critic of racial policies across the Empire who had visited South Africa during 1926. It was a first-person account of the narrator's experience with a group of English- and Afrikaans-speaking South Africans on an outing in the Transvaal, but parallels with *Voorslag* are too obvious to be coincidental. A member of the party speaks of his plans to publish 'The Voorloper', a bilingual 'monthly review, to be devoted to the art and literature of South Africa', and to be financed by a mine-owner.[46] Both titles suggest the necessity of spurring a somnolent culture into action, 'voorloper' being Afrikaans for the leader of a team of wagon-oxen.[47]

Surrounded by a wide variety of miscellaneous material, 'Tristan da Cunha' appeared in the midst of highly aesthetic – and high-aesthetic – discourse in the *New Statesman*, between MacCarthy's review of Russian theatre in London and a feature on the National Memorial Theatre.[48] The issue also carried reports of international politics, British trade union activities and the political parties' conference season. The paper, of course, since its inception in 1913 had been associated with Fabians and socialists, although, while its ties to the socialist cause remained strong, it was never aimed at the working classes.[49] Its political sympathies and artistic pretensions create a field of tension which foregrounds similar tensions in a reading of 'Tristan da Cunha', in which the poet–speaker is apparently alienated from his society, despite needing to find an audience among its members. The *New Statesman*'s coverage of South Africa was consistently critical of segregation, and in the context of the paper's portrayal of South Africa the angst-ridden relationship evident in 'Tristan da Cunha' between critical poet and a society in which he feels out of place would certainly have been emphasised.[50]

The poem's appearance in print in Britain attracted attention from, among others, T. S. Eliot, whose appreciative letter to the editor in the paper's next issue congratulated Campbell on his 'remarkable' metrical control, and 'stronger and less flamboyant' language compared to 'some of his earlier work'.[51] South African commentators were similarly impressed, a critic in the *Cape Times* suggesting that 'Tristan da Cunha' showed the 'real measure of Mr. Campbell's growth since the immature magnificences of "The Flaming Terrapin"'.[52] Cape had published the *Terrapin*, and Campbell sent the publisher the manuscript of his next collection, including 'Tristan da Cunha', but Edward Garnett, Cape's reader, thought it 'not up to [his] best standard'.[53] Cape thought Campbell should send the poems to Nancy Cunard, but her small Hours Press had gone out of business, so he sent them to T. S. Eliot – whom he considered a friend – at Faber & Faber.[54] Faber duly published *Adamastor*, on 8 April 1930; it sold for 5 shillings, and went through 3 editions within 2 months of publication. There was also a special edition of 90 signed and numbered copies, and a further 90 out of series copies, which sold out at once. In 1932, it was reissued in a smaller format and new binding (green rather than red-brown), as number ten in 'The Faber Library'.[55]

'Tristan da Cunha' is positioned structurally at the mid-point of the collection, the fourteenth poem of twenty eight in the middle section, 'Adamastor'. It is arguably also the last of the African poems in this section. While the mythical Adamastor, spirit of the Cape, appears in 'Rounding the Cape', that poem is *not* included in the 'Adamastor' section; it is 'Tristan da Cunha' which stands at the heart of the volume.[56] Its appearance in *Adamastor* was the first of at least twelve further appearances in different collections in the ensuing decade, more than any other of Campbell's poems during this period. All of Campbell's editors and anthologists, whether admitting to prejudice or not, exercised their designs on the work, both in choosing it and in choosing how to present its text and information about its author's poetic and national identity. [57] Even before it was included in *Adamastor*, the poem appeared in two anthologies, Thomas Moult's selection of *The Best Poems of 1928* and Harold Monro's selection for Chatto & Windus's *Twentieth-Century Poetry* (1929). After *Adamastor*, it was reproduced in Britain in a Hogarth Press anthology edited by Dorothy Wellesley, in a short selection of Campbell's poems published by Ernest Benn (1931), in J. C. Squire's *Younger Poets of Today* (1932), the English Association's *The Modern Muse* and A. S. Cairncross's *Longer Poems Old and New* (both 1934), R. L. Mégroz's *Treasury of Modern Poetry* (1936), Maurice Wollman's *Poems of Twenty Years* (1938) and at least two anthologies in 1945: Margaret and Ronald Bottrall's *Collected English Verse*; and Francis Carey Slater's *New Centenary Book of South African Verse*.[58] There were doubtless many other appearances. Following the poem through some of the most interesting of these sites reveals a great deal about the way

Campbell's reputation, and the idea of a 'South African' literary tradition, was being constructed in different fields during the period.

Its inclusion in Moult's annual selection from British, Irish and American newspapers presented 'Tristan da Cunha' alongside poems by a relatively conservative group of poets, including Katherine Tynan, Harold Monro, John Drinkwater, John Gould Fletcher, Alfred Noyes, Walter de la Mare, Siegfried Sassoon and Vita Sackville-West.[59] In a letter to an editor at Cape in 1930, Campbell declined permission for Moult to use other of his poems in a new selection, and while the reasons are open to speculation this suggests that he may have had second thoughts about appearing in the 1928 selection. We might speculate about the inclusion of Sackville-West; her affair with Campbell's wife, Mary, had soured relations with the Nicolsons by this time.[60] However, Moult also included poems by Vachel Lindsay, Edmund Blunden and Edith Sitwell, whom Campbell admired. It is most likely that, by 1930, Campbell regarded a selection of poems culled from newspapers to be potentially a mere collection of ephemera. Later collections in which his work appeared tended to emphasise its energy, and perhaps the other poems in Moult's earlier selection had not seemed conducive to this reading.

The poem appeared in Monro's 1929 Phoenix Library selection *Twentieth-Century Poetry*, flanked by poems by Ford Madox Ford (formerly, Hueffer) and T. S. Eliot ('Whispers of Immortality'), a frame of which Campbell no doubt would have approved. Endorsement from Monro, the founder of the Poetry Bookshop, editor of *The Chapbook* and among the most influential figures in English poetry during the 1920s, was potentially significant, too.[61] Campbell had suggested in *Voorslag* that the poetry-reading public was, by the end of the 1920s, 'tired of the concentrated saccharine of the "Georgians"', often championed by Monro (he published Edward Marsh's *Georgian Poetry* anthologies), but it is clear that there was no bad blood between them on that account.[62] Monro introduced his selection by claiming that he wished to offer a balanced view of the best, most representative poetry of the first three decades of the century, and Campbell was judged important enough for such a selection.[63] Nevertheless, despite what he called its 'mild chronological tendency', Monro's organisation of poems presents little sense of poetry's development during the period, and the selection was overtly cautious: Monro gestured tentatively at experimental poetry, but declined to entertain 'discussion of what is known as *free verse*', claiming that it was 'controversial and subject to much misunderstanding'.[64] Monro's review of *Adamastor* in *Criterion* in 1931 would lay great emphasis on Campbell's identity as a colonial, declaring his 'metaphorical equipment' largely 'colonial, and, in many instances, explosive, rackety, or far-fetched and disturbing'.[65] The category of 'colonial' here is not a national category, rather marking a sense of difference from a metropolitan standard. Monro doubtless chose 'Tristan da Cunha' for his 1929 anthology because it fitted most easily into the category of 'British' poetry because it was not too noisily or unremittingly colonial, and did not challenge Monro's idea of poetry 'intrinsic' to the period.[66]

The complexity of the construction of Campbell's national identity is noticeable in his biographical note in the slim, paper-covered volume of his *Poems* published in Ernest Benn's 'Augustan Books of Poetry' series in 1931. Declaring Campbell's 'the one reputation made in poetry since the war' which was 'safe on the work already published', it described him as a 'Briton', but also with 'the advantage of coming from outside our life, with knowledge of the storm that is beating up in South Africa'.[67] A 'poet of ... vigour', Campbell was able to depict supposedly primitive energies sympathetically:

> [H]is verse is as equal to conveying the power couched within man's engines as to suggesting the primitive force stirring in a Zulu woman or (if I may be forgiven the collocation) a zebra or a cobra. Things that to our poets are 'local colour', eagerly picked up from books or hearsay and brought into poetry, to him are potentialities experienced from the inside.[68]

For many critics and editors, South African elements in Campbell's poetry, as well as the very fact of his colonial birth and his own self-consciously mythologised physicality (in published interviews, letters and his memoirs), emphasised the potentially reinvigorating potential of his poetry for a British tradition.[69] Many continued to view the poets of the dominions as being in the best position to offer an antidote to what some regarded as a contemporary 'formlessness' in metropolitan writing, and the posture of a poet writing in a traditional idiom, abjuring facile experimentation for its own sake in an attempt to reinvigorate poetry, was certainly one which Campbell was keen to affect.[70]

Cairncross's *Longer Poems Old and New,* in which 'Tristan da Cunha' concludes a collection beginning with Chaucer, likewise claimed that Campbell's poetry possessed a 'rebellious ... energy'. Notes indicate that Campbell was born in Durban, but do not suggest that he is anything other than British, like the other poets in the collection.[71] The English Association's *Modern Muse: Poems of To-Day, British and American,* published in the same year, included work by a number of poets from Britain (71), the United States (25), Canada (11), South Africa (8), Australia (7), New Zealand (6), Ireland (3), Ceylon (2) and India (2), declared as its purpose to collect poems from across the Anglophone world to effect a 'quickening among these peoples [of] the sense of the greatness of their common heritage'.[72] Its Preface offered an interesting apology:

> While a standard of excellence has been kept in mind, the main aim has been to make the selection fully representative of the various countries. To this aim must be attributed the presence of poems which are unusual in form, structure, and subject-matter; and it should be remembered under what conditions, geographical, political, and social, they have been written.[73]

This anticipation that the implied reader would regard poetry from the margins of Empire as failing to meet metropolitan standards almost echoes Slater's apologetic Preface to the 1925 *Centenary Book of South African Verse*. Campbell's inclusion in *The Modern Muse*, alongside other Southern African poets, including Slater and a Rhodesian poet, A. S. Cripps, worked to stress the shared qualities of their poems and to suggest that Campbell's poetry ('Tristan da Cunha' and an extract from *The Flaming Terrapin*) may be read as belonging both to a regional and global 'English' poetic identity.[74] Campbell's South African origins are fore-grounded, in other words, but the editors, in explaining that the alphabetical arrangement of poets is such that a 'South African writer, for instance, may be found rubbing shoulders with his fellow from the Homeland', never allows the reader to lose sight of the standard by which one ought to judge all writing in English: that of the metropolitan centre of the Empire.[75]

The category of 'South African literature' unsettles the relationship between nation and culture. The 1931 Statute of Westminster confirmed the relative sovereignty of the dominions, but that position was not often reflected in the fields of literary and popular culture, where the relative position of Britain and the individual dominions was less nuanced.[76] Osbert Sitwell was quoted in *Harper's Bazaar* in July 1932 claiming an abiding interest in Campbell's work: 'He seems to have all the good points that a colonial poet should have. His lack of subtlety is often atoned by the jolly bumping of his verse. I wish Australia and Canada would produce similar poets.'[77] Sitwell thinks of Campbell as colonial, and immediately thinks of Canada and Australia, as if the colonies – or, rather, dominions – are homogenous. For some editors and commentators, then, he was, first and foremost, a colonial. For most of them, he seems to have been indistinguishably so – he could have come from any of the colonies. For others, despite being colonial in origin, Campbell was British, and not merely because citizens of dominions were automatically so: from the metropolitan perspective, the dissociation of a distinct, proto-national, South African, cultural identity from a more general 'colonial' one had not yet taken place, at least not in cultural discourse.[78]

Doubly involved: Plomer on the margins and in the metropole

How did these debates and position-takings affect Plomer's reputation? Looking back on his youth in South Africa, he observed later that the 'successive volumes of *Georgian Poetry*, breaking in upon the late Post-Victorian twilight, had been as quickening to many of my generation, believe it or not, as a display of fireworks'.[79] Plomer's early models, in other words, were, as might be expected, just as *metropolitan* as Campbell's. In fact, he sent an early poem called 'Symphony' to the *English Review* in 1921, and, before leaving Johannesburg for the Eastern

Cape (where he wrote *Turbott Wolfe*), wrote to Harold Monro in April 1921, initiating a correspondence which lasted for some time – Plomer even signed one of his letters 'Your literary godson'.[80] One of the earliest sites in which Plomer's poems appeared was in South Africa, in a journal about as different from the *English Review* as it is possible to imagine: 'Three Folk Poems' was published, under a pseudonym, in John L. Dube's Zulu newspaper *Ilange Lase Natal*, on 14 March 1924, accompanied by an author's note expressing the hope 'that these simple verses may help to serve as an early movement towards our own literature. A national literature can only be built up of many parts, and with infinite pains, but if we can plainly express now some of the true feelings of our people, however simple, we may be able to lay a secure foundation.'[81] While early attempts to bring his work to a wider British audience demonstrate the extent to which he kept abreast of literary developments in London and desired metropolitan validation for his work, Plomer clearly simultaneously entertained an incipient South African – perhaps even African nationalist – sense of national and literary identity.

This wish for an indigenous South African literature was partially echoed in Plomer's response to comments about *Turbott Wolfe* in the *South African Nation* in July 1926. T. E. Clarkson had charged that Campbell's defence of the novel in *Voorslag* gave it undue attention: Campbell had '[put] his subject definitively into South African "literature"' where he might otherwise not have been.[82] Plomer replied that he would not be '"put into" South African literature', which he called 'a cottage hospital full of lady novelists suffering from anaemia, and of facetious journalists suffering from home-sickness'.[83] He was careful, nonetheless, to identify himself with South Africa and not appear a colonial suffering 'home-sickness' for Britain, stressing that he had not visited England since childhood.[84] Despite the posturing in a letter judged carefully to respond violently enough without disqualifying himself on his own terms, Plomer clearly did regard a repudiation of white South African society as compatible with a claim to be South African, in fact to be the progenitor of the first genuinely and identifiably South African literature. His response drew attention to the lack of national self-consciousness of much writing produced in South Africa in its refusal to confront the realities of the colonial situation. Many years later he would state in a review of New Zealand writing that literature produced in the dominions abdicated the onerous task of grappling with new and challenging environments: 'Too many looked to London and the lanes of Devonshire, known or imagined, as the scene of a Golden Age to which it was infinitely desirable to return ... Only a few caught and held deep feelings about their new world in new arrangements of words.'[85] They were, in other words, like the Fotheringhays, characters in *Turbott Wolfe* who, 'although they had spent nearly all their lives in Africa ... had never begun to think of Africa'.[86]

By the time Plomer arrived in Britain from Japan in April 1929, four of his books – *Turbott Wolfe, I Speak of Africa* (1927), *Notes for Poems* (1928) and *Paper Houses* (1929) – had been published in London, all by the Hogarth Press. He was 26, and set about consolidating his reputation and reinventing himself as a serious *English* man of letters, even altering the pronunciation of his name.[87] Two works help to plot Plomer's negotiation of that position. The first is *I Speak of Africa*, his second book and the first published after his departure from South Africa in September 1926. Appearing in September 1927, while Plomer was in Japan, it consolidated his relationship with Hogarth and confirmed his temperamental distance from white South Africa. The second, the short poem 'The Scorpion', printed in the *Nation and Athenaeum* in May 1930, shows Plomer working through his relationship with Africa in a striking way. It later appeared in his third poetry collection, the publication of which he handled in a manner which reveals how he consciously tried to shape his metropolitan career at its most crucial stage.

I Speak of Africa comprised 7 short stories, 2 'plays for puppets' (masque-like satires on South African racial policies), and 3 'short novels': 'Portraits in the Nude', 'Ula Masondo', and 'Black Peril'. 'Portraits', an episodic sketch of a dysfunctional farm, reads like Plomer's modernist response to Schreiner's *The Story of an African Farm*; there is domestic abuse, hypocrisy and repression, and, in a chapter entitled 'A Black Christ', two brothers lynch a black servant while their demented father stands by ringing a church bell, his eyes half-closed in a religious trance. Perhaps the first attempt to portray under-interrogated aspects of the white South African – particularly the Afrikaner Calvinist – psyche, it is the forerunner of works like Coetzee's *In the Heart of the Country*. Plomer's collection made currency of the fact that it reproduced the unexpurgated version of 'Portraits'; the new editors of *Voorslag*, in which it was first serialised, had insisted on covering the nakedness of a character at the story's end. The other two long stories appeared independently of *I Speak of Africa* in British sites. 'Ula Masondo' is perhaps the initiator of a pervasive South African genre measuring the effects of labour migration on rural black South Africans. In 'Black Peril', a white woman appears to initiate a sexual encounter with a black servant, but subsequently dies of what her husband and community regard as shock from rape.

Hogarth sought to capitalise on *Turbott Wolfe*'s publicity in promoting *I Speak of Africa*, including extracts from its reviews at the end of the new book.[88] Four of the South African reviews praised the early novel's prophetic nature and 'insight into Native character', while two were less flattering: The *South African Nation* called it 'pornographic', the *Zululand Times* likened it to 'stinking fish'. Of the English reviews, those from the Bloomsbury-friendly *Nation and Athenaeum* and the *New Statesman* were, not surprisingly, placed at the head of the list. Nonetheless, the collection received mixed reviews in Britain. Orlo

Williams, writing in the *Criterion*, called it misguided negrophilia, its 'glorification of the black man' demonstrating that Plomer was in 'thrall to certain fashionable fallacies of our day'.[89] However, the *New Adelphi*'s review differed in every point from the *Criterion*'s, recognising that Plomer admitted to sympathy for oppressed 'native races', but arguing that the author remained 'very creditably objective' nonetheless.[90]

Winifred Holtby gave the collection a favourable review in *Time and Tide*, a magazine vocal in its criticism of injustice and highly sensitive to the complexities of identity politics in the dominions (particularly Canada and South Africa).[91] In 1926, Afrikaner nationalists had proposed a new flag for the Union and criticised as unpatriotic all who opposed replacing the British Union Jack. Both flags were eventually officially endorsed, after a compromise with the opposition in May 1927. At the time, *Time and Tide* perceived that the issue was about more than just a flag: 'Socially, it means the question of whether South Africa shall be an end in herself or a means to an end in Europe, whether she shall be the "home", in which men hope to die as well as to live, or a *suburb* of Greater London.'[92] Holtby's balanced review did not seek to pronounce on *I Speak of Africa* from an implicated, institutional position, however, but rather ended with the positive remark that, while the other authors reviewed merely described racial problems in Africa, Plomer attempted an exploration of its psychological causes and impact.[93]

The publication of Plomer's third volume of poetry *The Fivefold Screen* is significant for a number of reasons. The manner in which he demanded a particular kind of physical appearance indicates that he was becoming frustrated with the small-scale and very ordinary production of his books by the Hogarth Press. Only 450 copies of *Notes for Poems* had been printed in March 1928, and he felt that if he was not going to sell many copies, his publishers should at least promote his reputation in a particular way.[94] He was particularly eager that his new collection appear independently of any Hogarth series (*The Family Tree* had been published in the 'Hogarth Living Poets Series' in October 1929).[95] John Lehmann agreed, and the volume appeared in a limited edition of 450 numbered and signed copies (350 for sale in the UK, 100 in the USA) on good paper, at an expensive 10s 6d; it was, Lehmann thought, one of Hogarth's 'finest publications'.[96] It was, in other words, a highly collectable *coterie* publication, aimed at a discerning readership, and worked to consolidate Plomer's reputation as a writer of quality. It was also the last of Plomer's collections to include a substantial number of poems inspired by the author's South African experiences, grouped together in a section entitled 'African Landscape with Figures', dedicated to Laurens van der Post (who had collaborated with Plomer and Campbell on *Voorslag*). These include some of Plomer's most anthologised poems, most notably 'The Scorpion', which had appeared first in the *Nation and Athenaeum* on 10 May 1930, a powerful response to the Africa Plomer had left behind which shatters any lingering romantic illusions of the continent in the European imagination.[97]

The poem's speaker reports on floods in the 'Limpopo and Tugela', rivers far from one another and clearly meant as representatives of the country as a whole. He and companions observe

> The corpse of a young negress bruised
> By rocks, and rolling on the shore,
>
> Pushed by the waves of morning, rolled
> Impersonally among shells.
> With lolling breasts and bleeding eyes.[98]

This Africa is an anti-pastoral space, not the promising, vacant vastness so often celebrated in writing about the dominions, and South Africa in particular. This, he declares in the poem's final stanza, 'was the Africa we knew',

> Where, wandering alone,
> We saw, heraldic in the heat,
> A scorpion on a stone.[99]

Ill at ease in the landscape, mere observers, the speaker and his companions are alienated from a landscape whose meaning is bound up in unyielding and dangerous ciphers – a scorpion, a stone – which declare a heraldry and genealogy illegible to the Western imagination. It presents a space of fascination which invites involvement, but is simultaneously unknowable. 'The Scorpion' enacts powerfully Plomer's double attachment and displacement; it is as if, having failed to whip South Africa into order with *Voorslag* (whiplash), his valediction to the country is to condemn it to the fate of the poisonous scorpion's tail.

This poem was much anthologised during the ensuing decade, for example in Yeats's *Oxford Book of Modern Verse* (1936), Maurice Wollman's *Poems of Twenty Years: An Anthology, 1918–1938* (1938), and Phyllis Jones's 1941 Oxford World's Classics *Modern Verse: 1900–1940*.[100] More significant, perhaps, is its appearance in a curious compendium published by the wealthy heiress, *provocatrice* and patron of the arts Nancy Cunard, in 1934. Cunard's *Negro: An Anthology*, published privately in limited numbers, was intended as an affirmative showpiece for cultural production from across the African diaspora. Plomer was happy to provide two contributions, a collection of aphoristic notes entitled 'From an African Notebook', and 'The Scorpion'. The latter appeared, however, in an altered version. Not insignificantly, the corpse became that of 'a young Negro' with 'broken lips' instead of 'lolling breasts'. The poem's Wordsworthian echoes (the negress as Lucy in a revision of Wordsworth's 'A Slumber Did My Spirit Seal') are lost, but it is not clear whether Plomer himself made the amendments or whether Cunard insisted on them to make the poem engage more directly with the title of her collection or because 'negro' was considered more symbolic or representative than the feminine.[101] Plomer mentions Cunard when writing about negrophilia in British intelligentsia in the late 1920s and early 1930s, but *Negro* was intended as something more provocative, as a political statement about racism and bigotry.[102]

Cunard espoused a radical politics, and fell out with several recognised African-American leaders in the USA because of her support for communist revolution to effect African liberation.[103] Plomer's reputation for socially responsible writing critical of racial discrimination could be enlisted on Cunard's side; his work lent itself to suggestive extension beyond the tame socialism of the *Nation and Athenaeum* and the *New Statesman* to the kind of oppositional calls for change with which he had been associated in South Africa. While *Negro* reached a small but appreciative audience, Plomer's inclusion confirmed his reputation as an anti-imperialist writer. It is clear that this aspect of his public persona, established in *Turbott Wolfe* and *I Speak of Africa*, was being privileged in several of the sites in which his work was reproduced in Britain. He also published a pot-boiler biography of Cecil Rhodes, in 1933, which condemned the imperialist for his exploitation of the indigenous peoples in Rhodesia, and the kind of British imperialism to which Rhodes contributed for making both the Boer War and the First World War possible.

Negro was not the only site in which Plomer's work was potentially assimilated to such a position. Two poems which would be included in *The Fivefold Screen*, 'Epitaph for a Contemporary' and 'The Russian Lover', were included in Michael Roberts's *New Signatures: Poems by Various Hands*, published by Hogarth in February 1932.[104] This was the first time that Auden, Spender and Day-Lewis appeared together in print, and many observers, including Leonard Woolf, regarded it as the 'generation's manifesto', although critics have since sought to downplay its importance or coherence.[105] In his Preface, Roberts claimed that the selected poems represented 'a clear reaction against esoteric poetry in which it is necessary for the reader to catch each recondite allusion'. He also noted that the contributors all accepted 'that the alleviation of suffering is good', acknowledging that these altruistic concerns may 'sometimes lead to what appears to be the essence of the communist attitude'.[106] Inclusion in this site projected Plomer as part of a new wave of young, socially concerned, radical intellectuals. Initially only 600 copies of *New Signatures* were printed, but sales were good enough for a reprint of 750 by the following month, and another 1,025 in September 1934 and again in 1935, indicating sales which were unusual for a volume of poetry and which would have circulated Plomer to a wider audience than any of his other books to date – except the immensely successful novel *The Case Is Altered*, a Book Society choice in 1932, but which had nothing to do with South Africa.[107]

A year later, Roberts edited a more significant anthology, *New Country: Prose and Poetry by the Authors of New Signatures*, with a Preface more polemical than before, exhorting readers to take a stance on action for revolutionary change: 'It is time that those who would conserve something which is still valuable in England began to see that only a revolution can save their standards.'[108] Included was poetry and prose by, among others, Auden (including 'A Communist to Others'), Day-Lewis (poems and 'Letter to a Young Revolutionary'), Spender ('Poetry and Revolution'), Isherwood and Upward. And in the midst of these statements of generational angst and communist exhortation was Plomer's short story 'The Child of Queen Victoria', a reworking of themes from *Turbott Wolfe*.[109] The effect of its inclusion was to illustrate the extent to which problems for which decisive action was sought in Britain extended to other parts of a diseased Empire; no mention was made of Plomer's South African background, however. Although he would not be regarded as one of the Auden generation, *New Signatures* and *New Country* are significant in their demonstration of Plomer's level of assimilation into politically progressive British circles only a few years after settling there. From the 'new countries' Plomer had, it seems, been accepted into the literary life of a 'new country'.

Doubly detached: diverging reputations

Michael Roberts went on to edit one of the most important – and polemical – anthologies of the period, *The Faber Book of Modern Verse*, in 1936; Chris Baldick calls it 'the most avant-gardist to the point of sectarianism'.[110] Roberts was typically outspoken in his justification for excluding poetry which, while not insignificant, did not contribute to 'any notable development of poetic technique'.[111] Specifically, he excluded Charles Sorley, Walter de la Mare, Edmund Blunden, Edwin Muir – and Roy Campbell and William Plomer. Plomer's exclusion might seem odd: he had, after all, been included in Roberts's two earlier groundbreaking anthologies, but anthology-making is a fickle business. Campbell's exclusion makes some sense on ideological grounds given his notorious differences with the left-wing poets to whom he gave the collective name 'MacSpaunday' (MacNeice, Spender, Auden, Day-Lewis), and the partisan nature of Roberts's anthology. However, Campbell was still, by Baldick's rough calculation, in the top-twenty most anthologised and recognised poets in Britain in the 1930s, among 'the most often read, the most widely studied, recited, and admired'.[112]

There is evidence that there may also have been a more mundane reason for Campbell's exclusion from Roberts's *Faber Book*, which confirms the fragility of reputation and the power of the reputation-makers. It seems almost certain that Roberts approached Campbell in mid-1934 for permission to include several of his poems in his anthology, making his high-minded justifications for Campbell's exclusion appear shaky. Campbell wrote to Roberts from Altea, in Spain (where he lived between May 1934 and June 1935), that his anthology fees were fixed at £2 2s for extracts under 40 lines, and £5 5s for anything longer.[113] Maurice Wollman had included five of Campbell's shorter African and Provençal poems in a 1934 anthology, *Modern Poetry, 1922–1934*, and Campbell's correspondence with Wollman preliminary to this anthology reveals a similarly hard-nosed attitude to anthology fees. He was particularly impecunious during this period, and gave Wollman a similar response when he wanted to include 'Tristan da Cunha', among other poems, in *Poems of Twenty Years*.[114]

As it turned out, 1936 was a watershed year for Campbell's reputation. He left Spain in August, during the height of the Civil War, and in October published his longest single collection, *Mithraic Emblems*, which developed a personal mythology drawing on the ancient cult of Mithras (which he encountered in Provence) and Catholic peasant life in Spain. The collection received very few, and very mixed, reviews.[115] Nonetheless, and despite his exclusion from Roberts's anthology, four of Campbell's best-known lyrical poems were included in *The Oxford Book of Modern Verse 1892–1935*, edited by W. B. Yeats, which sold 15,000 copies within 3 months of publication.[116]

In 1936, Campbell's work, including 'Tristan da Cunha', also appeared in R. L. Mégroz's *Treasury of Modern Poetry*.[117] In response to Mégroz's request for permission to include the poems, Campbell had told him in July 1935 that he could use any of the poems for a flat fee of 4 guineas; had he insisted – as he did with Roberts and Wollman just one year previously – on 2 guineas for poems under 40 lines, and 5 guineas for poems over, Mégroz would have had to pay him 16 guineas (£16 16s).[118] Money was tight in the mid-1930s – Campbell declared in 1936 that his 'only problem [was] cash' – so his willingness to accept a quarter of what he would have demanded from other anthologists is noteworthy.[119] Its likely reason is evident from the tone of Mégroz's reply to Campbell, which employed flattery ('Knowing I could not get enough for proper fees I was very worried about my favourite living poets, especially you'), and indulged in the kind of literary politics with which Campbell was highly sympathetic, attacking establishment figures ('So the Squires and whatnot can go to hell if they won't give me anything without a fee') and other anthologists with whom Campbell had already had unsatisfactory dealings ('that ineffable collector of names, Wollman').[120]

Campbell had come to feel increasingly persecuted by what he perceived to be a liberal English critical establishment, sympathetic to his Bloomsbury enemies. *Mithraic Emblems* contained many strident attacks on 'Charlies' and 'Pommies' as Campbell lashed out at left-wing poets and critics in a country from which he felt an increasing temperamental distance. It also included a vicious attack in verse on William Plomer,

'Creeping Jesus', as Campbell increasingly resented his erstwhile friend's eminence in left-wing literary circles.[121] By the mid-1930s, the erstwhile colleagues and collaborators had come to occupy very different positions in the literary field, their 'South African' origins and supposed characteristics differently interpreted, employed or elided.

The wide variety of publications in which Campbell and Plomer's writing appeared, and the implications of each site of publication, evidence the volatility of literary reputation and of national cultural identities during the period. In a BBC talk on South African poetry in 1953, Plomer described Campbell as 'a South African poet, and an English poet, and a European poet as well', one of many who had left and found 'some new vision' of South Africa away from the country, but the most outstanding of all its expatriate writers and the only one with an international reputation.[122] Plomer described himself, during a conference address on his only return visit to South Africa three years later, as a 'sort of doubly displaced person', 'simultaneously a South African writer and an English reader, but also an English writer and a South African reader'.[123] Both writers were expatriates with hybrid cultural identities amenable to many different constructions. Both contributed to an international, trans-national, decidedly diffuse, modern moment in the English-language, the British metropolitan, and the South African colonial and proto-postcolonial literary fields during the first half of the twentieth century. These descriptions highlight the positions both occupied years after their removal from South Africa, and which continue to characterise their reputations: of and between two sites of cultural politics, identification and production, '[d]oubly involved and doubly detached', in a period in which a discrete (white) 'South African' cultural identity was beginning, haltingly, to emerge.[124]

Notes

1 Slater, Preface, *Centenary Book*, vii, viii; on Slater (1876–1958), prolific poet, editor and amateur anthropologist, see Smith, *Grounds*, 45–7.

2 Nathan, *South African Literature*, 18; Slater, Preface, *Centenary Book*, viii.

3 Slater, Preface, *New Centenary Book*, v.

4 The best biography is Alexander, *Campbell*; Pearce's *Bloomsbury and Beyond* is inadequately referenced and stridently hagiographic; see *Oxford English Dictionary*, *OED Online*, 'voorslag, *n.*'.

5 Cunningham, *British Writers*, 420; see Ferguson, Salter and Stallworthy (eds), *Norton Anthology*, 1325–8.

6 See Plomer, *Double Lives*, 9.

7 Wilhelm, 'The Single-Dreamer', 25.

8 Plomer, 'Three Letters', 131.

9 Smith, *Grounds*, 47.

10 Chapman (ed.), *Century*, 21, 29; Chapman, *South African English Poetry*, 63.

11 Gordimer, 'Last Colonial Poet?', 1–2; Cronin, 'Turning around'.

12 Chapman, 'A Defence', 79, 84; Chapman, *Southern African Literatures*, 182; see Crewe 'Specter of Adamastor'.

13 Plomer, *Visiting the Caves*, 14–16.

14 Chapman, *Southern African Literatures*, 183.

15 NELM, Doc. 98.30.2.33, Campbell to Lewis. All unpublished Campbell correspondence with permission, Ms Theresa Campbell.

16 Quoted in Ethel Campbell, *Sam Campbell*, 355.

17 See Pajalich, 'Influences of Vorticism'; Parsons, 'Campbell and Wyndham Lewis'.

18 Campbell, *Terrapin*, 45; Carey, *Intellectuals and the Masses*, chapter 2.

19 Campbell, *Terrapin*, 94; on his debt to Nietzsche, see Campbell, 'Modern Poetry' in *Collected Works*, vol. 4, 173–86.

20 Coppard, 'Ark Afloat', 172; Newbolt (ed.), *New Paths*, 410.

21 Young, *Colonial Desire*, 52.

22 Campbell, *Terrapin*, 56, 57, 90, 79–80.

23 Jonathan Cape, 'Threshing'.

24 Anon., 'Land of Gold and Sunshine', 60.

25 Mortimer, 'New Books', 94.

26 Knight and Sabey, *Lion Roars*, 18, 67–9.

27 Sitwell, 'British Empire Exhibition', 44.

28 Bhagat, 'The Poetics of Belonging'.

29 Anon., 'She Was Our South Africa', 76.

30 Anon., Review of *The Flaming Terrapin*, 4.

31 Slater, Preface, *Centenary Book*, xii.

32 Miles, Review of *The Flaming Terrapin*, 423.

33 Monro, Review of *The Flaming Terrapin*, 147, 148.

34 See Alexander, *Campbell*, 45, 48, 54–5, 67–8; Alexander, *Plomer*, chapter 6.

35 Millin, 'South African Magazine', 8.

36 Anon., '*Voorslag*', 8; Clarkson, 'A Lash', 21.

37 Lewis, 'The State of Literature'.

38 Waugh, *Ninety-Two Days*, 16.

39 Campbell, *Adamastor*, 74 (lines 67–8, 75–6).

40 *Ibid.*, 75 (lines 100–3).

41 National Library of South Africa, Cape Town (NLSA), MSB 76, 1/192, MS Tristan, Campbell, 'Tristan da Cunha'; see Plomer, '*Voorslag* Days', 50; Alexander (ed.), Introduction, xiv; Alexander, *Campbell*, 62.

42 Campbell, 'Tristan', *Waste Paper Basket*, 4–7; Wilson to Van der Vlies, private correspondence.

43 Alexander, *Campbell*, 34.

44 Campbell, 'Zulu Girl', 'The Serf'; see Pearce, *Bloomsbury and Beyond*, 79.

45 Campbell, *Adamastor*, 41 (line 11); several other of Campbell's poems appeared in the paper between 1928 and 1930.

46 Holtby, 'Voorloper Group', 568–9.

47 *Oxford English Dictionary*, OED Online, 'voorloper, *n.*'.

48 Campbell, 'Tristan', *New Statesman*.

49 Sullivan (ed.), *Victorian and Edwardian Age*, 263.

50 See, for example, Anon., '"Solving" the South African Native Problem'; and Anon., 'South Africa's "White" Problem'. Plomer's Mabel van der Horst

makes a similar observation in *Turbott Wolfe*: 'My good man, there is no native question. It isn't a question. It's an answer' (122).

51 Eliot, 'Tristan da Cunha'.

52 See 'Om', 'The Poetry of Roy Campbell'.

53 Jonathan Cape Archive (RUL Cape), A Files, Thompson to Campbell. All Jonathan Cape Archive, University of Reading material quoted with permission, Random House.

54 RUL Cape, A Files, Campbell to Thompson.

55 See Parsons, *Bibliography*, 7–12.

56 On the significance of the myth of Adamastor, the black Titan who was the hostile presiding spirit of the Cape in *Os Lusiadas* (*The Lusiads*), the epic by sixteenth-century Portuguese poet Luis Vaz de Camões (Camoens), see Gray, 'Myth of Adamastor'; Alexander, *Campbell*, 74; Smith, *Grounds*, 49–50.

57 Parsons includes an invaluable list of anthologies, to 1981, which included Campbell's poems; see Parsons, *Bibliography*, 105–17. For an account of variations in the text of the poem collected in different anthologies, and an edition of the poem enumerating these variations, see Van der Vlies, '"Your Passage Leaves its Track of . . . Change"'.

58 See under Campbell's 'Tristan da Cunha', in Bibliography.

59 Campbell, 'Tristan', *Best Poems of 1928*.

60 See Alexander, *Campbell*, 78–86.

61 Sullivan (ed.), *Modern Age*, 69–77, 313–20; see Hibberd, *Monro*.

62 Campbell (as Marston), 'Eunuch Arden', 33.

63 Monro (ed.), Introduction, 7.

64 *Ibid.*, 10, 11.

65 Monro, Review of *Adamastor*, 352–3.

66 Monro's selection included a wide range of mostly established and many Georgian and First World War poets, including Flint, Mew, Bridges, Davidson, Blunt, Meynell, Housman, Thomas, de la Mare, Aldington, Wolfe, Binyon, Graves, Rosenberg, Sassoon, Owen, Quennell, Noyes, Squire, Chesterton, Hardy, Hopkins, Yeats, Eliot, H. D., Joyce, Pound and Lawrence.

67 'Roy Campbell, 1902–', in Campbell, *Poems* (1931), iii.

68 *Ibid.*

69 See Campbell, *Broken Record* and *Light on a Dark Horse*.

70 Slater, Preface, *Centenary Book*, vii–viii, xii.

71 Campbell, 'Tristan', *Longer Poems*, 236–9; and Cairncross (ed.), *Longer Poems*, 292, 304.

72 *Modern Muse*, vii.

73 *Ibid.*

74 Campbell, 'Tristan', *Modern Muse*, 56–9. Arthur Shearly Cripps was a radical Anglican missionary in southern Rhodesia, author of the controversial *The Black Christ* (1902); see Chapman, *Southern African Literatures*, 159–60.

75 *Modern Muse*, viii.

76 See Davenport and Saunders, *South Africa*, 291, 320, 334; Macnab, *South Africa House*, 88, 93.

77 Patmore, 'Florentine Interlude', 84.

78 See also Lambert, 'South African British?', 203–5, 208–9.

79 Plomer, 'Coming to London', 21.
80 NELM, William Plomer files, Plomer to Monro, 14 January 1922; see also *ibid.*, 2 October 1921. Both letters quoted with permission, NELM, and copyright the William Plomer Trust. See Alexander, *Plomer*, 60–6, 74–5, 343.
81 See Plomer, *Selected Poems*, 16.
82 Clarkson, 'A Lash'; see Campbell, 'The Significance of *Turbott Wolfe*'.
83 Plomer, 'Pop!'
84 *Ibid.*
85 Plomer, 'Some Books', 55.
86 Plomer, *Turbott Wolfe*, 89.
87 Alexander, *Plomer*, 149–58; Plomer, 'Coming to London', 18–19; Plomer, *At Home*, chapters 3 and 4. Instead of rhyming with 'Homer', his name was to rhyme with 'bloomer'.
88 Plomer, *I Speak*, 259–60.
89 Williams, Review of *I Speak of Africa*.
90 Anon., 'More Fiction', 191.
91 See Sullivan (ed.), *Modern Age*, 441–53.
92 Anon., 'Illumination'; see Davenport and Saunders, *South Africa*, 303–4; Campbell, 'Fetish Worship', 16.
93 Holtby, 'They Speak of Africa'.
94 Woolmer, *Checklist*, 60, 57.
95 Hogarth Press Archive (RUL Hogarth), MS 2750, 342, Plomer to Lehmann. All Hogarth Press Archive, University of Reading material quoted with permission, Random House.
96 Woolmer, *Checklist*, 106; RUL Hogarth, MS 2750, 342, Lehmann to Clarke.
97 Plomer, 'Scorpion', *Nation and Athenaeum*, 170.
98 Plomer, *Fivefold Screen*, 40 (lines 7–11).
99 *Ibid.* (13–16).
100 See Bibliography further.
101 Plomer, 'The Scorpion', *Negro*, 268.
102 Plomer, *At Home*, 102.
103 Chisholm, *Nancy Cunard*, 214.
104 See Plomer's 'Epitaph' and 'Russian Lover', in Roberts (ed.), *New Signatures*, 78–85.
105 Woolf, *Downhill*, 174; see Baldick, *The Modern Movement*, 92, 108; Haffenden, *William Empson*, 263.
106 Roberts (ed.), *New Signatures*, 12–13, 18.
107 Woolmer, *Checklist*, 107. *The Case Is Altered* sold 11,308 copies in its first 6 months; see Willis, *Hogarth Press*, 202–4; Van der Vlies, 'William Plomer', 221–3.
108 Roberts, Preface, *New Country*, 11.
109 Plomer, 'Child of Queen Victoria', in Roberts (ed.), *New Country*, 111–54; it was included later that year in Plomer's *The Child of Queen Victoria*.
110 Baldick, *The Modern Movement*, 76.
111 Roberts, Introduction, *Faber Book*, 1.
112 Baldick's representative comparison of major anthologies – including several in which 'Tristan da Cunha' appeared – reveals that Campbell was the nineteenth-most represented poet (of Baldick's thirty-five listed): *The Modern Movement*, 111.

113 BL, MS Add. 58079J, Campbell to Roberts. See Alexander, *Campbell*, 149, 155, 133.

114 State University of New York, Buffalo (SUNY), Campbell to Wollman (February 1934 and late 1936). With permission, Poetry Collection, University Libraries, SUNY, Buffalo.

115 See Alexander, *Campbell*, 167.

116 'The Serf', 'The Zulu Girl', 'The Sisters' and 'Autumn', in Yeats (ed.), *Oxford Book*, 393–6; Yeats, *Letters on Poetry*, 147.

117 Other poems included were 'The Palm', 'The Zulu Girl', 'Mass at Dawn' and 'African Moonrise'; see University of Reading, 'Papers of R. L. Mégroz' (online).

118 RUL Hogarth, MS 1979, Campbell to Mégroz.

119 Campbell, 'A Yarn with Old Woodley', in *Collected Works*, vol. 4, 270.

120 RUL Hogarth, MS 1979, Mégroz to Campbell. With permission, Mrs A. Mégroz Lord.

121 See Campbell, *Mithraic*, 132–4; Alexander, *Campbell*, 113–14, 168, 264; Alexander, *Plomer*, 157–8, 164, 199–200.

122 NELM, 091 PLO 530/35–36, Plomer, 'South African Poetry'. Copyright: the William Plomer Trust.

123 Plomer, 'South African Writers', 55.

124 *Ibid.*

4

Whose *Beloved Country*? Alan Paton and the hypercanonical

I do not remember precisely when I first read Alan Paton's novel, *Cry, the Beloved Country: A Story of Comfort in Desolation*, although it was probably late in my primary-school career. I do, however, have vivid memories of two later engagements with the novel which speak to this chapter's attempt to account for its remarkable biography. I bought a copy of the new Penguin Twentieth-Century Classics edition at Fogarty's Bookshop on Main Street, in downtown Port Elizabeth, in late 1991. Before leaving the store, I recognised another customer, an elderly black man, as the recently released political prisoner Govan Mbeki (father of President Thabo Mbeki), and asked nervously for his autograph, which he gave graciously. I pasted it into my copy of *Cry, the Beloved Country*. The novel's emotional energies clearly worked on a white youth of 17, attuned to the politics of the interregnum – Mandela had been released, negotiations were underway, the television news reported violence engineered by mysterious 'third forces' – but feeling marooned (in hindsight, self-right-eously) in white suburbia. Had I been identifying Mbeki with the long-suffering Stephen Kumalo, and myself with Arthur's child, the young white boy pleased with his contact with a real African? I remember recall-ing that encounter when the post-apartheid City Council renamed Main Street as Govan Mbeki Avenue.

The second memory is of my first train journey to Johannesburg, in January 1996. Initially, I shared a second-class compartment with a former Umkhonto we Sizwe (the ANC's armed wing) cadre, but he disem-barked at Bloemfontein to rejoin his National Defence Force unit, and with the compartment to myself, I opened the blinds as the train crossed the Vaal River and read Paton's description of Kumalo's train journey to Johannesburg. Despite my 21-year-old self's cynicism about Paton's Christian paternalism, I still found the novel immensely moving: two years into the New South Africa, it seemed we hadn't all turned to hating, as Stephen Kumalo, at the end of the novel, recalls his friend Msimangu fearing.

These two moments attest to the strange and enduring power of *Cry, the Beloved Country*, despite many of the justifiable criticisms levelled against it. They support Dan Jacobson's claim, in a tribute on Paton's death, that the book had achieved a 'proverbial' status, that for South Africans it evaded adequate assessment in exclusively political or aesthetic terms, instead becoming 'part of a common stock of reference and of modes of self-recognition'.[1] At the time of Paton's death in 1988, his most famous novel had sold 15 million copies in 20 languages, and was still selling some 100,000 a year.[2] Repackaged in book club, college and school editions, sometimes in shortened or simplified 'versions', serialised and abridged, filmed, dramatised and staged as a jazz opera on Broadway, *Cry, the Beloved Country* qualifies as what Rob Nixon calls 'the only blockbuster in the annals of anti-apartheid literature'.[3]

Its remarkable afterlife continues, it seems fair to say, because it has satisfied an array of ever-changing context- and period-specific desires. Its model of Christian humanism, trusteeship and reconciliation spoke to white, middle-class, American readers, anxious about racial tensions in their own country. Paton's novel seemed to offer something to many in post-war Labourite Britain, too, capitalising on interest in social conditions across the Commonwealth, while touching on a sense of crisis in white British identities as the Empire ebbed away. In a letter in May 1948, Paton mused about the possible reception of the novel in South Africa, fearing that it would 'be very different from the American', that it would 'arouse unconscious antagonism' and that, 'instead of attacking the cause of their antagonism', his critics would 'attack ... its art'.[4] While there was immediate scorn for the novel's politics from activists and writers on the left of the political spectrum in South Africa, hostile to Paton's apparent answers to the country's racial injustices, he need not have worried.[5] Readers there, their sense of cultural nationalism both encouraged and piqued by the fact of the novel's Anglo-American publication and the nature of its reception abroad, encountered a text whose local pre-publication advertising declared it already a masterpiece, a classic-in-the-making. Only a very few dared comment on its 'art', and then, usually, only to praise what had already been validated by critical acclaim in the capitals of northern aesthetic judgement. The coincidence of the novel's appearance in the same year as the May 1948 election victory of the National Party, with its programme of apartheid policies, created a climate in which Paton's prognostications on the country assumed near prophetic status.[6]

Endorsements by prominent South African public figures (significantly, both white) on the back cover of a recent Penguin edition suggest its continuing national and international construction: Nadine Gordimer calls it the 'most influential South African novel ever written'; the late Donald Woods thought that '[n]o book since *Uncle Tom's Cabin*' had a comparable impact 'on international opinion on the issue of race'.[7] Both comments indicate the extent to which *Cry, the Beloved Country* has come to be revered both as an important – and specifically 'South African' – social *document* and also a work of *literature*. It has been and remains a

multimedia phenomenon unparalleled in the history of the country's literary and cultural production, undoubtedly its best example of the demands
and dividends of *canonisation*; one might call it 'hypercanonical', following Jonathan Arac's description of the mid-twentieth-century contestation
and elevation of Mark Twain's *Huckleberry Finn*, which is both among
the most banned texts by American school boards, but also a premiere
text in discourses about American national literary identity.[8] Paton's novel
continues to be taught in schools around the world, its most recent film
adaptation was as late as 1996 and, in 2003, it was featured on Oprah
Winfrey's Book Club, touted by no less than Bill Clinton, Alicia Keys and
Charlize Theron.[9] In this chapter I seek to account for some of the ways
in which the novel's political energies have been modified or elided by the
material conditions of different instances of publication. I consider its
reception in the USA, Britain and South Africa after publication in 1948,
some exemplary appropriations of the novel published during the 1950s
and 1960s and its promotion as an educational text from the 1960s to the
1980s.

The 'exquisite pleasure' of 'moral indignation': America reads *Cry, the Beloved Country*

Paton was serving as warden of Diepkloof Reformatory, a borstal for
young, black, male offenders, when he began his novel. At the time,
September 1946, he was on a brief visit to Trondheim in Norway during
a study tour of reformatories and prisons in Europe and North America.
The manuscript was completed in California during the same trip, in late
December, and sample chapters dispatched to a dozen American publishers. Several expressed interest, but Paton chose Charles Scribner's Sons in
New York. In February 1947, the firm's Maxwell Perkins accepted the
novel for publication, and it appeared on 1 February 1948.

It is chiefly to its reception in the USA that *Cry, the Beloved Country*
owes its remarkable success. Six impressions of the Scribner's edition
appeared within three months of first publication, and sales since have
been consistently impressive.[10] Early success was not an accident:
Scribner's sent advance copies to the *New York Times* and *New York
Herald Tribune*, where the novel would be noticed by book club editors,
and library and school advisers. A favourable notice from the *Christian
Herald* was sent to forty religious bookshops, too, to excite attention
from retailers thought likely to respond well to Paton's message.[11]
Advertisements in the trade journal *Publishers' Weekly* quoted ringing
endorsements from three constituencies – critics, clergy and booksellers –
suggesting the qualities which Scribner's sought to emphasise, and which
would be rehearsed repeatedly in the novel's very many American reviews:
its 'strong inspirational appeal', its nature as a 'penetrating and timely
study of a pressing social problem' and its 'unique, beautiful, and moving

writing'.[12] The tone of the blurb on the first edition's cover expressly invokes all three categories of judgement: Kumalo's journey to Johannesburg is to 'the city of evil', his search for 'his only son' is 'long and sorrowful', reaching a 'height of tragedy which has seldom been equalled in contemporary fiction', and although it is 'a sad book', it is also 'beautifully wrought with high poetic compassion'; it is 'the story' of South Africa's 'landscape, its people, its bitter racial ferment and unrest'.[13] Whether in mass circulation dailies or rural weeklies, *Cry, the Beloved Country* was read as all of these things: an affecting narrative, a documentary and also a work of art.

On the day preceding publication, the Sunday edition of the *New York Times* carried an advance notice by Richard Sullivan calling it 'beautiful', a 'rich, firm and moving piece of prose' and 'poetic and profound spiritual drama' which 'in other hands might have made merely an interesting sociological document'.[14] The Monday edition of the same newspaper carried Orville Prescott's description of it as 'creative fiction of a high order' demonstrating that 'a thesis novel' need not sacrifice 'artistic integrity'. Paton did not mount a 'soap box to orate at the expense of his novel as a work of fiction', Prescott argued: the novel was a documentary record *and* a work of art.[15] Harry Hansen's review in New York's *Survey Graphic* in March 1948, 'A Gentle Protest', commended it, too, as an 'outstanding example of a creative effort embodying social comment', expressly not '[p]ropaganda', 'a word that novelists detest'.[16]

The discussion of the novel's characters both as dignified individuals and as types acting out a psycho-drama, the universal resonances of which prevented the novel from being viewed as propaganda, was widespread. Adrienne Koch's suggestion in New York's *Saturday Review of Literature* that Kumalo's 'pilgrimage' was an 'objective correlative for one of the central problems of our time – how to resolve belief in the dignity and integrity of the individual with the needs of modern industrialized society' is exemplary.[17] Kumalo was seen as 'a complete human being' and the white characters as representative of 'white colonials anywhere'.[18] A reviewer in the African-American journal *Phylon* called it 'as ironic and detached as a fine Greek tragedy' and commended Paton's 'moving, human drama, that lifts this novel to the plane of great social vision, and, simultaneously, to the plane of great art'.[19] In its apparent representation of universal human values, then, the novel was regarded in the USA as having avoided the pitfalls of social protest literature, in a period in which 'protest' was widely distrusted in literary circles. In a 1939 *Partisan Review* symposium, for example, Lionel Trilling called 'protest' damaging; despite legitimately intending to arouse 'pity and anger', as a genre it was merely a form of 'escapism', 'subtle flattery by which the progressive middle-class reader is cockered up with a sense of his own virtue';[20] 'moral indignation', Trilling observed in his 1947 essay 'Manners, Morals and the Novel', 'may be in itself an exquisite pleasure'.[21] The public was not convinced by the aesthetic merits of works which held up 'some image of society to consider and condemn', he argued, and, if 'the question of quality' was raised, readers were likely to declare these books 'not great ... not imaginative ... not "literature"'.[22] Jonathan Arac also identifies Trilling – particularly his Introduction to Rinehart's 1948 college edition – as the most important critical voice whose endorsement precipitated the hypercanonisation of Twain's *Huckleberry Finn* in the latter half of the twentieth century.[23] I suggest that, while there is no similarly identifiable, single, authoritative, critical intervention in the reception of *Cry, the Beloved Country*, liberal critical discourses of the type of which Trilling's is exemplary explain, at least in part, the widespread celebration of the novel in America, a celebration which set the scene for the novel's positive British and South African reception.

Cry, the Beloved Country was, of course, amenable to this reading. A response which absolves the state of the responsibility to eliminate discrimination is mystificatory and encourages a revisionist history of oppression; reading Paton's novel as a tale with universal appeal and application by focusing on individual characters as representative human types marginalised the novel's undeniable critique of institutionalised racial discrimination, no matter how retrograde Paton's representations of black characters would, in themselves, be regarded by some more radical readers. It should be noted that not all critics were so easily won over, however. The reviewer in the *Chicago Tribune* agreed that *Cry, the Beloved Country* was valuable as a 'revelation of conditions in South Africa', but suggested that it was 'unfortunately ... more of a tract than a novel', its characters 'simply dummies pushed around for the sake of the plot', 'types without any individuating traits whatever'.[24]

It is clear, however, that Paton's novel played to a particular anxiety in the USA. A review by Aubrey Burns, in whose home in California Paton had finished the manuscript, suggests its clear parallels for America: Burns called *Cry, the Beloved Country* 'a mirror in which the American South may be seen reflected in dispassionate perspective', and claimed that it offered 'the most acceptable and effective expression on the subject of race relations for American readers'.[25] Cannily, perhaps, or perhaps inadvertently, the jacket blurb of the Scribner's edition refers to James Jarvis having a 'great plantation', a southern term by then current across America (especially after *Gone With The Wind*), but a term which is not used in the same way in South Africa. It comes as no surprise that Paton came to enjoy the status of a sage in the USA on the issue of racial conflict, touring the country for *Collier's Magazine* in 1954 to write two articles on the position of African-Americans.[26] *Cry, the Beloved Country* received the Ebony Award 'for the best book improving racial understanding' in 1948, and won $1,000 in the Anisfield–Wolf Awards for Books on Racial Relations in 1949.[27]

Paton's novel suggested to an American audience that a non-confrontational, non-communist solution could be found also for that country's racial inequalities and discrimination. Lesley Cowling suggests that it 'allowed for a collective imagining of a narrative of race, trauma and Christian reconciliation in an imagined world (the beloved country) that was not [Americans'] own', that the 'thorny problem of racism in their own context could be displaced and resolved in the imagined world of the book'.[28] It was right for its time. Diana Trilling confessed, tellingly, in *The Nation* in 1948: 'I suppose if Alan Paton had written about the American Negro or even about the American Indian in the idyllic vein in which he writes about the Zulus, I would be quick to dismiss him as a sentimentalist.'[29] Paton's is not the only South African writing which has appealed in this way to American audiences, of course: Athol Fugard's plays have proved consistently popular over the past thirty years precisely because they, too, can be construed as participating in the ongoing 'agonized conversations about race in America', Fugard's white South African characters seeming, American academic Jeanne Colleran suggests, 'like long-lost cousins who have reappeared just in time to remind us that despite our tepid political response to both apartheid and to domestic racism, our capacity for moral outrage is still intact'.[30]

A novel guide: Britain reads *Cry, the Beloved Country*

Not long after Scribner's had accepted the manuscript, British publisher Jonathan Cape, on business in New York, called on Maxwell Perkins and was offered the British rights to the novel.[31] Paton always claimed that Cape accepted *Cry, the Beloved Country* without hesitation, and that Plomer, the firm's chief reader, was 'immediately enthusiastic' about the manuscript.[32] This, however, was not the case. The reader's report, long presumed lost, actually survives among Paton's papers and shows that Plomer was far from confident that the novel was worthy of the firm's list. His report, dated 12 March 1947, also shows that he thought the author to be 'English by birth and South African by adoption', which might explain his less than glowing assessment that Paton had not been successful in 'the difficult task of trying to describe the natives from the inside'.[33] He was unable to portray convincing characters, Plomer suggested, because his was 'essentially a propagandist novel, intended to show the native in as favourable a light as possible and to influence white opinion'. While the novel had 'considerable merits' as a social commentary, it was unlikely to succeed, he felt: 'I have known better books of the kind flop, though they have had respectful reviews.'[34] It is ironic, of course, that Plomer's *Turbott Wolfe* and the stories in *I Speak of Africa* had been similarly construed by many British reviewers.

While Plomer had some difficulty deciding whether serious purpose should outweigh doubts about the novel's artistic merit, and concerns about it being propaganda, short reports from two other readers were more positive. Daniel Bunting noted that, while 'disposed to resist the urgent propaganda appeal' and the biblical style of the prose, the narrative was compelling, and readers would find 'its unusual theme and treatment ... of great interest'.[35] He reinforced that reading when reviewing the novel (as Daniel George) in the *Daily Express* in late September, describing it as having 'literary merits which must command universal respect'.[36] Bunting had recommended Orwell's *Animal Farm* to Jonathan Cape – in vain, it turned out – in 1944, and was clearly receptive to novels engaging with political issues.[37] Cape finally accepted Paton's novel, but post-war paper shortages meant it was unlikely to appear in Britain or South Africa, where Cape held the rights, before 1949. The novel's warm reception in America, however, encouraged Cape to hurry it out, and the British edition appeared on 27 September 1948.[38]

There are some differences between the British and American editions. Scribner's edition is dedicated to Aubrey and Marigold Burns (in whose Californian home Paton completed the manuscript), the Cape edition to Paton's wife and his mentor, United Party politician and jurist J. H. Hofmeyr.[39] Apart from the American and British English spelling variations, the American edition is divided into three 'books' with chapters numbered consecutively throughout, while chapter numbers in the British edition begin anew in each book.[40] There are several minor textual variations: one notable difference occurs in the passage in which Reverend Kumalo discusses his future with the bishop (the fifth chapter in Book Three) and a letter arrives from James Jarvis, acknowledging Kumalo's message of sympathy at his wife's death, and offering to build a new church. Kumalo declares it 'from God' but the bishop reads the letter and, in the American edition, declares gravely: 'That was a foolish jest. This is truly a letter from God.' The Cape and subsequent Penguin editions omit the final sentence, altering the tone of the bishop's response from that of a mild rebuke which affirms the divinely inspired providence of the help Jarvis offers to severe displeasure at Kumalo's insolence in suggesting that Jarvis is God-like (it reads, too, as pique at being excluded from unfamiliar cooperation between black and white).[41]

British reviewers repeated the anxious American representation of *Cry, the Beloved Country* as both social document *and* literature – and by virtue of being literary, more than mere social document, or propaganda. *Current Literature* called Paton 'too good an artist to descend to partisanship'.[42] The *Daily Telegraph*'s reviewer called it 'that rare treat, a novel with a social purpose which is also a good story and an artistic whole'.[43] The *British Weekly* ('A Journal of Christian and Social Progress') thought it 'social history in the form of great literature', and the *Manchester Guardian* called it 'as remarkable ... for its facts as for its truth', suggesting that truth was a function of the art which made the novel more than a presentation of fact.[44] Francis Brett Young – a prolific English writer and critic who lived in South Africa from 1945 until his death in 1954 and a passionate advocate of the country – wrote in the *Sunday Times* that *Cry, the Beloved Country* was 'not only a work of art but a "novel with a purpose"', 'sincere' and with 'moments of beauty and pitiful emotion' which marked it as 'a work of art'.[45] Extracts from that review were reproduced on the front inside jacket-flap of later impressions of the Cape edition, replacing the first British edition's more narrative blurb, which had stressed Paton's 'wide knowledge of local conditions', and his 'religious sense'.[46] For the few critics mildly sceptical of Paton's literary abilities it was the availability of universal themes in the novel which they chose to emphasise. Walter Allen in the *New Statesman and Nation*, for example, thought *Cry, the Beloved Country* 'amateurish' in some respects, but noted that in Stephen Kumalo Paton had created a 'moving and wholly acceptable symbol of human goodness'.[47] The *Tribune*'s reviewer found 'overwritten rhetorical musings', but suggested that, while it had 'weaknesses as a novel', it was 'a morality story, of course'.[48]

Some reviewers likened the purpose and potential impact of the novel to the work of Victorian condition-of-England novelists: the *British Africa Monthly* ventured that, 'like *Oliver Twist* and the other social tracts of the great Victorian novelist', it might 'let light into dark corners'.[49] In a similar vein, many regarded it as a kind of report on the situation in South Africa, but as more significant – and 'true'. In South Africa, the Government's Fagan Commission's report had also been published in February 1948, addressing many of the same issues as Paton's novel. It came too late to offer impetus for real change to the jittery United Party Government of Prime Minister Jan Smuts, soon to lose elections to D. F. Malan's revitalised National Party, but nonetheless raised the possibility of changes of which Paton would have approved: that black workers be allowed to bring their families with them to the cities; that more humane conditions be created on the new Orange Free State goldfields; that landlessness and deprivation in the tribal reserves be addressed and the pass system ameliorated.[50] The *British Africa Monthly* was no doubt correct in supposing that *Cry, the Beloved Country* would have greater appeal than a government report, but its suggestion that Paton's novel contained essentially the same material, possibly to greater effect, is intriguing. 'May it not be that Alan Paton in clothing the problem in flesh and blood by the creation of Africans and Europeans of goodwill has done something that will help to make it possible to keep alive the liberal spirit in South Africa', the reviewer asked.[51]

The third impression of Cape's edition had appeared in Britain within a month of publication. There were 18 Cape impressions by 1951, although each was of only 5,000 copies. At least half of these, about 45,000 copies, were sold in South Africa. There were 31 Cape impressions between 1948 and 1977, amounting to 178,000 copies, and the novel also sold 158,000 copies in the Reprint Society World Books series.[52] Exceptionally large sales of the novel in Britain and South Africa were achieved in its Penguin edition; Penguin had been anxious to acquire rights to the novel for several years before Cape decided to license a paperback edition in 1958, and there were new editions in 1959, 1988 and 2001.[53] Sales figures are sketchy, but the Penguin edition, for example, sold in excess of 30,000 copies in the 6 months to the end of December 1972 and the same number in the 6 months following.[54] Penguin's licence was extended regularly, earning Paton a considerable amount.[55]

'A great book in any [other] country': South Africans and *Cry, the Beloved Country*

The *Cape Times* noted on 24 March 1948 that American critics were praising Cry, *the Beloved Country* 'so enthusiastically that it [was] likely to move up into the ranks of the best sellers in that country', while South African readers had to 'wait impatiently for a British edition, available to booksellers in the Union, to be published'.[56] Once it had arrived, most English-language reviews in mainstream white papers were positive. A review in the *Daily Dispatch* in early October 1948, for example, agreed that while it was 'often not possible to rely too closely upon foreign opinion in estimates of their worth of books upon South Africa' ('works that might impress outside observers do not always stand up to the searchlight of local knowledge'), Paton's novel was indeed 'entitled to be called a great book in any country, anywhere'.[57] Advance advertisements in the country had drawn heavily on American notices and reviews, often repeating them almost exactly (as in the Central News Agency's advert in the *Rand Daily Mail* on 18 September).[58] This quoted 4 American endorsements, 3 directly from the *New York Times* advertisement, and encouraged readers to obtain a copy of a 'timeless story of modern South Africa'. The description draws on American endorsements which discover a universal appeal, while also suggesting that the novel was a document of contemporary, specifically South African, circumstances.

A review in the *Natal Mercury*, published in Paton's home province, echoed those sentiments, confirming that the novel was widely *expected* to become a best-seller. It claimed, too, that while foreign readers had judged it 'an outstanding piece of literature', South African readers would 'look at it differently' and be impressed chiefly by Paton's 'realistic understanding of some of the indigenous problems of this country'.[59] These by now familiar terms of engagement are clear from the *Daily Despatch* review: Paton's novel 'has deep truth, and simplicity and directness' which spoke of 'profound understanding'; it was not mere reportage. Furthermore, it suggested 'a forceful message that is concealed in the writing of it and that emerges indirectly and not at the insistence of the author'.[60] An anonymous reviewer in *Jewish Affairs* grappled with a concern that the novel was not great literature even if it seemed important documentary work. The novel was noticed in all the major South African

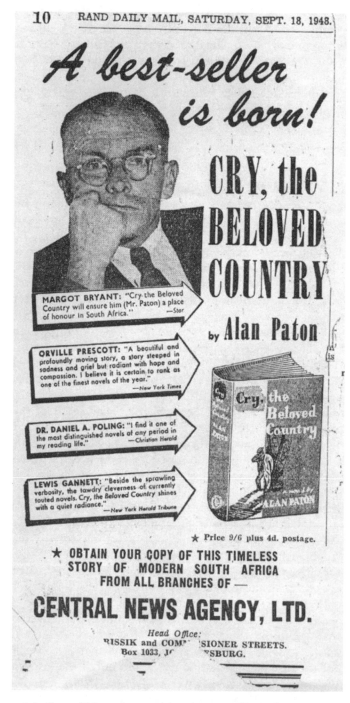

4.1 Central News Agency advertisement, September 1948

BOOKS *New York Times*
February 9, 1948 · 17

A best-seller is born!

The first printing was entirely sold out the day after publication.

Two days after publication translation rights for three foreign languages (French, Swedish, Italian) were sold.

A *large second printing* is now on press.

Here is the spontaneous chorus of praise that launched it!

ORVILLE PRESCOTT: "A beautiful and profoundly moving story, a story steeped in sadness and grief but radiant with hope and compassion. I believe it is certain to rank as one of the finest novels of the year."
—*New York Times*

LEWIS GANNETT: "Beside the sprawling verbosity, the tawdry cleverness of currently touted novels, Cry, the Beloved Country shines with a quiet radiance."
—*New York Herald Tribune*

HARRY HANSEN: "We need more such books, for the lift that they give the spirit."
—*New York World-Telegram*

CRY, the BELOVED COUNTRY by Alan Paton

CRY, the BELOVED COUNTRY by Alan Paton

DR. DANIEL A. POLING: "I find it one of the most distinguished novels of any period in my reading life."
—*Christian Herald*

W. G. ROGERS: "A grand and beautiful book."
—*Associated Press*

DR. RALPH W. SOCKMAN: "A memorable book—it has a haunting quality which lingers in the mind of the reader long after he has laid it down."

ADRIENNE KOCH: "A greatly moving and beautiful story." —*Saturday Review of Literature*

DR. JOSEPH R. SIZOO: "I cannot keep it out of my mind and I keep going back to it."

RICHARD SULLIVAN: "There is not much current writing that goes deeper than this."
—*New York Times Book Review*

MARGARET CARSON HUBBARD: "Not since The Story of an African Farm has a novel come out of South Africa which touches as truly and poignantly the turmoil and burning tragedy of that glad, sad country."
—*New York Herald Tribune Weekly Book Review*

DUDLEY JENKINS: "Here indeed is a book that is entitled to be called *distinguished*."
—*Philadelphia Bulletin*

G. W. WAKEFIELD: "A novel of love, not hate, of hope and courage springing from the dauntless spirit of man." —*Library Journal*

CRY, the BELOVED COUNTRY by Alan Paton

Have you discovered for yourself this timeless story of South Africa today?

4.2 Scribner's advertisement, February 1948

Jewish papers, all of which were very aware, in the early post-Holocaust years, of the urgent need to extend to other races in South Africa the recognition and tolerance which Jews demanded themselves.[61] Echoing in order to dismiss the suggestion that anyone with Paton's experience of 'African conditions' could have written the novel, the *Jewish Affairs* reviewer argued that '*Cry, the Beloved Country* looks so much like a document, so much like a presentation of facts, merely edited, that its literary merit tends to be overlooked', but literary merits it had, the reviewer thought. Paton 'contrived to import to what is essentially a work of fiction, an authenticity which gives it the validity of a document', the reviewer noted, but, while certainly a document, it was also 'a piece of creative art'.[62] For *Femina*, too, Paton's novel was a technically accomplished 'tour de force' as well as (or on account of being also) 'a statement, a documentary'.[63]

Operating with a limited conception of the category of 'the literary', one effected in large measure by metropolitan assumptions about a (British) literary standard, the horizon of expectations for many South African critics was challenged by Paton's novel – as it had been in a different manner by, for example, Schreiner's *The Story of an African Farm* and Plomer's *Turbott Wolfe*. To read the novel was 'to undertake a new step in our own education', declared the *Rand Daily Mail*'s reviewer, who suggested further that a 'very good preparation for reading it intelligently [was] to go down to Johannesburg station at nine o'clock in the morning and watch the Natal train come in and pour its passenger-load of problems on the platform'.[64] The veracity of Paton's representation of the problems attendant on urbanisation and detribalisation – which the reviewer uncomfortably, and perhaps tellingly, anthropomorphises in the persons of their victims – might be ascertained through social observation: 'This stream of humanity is so vividly heterogenous that you cannot fail to be shocked by it into a sudden, sharp realisation of the extent of Johannesburg's impact upon these people, and it is precisely this impact which is the theme and impulse of the book.'[65] Once again, discourses of the literary and the social documentary complement and qualify each other.

Almost all such reviews mirrored the paternal attitude to 'these people' which, many have argued, informed Paton's approach. The *Daily Despatch* reviewer called the novel 'a message of sympathy and kindliness towards a childlike people groping in the darkness'.[66] Joseph Sachs claimed in *Trek* that the reader of *Cry, the Beloved Country* witnessed 'the Natives whom we know as a people and a problem, shed their anonymity and emerge as ... human beings with feelings, passions, dimensions'.[67] But his discussion of Paton's representation of the cadences of the vernacular Zulu militated against any presentation of Africans as other than undifferentiated members of a primitive, pre-linguistic community: 'their discourse has the animistic flavour of the primitive; their ideas run to metaphor and personification', it is 'redolent of a primal symbolism', it 'vibrates with the living rhythms that stir their childlike minds'.[68] It was this portrayal of black characters which invited trenchant criticism on political grounds from black South African intellectuals.

A reviewer in the Cape Town-based periodical *The Torch*, which served a largely Coloured readership and was the mouthpiece of the Non-European Unity Movement (and so allied with South Africa's Trotskyist Left), took issue with the politics of *Cry, the Beloved Country* soon after its arrival in the country, rejecting what it took to be the novel's suggestion that the '[b]lack man's answer to oppression' ought to be 'long-suffering humility and gratitude for small mercies'. Such 'time-worn answers' were 'no longer acceptable to the Non-Europeans', *Torch* declared; they had rejected 'Christian trusteeship' and Paton's message had 'no validity for them to-day'.[69] There was a lively debate about the novel in *Torch*. A letter published on 29 November 1948 took issue with those who praised the 'humanity' of *Cry, the Beloved Country*. They ran into trouble, the correspondent suggested, because the 'politics of emancipation' was the only critical standard by which to measure 'the ideological side' of such a novel, and, in the final analysis Paton stood 'condemned' for 'preaching regressive policies in the name of progress'.[70]

Paton's novel gives little idea of any effectively organised black political opposition. Reverend Stephen Kumalo is quick to chide Napoleon Letsitsi, the agricultural instructor brought to Ndotsheni by James Jarvis, for suggesting that blacks should aspire to self-sufficiency, to refuse handouts from conscience-stricken whites.[71] John Kumalo is an inefficient, selfish, cowardly manipulator, and black South Africans are represented as incomplete: of the three important local black politicians, Msimangu tells Stephen, Tomlinson 'has the brains', John Kumalo 'the voice', while Dubula 'has the heart'. All lack something, and the intelligent one is Coloured – 'brown' – rather than black.[72] Predictably, Msimangu is full of praise for a white liberal who, of course, combined the talents of all three: 'Professor Hoernlé ... was the great fighter for us', with, significantly, 'Tomlinson's brains, and your brother's voice, and Dubula's heart, all in one man'.[73]

For Lewis Nkosi, Stephen Kumalo was a 'cunning expression of white liberal sentiment', his forbearance, humility and resignation suggesting that whites could evade responsibility for racial injustice. Paton's novel could envision only a 'distorted, sentimental' solution 'in which reconciliation consists of liberals supplying milk and helping build a dam in a Bantustan'.[74] For Ezekiel Mphahlele, too, Paton 'sentimentalized his black characters in order to prove the effectiveness of a liberal theory that he posed'.[75] Nat Nakasa dismisses the novel for its black characters' 'naïve confidence in the potential goodness of the next man and his religion'.[76] As Rob Nixon notes, *Cry, the Beloved Country* was a 'cardinal counter-text for the Sophiatown set – it was the book they wrote against'.[77] Their distaste for Paton's representation of black characters was given form in Lionel Rogosin's seminal film *Come Back, Africa* (1959), in which Blake Modisane, Can Themba and others 'expound on the inadequacy of Paton's account of urban African life'.[78]

Left-wing white critics were also generally dismissive of the novel. Murray Carlin, writing in Rhodes University's *Review*, declared that Paton's supposedly simple style was in fact 'highly artificial', and the novel as a whole 'too unskilled in technique and too false in feeling to be considered at all highly as a literary work'.[79] Some reviewers grounded a judgement of the novel's apparent literary merit in an appreciation of the manner in which Paton conveyed the impression of a transposed and translated Zulu idiom.[80] The *Daily Despatch* reviewer suggested that through its use Paton achieved 'an atmosphere of realism and effect that would probably not be secured in any other way'.[81] Interestingly, J. M. Coetzee would repeat many of Carlin's criticisms of the novel's artifice in *White Writing*, even uncannily using the same examples of Paton's unnecessarily awkward and childlike Zulu usage. This language, Coetzee asserts, is a 'phantom Zulu', less a medium through which characters speak than 'part of the interpretation Paton wishes us to make of them', marking them as belonging to an 'old-fashioned context of direct (i.e. unmediated) personal relations based on respect, obedience, and fidelity'.[82] Carlin found *Cry, the Beloved Country* wanting as a 'social document'. He called Paton's 'the Christian viewpoint', but remarked that it was 'also the sentimental, the compliant, and, worst of all, the ignorant viewpoint'; the novel glossed over 'the real savagery of the situation in South Africa', a failing which, Carlin noted sharply, was undoubtedly a reason for the novel's success.[83]

Carlin claimed that other reasons for its popularity included the 'reigning artistic-patriotic fervour' – 'whereby anything South African [was] automatically good' – and 'confusion in loyal minds between literary and political standards, between Paton the novelist and Paton the Liberal'.[84] It is certainly true that the real subject of appreciative – and defensive – South African reviews was 'Paton the Liberal', rather than his novel. Liberal assumptions are paramount, for example, in Sachs's review in *Trek*, which casts Paton as speaking for the speechless. Yet it was this interpellation which Nkosi and his contemporaries found most disturbing, and its assumptions evidence what Bhabha and others have usefully described as '*processes of subjectification* made possible (and plausible) through stereotypical discourse', processes which are part of the 'productivity of colonial power', and which construct colonial subjects – in this case the black characters in Paton's novel and, by extrapolation, black South Africans in general – as paradoxically both *other* and *knowable*.[85] Said suggests that the 'general liberal consensus that "true" knowledge is fundamentally non-political (and conversely, that overly political knowledge is not "true" knowledge) obscures the highly if obscurely organized political circumstances obtaining when knowledge is produced'.[86] Paton's *artful* representation of socio-political conditions in South Africa had the appearance of document for many reviewers, but masked a clear political programme: Christian, liberal, humanist trusteeship.

'White Man, Do Not Deceive Yourself': Paton and the *African Drum*

Given the hostility to the novel among black intellectuals, what are we to make of the fact that *Cry, the Beloved Country* was serialised, in 1951 and early 1952, in the first thirteen issues of *The African Drum*, a journal aimed at a black readership?[87] The changing content of the magazine provided a context which commented on Paton's novel in oblique but fascinating ways: where the first instalment appeared alongside African-American poet Countee Cullen's 'Heritage', a poem expressing a similar Christian idealism and nostalgia for a rural, archaic, African identity and similarly able to be adduced to a non-confrontational political ethic, later instalments appeared alongside reports on rival conferences of African liberation organisations and an article on forced removals under the Group Areas Act.[88]

An editorial in the second issue quoted a letter from a reader, Mr Zondi, approving of the young magazine's disavowal of politics. While 'as black as ebony and an African of the first water', Zondi wrote, he had been sceptical of the magazine, which he initially expected to be another 'call to arms for our political rights', a cause on which he was reluctant to 'waste time'. He had expected 'photographs of gargantuan political gatherings and doubtful patriots with corpulent tummies delivering orations with voices that shake the very air and sway the masses', but was delighted to find that the magazine's editors had 'decided to shun the political field which is strewn with partisanship, hate and controversy'.[89] The second issue also included, unabridged, Chapters Six, Seven and Eight of Book One of *Cry, the Beloved Country*, including Stephen Kumalo's meeting with his brother John, the latter portrayed in Paton's description and in the accompanying illustration, as every bit one of the corpulent demagogues Mr Zondi despised.[90] John had 'grown fat', his brother notices, and sits 'with his hands on his knees like a chief', suggesting that he is acting above his station. He is dangerously beguiling, swaying 'to and fro' as if addressing an absent crowd, and speaks in a 'strange voice'. Paton's is a distinctly unflattering portrait, and one which was in accord with *The African Drum*'s dismissal of 'dubious patriots' who stirred up violence.[91]

By contrast, later in 1951, the October issue included, with English translation, a Zulu poem, 'Mlung' Ungazikhohlisi' (White Man, Do Not Deceive Yourself), which invited the 'white man' to consider that education and acceptance of Western dress and habits did not mean that a black person had been subjugated or assimilated. The poem was by 'Bulima Ngiyeke', a pseudonym which can be translated as 'stupidity leave me

He was not speaking to them, he was speaking to people who were not there.

4.3 Illustration from *The African Drum* (April 1951)

alone'. Cutting sarcasm suggests an ironic and knowing mimicry, which, in Bhabha's formulation of the positive tension of mimicry as a strategy to subvert oppression and stereotype, turns the 'gaze of the discriminated back upon the eye of power'.[92] The speaker warns in conclusion:

> If I pretend to be like you, Prince,
> Apeing you, I know what I am about
> I know what I brought with me
> I know what I will take away with me
> I know well what is in my gourd,
> How could I forget, this is my birthright
> White Man, do not deceive yourself.[93]

Deference and submission to the multiple indignities of segregationist legislation, and apparent adoption of, or aspiration to adopt, the trappings of Western civilisation, did not negate a black African identity, the poem suggests. Paton's young Johannesburg priest Theophilus Msimangu, marked by his name as loving (the white man's) God, by consciously and sincerely mimicking the 'European' in dress and metaphysics, does not, however, apparently intend to return the gaze of the oppressor: Paton has him state explicitly that he is grateful that missionaries brought his 'father out of darkness'.[94]

Edited initially by whites who wholly endorsed Paton's novel's (apparent) model of humanitarian trusteeship, *The African Drum* did not sell well, although those who bought it thought highly of the novel: it received the most nominations in a poll to rank regular features, with nearly 2,000 'votes' compared with 1,360 for the least favourite feature, 'Music of the Tribes'. The editors wondered, in response to the latter item's poor showing, whether 'the African of to-day [is] too much concerned with the 20th century and ... juke boxes to be interested in his tribal antecedents and environment'.[95] Paranoia about detribalisation constantly exercised the magazine's white managers, but articles on tribal customs and music did not appeal to an increasingly sophisticated, urbanised readership, and within a year the magazine was transformed into *Drum* under a new editor, Anthony Sampson. With talented writers and polemicists like Nat Nakasa, Can Themba, Ezekiel Mphahlele, Todd Matshikiza and Lewis Nkosi, *Drum* soon became the mouthpiece of vibrant, black, Johannesburg culture, publishing articles on crime, jazz, sports and celebrities.[96] Early instalments of Paton's novel appeared under a banner illustration juxtaposing a rural scene with the city. Under the new team, drawings casting the city in a negative light and romanticising the country gave way to photographs of the actors starring in the 1951 London Films version of the novel.[97]

Early instalments of *Cry, the Beloved Country* were unabridged, but as the tone and editorial direction of the magazine changed, Paton's novel was no longer the only fiction it published. The issue for September 1951 included other fiction for the first time: a short story by Bloke Modisane, 'The Dignity of Begging', involving a courtroom scene which, unlike those the reader was still to encounter in the serialisation of *Cry, the Beloved Country*, was satirical, humorous at the expense of whites.[98] By early 1952, under its new editor, *Drum*'s pages were crammed with popular culture stories, competitions and photo essays, and there is a very real sense that Paton's text was outstaying its welcome; the serialisation continued only because it was so nearly completed, one suggests, but the final instalments are heavily abridged. In the issue for September 1951, all but the final two sentences of the excerpt which James Jarvis reads from his son's essay (in Chapter Twenty-One), are omitted, significantly shortening Arthur's bitter indictment of the hypocrisy of a supposedly religious white society.[99] Much of the twenty-third chapter (the discovery of gold at Odendaalsrust) and all of the chapter following (Jarvis re-visiting his son's study) are omitted from the October issue, reducing further the extent to which Arthur Jarvis's liberal dilemma is dwelt on in the *Drum* text.[100]

Both of these instalments appeared under the old editorial team, and their care to ameliorate, or circumscribe, potentially negative representations of whites is clear. In the February 1952 instalment, which included the first chapter of Book Three (Kumalo's return to Ndotsheni), the section in which the new schoolteacher wishes to sing *Nkosi Sikelel' iAfrika*, a prayer for Africa and an anthem long associated with black South African nationalism, but finds the people do not know the words, is omitted. This appeared after Sampson's assumption of the editorship, and he may have thought that the villagers' ignorance ought not to be represented.[101]

The March 1952 instalment omits the faintly comical portrait of the chief's attempts to help the surveyors mark out the site for the dam, in the third chapter of Book Three.[102] Restricting representation of the chief's slowness to understand the advances planned for the valley effectively circumscribes implied criticism of traditional leadership structures (which *African Drum* had been keen to promote). In the context of its new editorial policy, it may have been that this portrayal was excluded as a negative and potentially politically reactionary presentation by a white writer of a black character (as excessively naive). Many of the omissions work to limit Paton's criticism of black political activity. In the final instalment, the novel's penultimate chapter is omitted in its entirety, and all of Kumalo's discussion with Letsitsi, and Paton's implicit critique, through Kumalo, of Letsitsi's pan-Africanism, are consequently lost.[103] These tensions between the abridged text of Paton's novel and its context in *Drum* suggest both how amenable the work was to appropriation by liberal attitudes of trusteeship and how it was received sceptically by a sophisticated, politicised, urban, black readership.

Condensed and digested: abridging *Cry, the Beloved Country*

The serialised and abridged version of Paton's novel in *Drum* was not its only appearance in such a highly charged context. In the wake of the early success of Scribner's edition in the USA, and the positive tone of almost all the American reviews, *Cry, the Beloved Country* had been selected as an alternative choice for the American Book-of-the-Month Club as early as April 1948.[104] Janice Radway suggests that judges for the Club's list were especially keen on texts which appeared to them 'to combat despair with sympathy and affiliation'.[105] A similar endorsement of individualism and forbearance was propagated by the *Reader's Digest* magazine which, from its inception in 1922, but particularly during the Cold War, played a significant role in the construction of a popular American national identity through accessible, widely read, 'middlebrow' publications, its flagship magazine consistently presenting itself as a guardian and promoter of the 'American' virtues of individualism and optimism.[106] In 1950, *Reader's Digest* launched its 'Condensed Books' series and the very first volume, which went on to sell half a million copies by 1957, contained an abridged version of *Cry, the Beloved Country*. This abridged text was included, in 1956, in the second volume of the Canadian 'Condensed Books' series, and, with some variations, in a British 'Condensed Books' volume of at least 250,000 copies, also marketed in Australia and South Africa, in early 1958.[107]

The other abridged texts in the American volume had a popular appeal and emphasised similar values of individual perseverance in the face of adversity: *The Show Must Go On*, by prolific dramatist Elmer Rice; Morton Thompson's *The Cry and the Covenant*, about a Hungarian medical innovator; and the autobiography of the much-loved cowboy entertainer Will Rogers. Other abridgements in the Canadian and British 'Condensed Books' volumes were similarly popular 'middlebrow' novels: in Canada, Herman Wouk's best-selling war novel *The Caine Mutiny* and Irving Stone's *The President's Lady*; and in Britain *The Enemy Below*, *Minding Our Own Business* and Edna Ferber's *Giant*, which partially dealt with white–Mexican contact in Texas, the film adaptation of which, starring James Dean, had been released by Warner Brothers in 1956.

Publication in a series aimed at the 'middlebrow' readers of a culturally and politically conservative magazine in the early years of the Cold War constitutes a revealing appropriation of Paton's text in a fascinating *local*, but globally conscious, context. Joseph Grigely prefaces an analysis of a simplified and abridged *Reader's Digest* version of *Tom Sawyer* with the observation that while '[f]ew people would consider a *Reader's Digest* condensed text an important text worth scholarly attention', the existence and popularity of such items witness to the fact that 'the vicissitudes of culture are not in the end dictated by the intentions of artists alone'.[108] The text of the *Reader's Digest* version of *Cry, the Beloved Country* is even more amenable than Paton's original to being read as a Christian morality tale of the corrupting effects of the city on *simple* peoples, with potentially universal application.

A prefatory note, surrounded by a border featuring sketches of black workers with spades and other implements, and Zulu warriors brandishing shields and assegais, describes the narrative as moving from 'semi-primitive tribal life in the green hills of Natal to the Shanty Town warrens of Johannesburg's slums, breeding ground of racial tensions and violent crime'.[109] Attention is drawn thematically and visually to the contrast between the corrupting city and rural life, although in the text itself much of the original novel's detailed descriptions of rural and urban conditions is omitted, with the cumulative effect of lessening the novel's constant emphasis on the disparities between the social conditions of whites and blacks.[110] Many passages containing material which could be read as critical of whites, or which detail political injustice or repression, are cut from the *Reader's Digest* text.[111] Chapters Nine and Thirteen are omitted in their entirety; the absence of the first lessens the novel's indictment of appalling township conditions and eliminates the multiple voices of the nameless black residents who act in Paton's original text as a kind of chorus. By contrast Chapter Twelve, which presents numerous voices of *white* Johannesburg residents, is significantly retained largely unchanged.[112]

Several chapters in Book Two are omitted in their entirety, of which the ninth, in which John Kumalo addresses a gathering in support of the 1946 miners' strike, is the most significant. The conversation about politics between Stephen and John in Book One (Chapter Seven) is also severely edited, but the representation of John as a demagogue, corpulent and duplicitous, remains relatively unaffected, although Msimangu's subsequent discussion of his failings (in the same chapter) is shortened to omit a critique of blacks who break the law, however unjust or immoral.[113] The *Reader's Digest* version appears, then, to mitigate what many have read as Paton's implicit dismissal of black political activists, by omitting negative portrayals of those activists. The original text is, however, more complex than is sometimes acknowledged. Often overlooked descriptions of John's effective self-censoring, lost in the omission of the ninth chapter in Book Two (chapter twenty-six in consecutive numbering), may appear redundant, but offer a notional point of comparison with another kind of black political aspiration which Paton's novel posits, even if perhaps unintentionally. In the original text of the novel, the experienced policemen listening to John's speech know he is 'afraid' of his own rhetoric, and that he does not address his audience on pan-African resistance. Paton could be argued implicitly to be acknowledging the force of this alternative politics in stressing John's failure to exploit its possibilities.[114] As such, the omission of these passages from the *Reader's Digest* text might be regarded as marginalising all black political opinion more comprehensively than Paton can be accused of doing.

A similar subtext of pan-Africanism is to be found in the original text's numerous references to the singing of *Nkosi Sikelel' iAfrika*. With one exception, all references to it, and so (obliquely) to pan-Africanist discourse, are omitted from the *Reader's Digest* text. In Paton's novel, it is sung in the shantytown scene, while in the first chapter of Book Three the new teacher calls for it to be sung, but is rebuked by the old teacher, who dislikes politics and is ashamed at not knowing the words. In the penultimate chapter, when Kumalo asks why Letsitsi insists that all who are intent on regenerating the land must work for *Africa*, not South Africa, he replies: 'We speak as we sing ... for we sing *Nkosi Sikelel' iAfrika*'.[115] Kumalo's extreme disquiet at Letsitsi's attitude to Jarvis's magnanimity, and Letsitsi's claim that white largesse is the least that is owed by whites for having stolen the land, are also omitted. All criticism of Jarvis is removed, and Paton's powerfully ambivalent portrayal of the conflicting imperatives of Kumalo's Christian humanism and Letsitsi's pan-Africanist socialism is lost. Paton's original text does, at least, admit of the complexity of socio-political alternatives. The one reference to *Nkosi Sikelel' iAfrika* which is retained occurs in the final chapter of the novel. Alone on the mountain on the morning of his son's execution, Kumalo prays 'for all the people of Africa, the beloved country. *Nkosi Sikelel' iAfrika*, God save Africa.' The British (but not Canadian and American) *Reader's Digest* text adds brackets, arguably depoliticising the reference by making the Xhosa title merely the translation of a prayer, '(God save Africa)', rather than the name of the anthem of black nationalism.[116]

Similarly, extensive excisions from the courtroom scenes render Paton's emphasis on the importance of the rule of law considerably less qualified than in the original text, which highlights, not entirely unintentionally, the precarious inscrutability of the court. There are many other omissions. Some are likely to have been informed by the abridgers' sense of the likely audience's religious sentiments – for example those emphasising Stephen Kumalo's virtue by removing all reference to 'flaws' in his character (including his cruelty to Absalom's girlfriend, the religious doubts and anger he expresses to Father Vincent, and the lie he tells to hurt his brother).[117] Others mediate the complexities of the South African situation for the intended audience of the abridged version, the average American reader not conversant with many facts about the country or its history, and subsequently similar readerships in Canada and elsewhere in the Commonwealth. Consequently, many of the subtleties of the South African situation depicted with considerable care in Paton's novel are lost. More significantly, the author's implied socio-religious programme for addressing the disparities between a first world and (not inconsequentially) largely white society, on the one hand, and an intentionally undeveloped or under-developed black population, on the other, would have appealed to white American readers in an age in which, Ralph Ellison argues, America's 'so-called race problem' had 'lined up with the world problems of colonialism and the struggle of the West to gain the allegiance of the remaining non-white people who [had] thus far remained outside the Communist sphere'.[118]

'Preferably a bit simple': Paton in the classroom

If a process of therapeutic identification (or displacement) operated in the *Reader's Digest* abridgement of *Cry, the Beloved Country*, the novel's serialisation in the *African Drum* evidences modes of self-recognition as interpolated by a paternalistic, white, editorial regime, endorsed, then challenged, and ultimately displaced by the local demands of a black readership. The novel's wide uptake in school curricula in the USA and across the Commonwealth displays some of the same kinds of displacements, but also altogether more *local* – and economic – decisions.

The novel's suitability for American schools and colleges was discussed in educational magazines, including those concerned with African-American schools, as early as 1949. Gertrude Rivers wrote that year in the

Journal of Negro Education that it was a 'guide book' and an indictment of injustice, and compared it favourably with Richard Wright's *Native Son* and Lillian Smith's *Strange Fruit*, two influential studies of the injustices suffered by African-Americans.[119] Harold R. Collins suggested in *College English* in 1953 that *Cry, the Beloved Country* was a 'capsule history' of South Africa.[120] He argued that the novel's primary theme was detribalisation and the attendant 'loss of the old African moral order that gave purpose and meaning to African lives', but that it did 'what no discursive work in political science, sociology, economics, or anthropology could': it conveyed 'the "form and pressure" of life' in the country.[121] Both Rivers and Collins, then, advanced a reading of the novel as a guide to actual social conditions in South Africa, in much the same manner that many reviewers in Britain and America had done. School and college sales increasingly amounted to a large proportion of the novel's American sales. By 1959, it was selling between 6,000 and 8,000 copies annually to colleges, and around 3,000 a year in bookstores, and Scribner's published a paperback edition in 1959 to increase sales, particularly to colleges, where, as Charles Scribner Jr wrote to Paton, the novel had 'acquired the status of a classic'.[122]

Other interventions confirmed that part of the novel's attraction for many American readers was its Christian humanist message. Sheridan Baker argued in *College English* in 1957 that a specifically Christian 'moral geography' (valleys of despair, mountains of hope) mirrored the novel's depiction of 'the salvage of evil through love and suffering'.[123] He went on to edit an edition of *Cry, the Beloved Country* in the Scribner 'Research Anthology' series, billed as providing access to 'the Novel, the Critics, the Setting', in 1968. In addition to the full text of the novel, this volume included responses to the work (including Collins's and Baker's essays) and a range of documents, by Paton and others, on social and political conditions in South Africa, including extracts from anthropological studies and discussions of the effects of apartheid (including crusading anti-apartheid British cleric Trevor Huddleston's memoir, *Naught for Your Comfort*, and the defensive riposte by the Director of Information at South Africa's British Embassy).[124]

Baker claims in his Introduction that *Cry, the Beloved Country* is 'an important twentieth-century novel' which merits 'close analysis in its own right'. But its value is also that it 'evokes a specific time and place, South Africa in 1946', and opens 'a world outside the novel for investigation'. The criterion of literariness hovering on the edges of Baker's discourse is that the literary 'springs from a deep private response to the social sense', that 'particulars must convey some universal implications'; Paton's novel satisfies this requirement, demonstrating 'uncommonly well the fundamental nature of literature'.[125] Confirming an implicit recognition in many earlier reviews and assessments, Baker concedes tellingly that the 'most significant reason for the novel's strange power' over American readers is that it 'speaks with immediacy to analogues within our own society and our individual experience'.[126] Universality opens eyes to the world, and to the world at home. The date of this volume's publication, 1968, is significant, too, coinciding with the Reverend Martin Luther King Jr's assassination and the Democratic National Convention riots in Chicago, in the midst of a heated period of protests for civil rights and against the Vietnam War.

The earliest example of the effect of a judgement about the suitability of Paton's novel for use in the classroom in Britain and the Commonwealth is an abridged and 'very lightly' simplified edition published by Longmans, Green & Co. in 1953. This was the first of several school editions or versions of the novel published by the firm and its successors over the next forty years. Each made intriguing decisions about the presentation of the work and sometimes revealing changes to its text. Some of these are now considered in turn.

The 1953 series aimed to provide reading material for students with a limited vocabulary and little grasp of '*English* thought and ways of life', and who had completed a simplified course in the language.[127] All titles in the series – which included *Nicholas Nickleby*, *Great Expectations*, Sherlock Holmes stories, selections of one-act plays and various prose anthologies – started from a 3,000-word vocabulary, introducing suitably glossed new words to a limit of 7,000 words.[128] There are many omissions from Paton's original text, most simplifying the novel's politics and emphasising its presentation of black South Africans' conditions as tragic – rather than the result of the white rulers' policies or neglect. Relatively few words in the remaining text appear to have been changed. In the opening paragraphs, for example, 'matted' is changed to 'thick', 'well-tended' becomes 'well looked after', 'unshod' becomes 'barefoot' and 'kloof' is translated as 'small valley'.[129] The Afrikaans *kloof* – like *koppie*, in its Dutch form *kopje* – had almost certainly become familiar to British readers from nineteenth- and early twentieth-century colonial adventure stories and reportage from the Anglo-Boer War, but the simplified abridgement (and the series as a whole) was clearly intended for a different set of readers: second-language speakers, many in the same kind of social and economic circumstances as Paton's novel's poor rural and shantytown black communities.

This simplified version did well enough for Longmans, Green & Co. to publish an abridged edition of the original text in 1962, aimed at younger native speakers or older, more accomplished students of English, in Britain and the Commonwealth, in a series which included established set-texts like *A Tale of Two Cities*, *Wuthering Heights* and *Pride and Prejudice*. An introduction argued that *Cry, the Beloved Country* had universal appeal, and sought to position it in the context of 'big problems that hit the headlines of the world: colonialism, the colour problem, bad farming', and 'swift and careless industrialism'; it also suggested that the novel was a guide to the 'helpless confusion of African affairs'.[130] Almost every reference to prostitution, pregnancy out of wedlock and common-law marriage – sensitive topics in a text aimed at a school market across the Commonwealth – is omitted from the abridged text. One can only speculate on whether it was cultural and religious sensibilities that prompted the omissions or a paternalistic concern for morals amongst likely readers who were often constructed in imperial and liberal discourse as childlike and easily influenced.[131] The novel's political discourse is also radically circumscribed: selective editing of the judge's summation at the end of Absalom's murder trial curtails discussion of the concepts of the *law* and *justice* in an unjust society; all representations of rural ignorance or naivety are cut, as are many of the chorus-like passages conveying the anonymous and politically inflected voices of black and white Johannesburg. The novel's moral, as paraphrased by the editor, is clearly served by all of these changes: 'If the greed and hatred could be turned to love and co-operation, Paton believes the land could be nursed to an abundant fertility and every human enterprise could flourish.'[132]

Longman published an unabridged edition of *Cry, the Beloved Country* for school use, primarily in Britain, in 1966, in its 'Heritage of Literature' series. The apparatus provided in this edition presents it as a social-problem novel: the Introduction discusses urbanisation and the effects of industrialisation, describing detribalised Africans problematically, as having crowded into cities, 'where they were responsible for some of the social problems described in *Cry, the Beloved Country*'.[133] Themes of personal tragedy and the triumph of personal faith are highlighted, as is Paton's 'style', which is described as biblical and as conveying the 'symbolic, poetic quality of the Zulu language'.[134] The editor reinforces the novel's depiction of John Kumalo as one of 'those Africans who have learnt from the Europeans but who have abandoned the ideals and tradi-tions of their own people and found nothing to put in their place'.[135] Young readers are encouraged to read the novel as an endorsement of trusteeship, as exactly the kind of text black South African intellectuals criticised.

Cry, the Beloved Country was widely prescribed by Britain's domestic examining bodies in the 1970s and 1980s. It appeared on many approved reading lists for schools, and many will have used Longman's 1966 edition, which went through sixty-six impressions and had never been out of print when the company included it in another series, 'Study Texts', aimed at the 'O' and 'A' levels market and launched in 1983.[136] The fact that Longman could reprint the novel seems largely to explain why it did so: there being no pattern for selecting set texts, publishers generally played to the sets of books teachers already had in their book cupboards. The series editor, Richard Adams, a chief examiner for the Oxford Board, invited Mark Spencer Ellis, an English master at the independent Forest School in London, to provide new prefatory and paratextual material to accompany the 1966 typesetting for the 'second wave' of titles in the series, in 1986.[137] Ellis's Introduction situates the novel specifically in the history of South African protest literature, providing extensive context for students to evaluate the veracity of Paton's portrayal of legalised injustices, and placing it in perhaps the most overtly political context of all the novel's editions to date. Paton had to approve new editorial matter, which he did, doubtless flattered at the political incisiveness attributed to his work nearly forty years after its first appearance.[138]

Ellis seeks to negotiate a means of reading *Cry, the Beloved Country* less as a novel of liberal reaction than a text remade through an act of perceptive reading. He attempts, in effect, to save Paton from his own book, suggesting that if one's 'assessment of *Cry, the Beloved Country* is that it reveals a world which can only be put right through revolution', then it appears to be 'a revolutionary text, irrespective of the peaceful humility of the principal characters'. Ameliorating Paton's presentation of black political activists, Ellis argues that an 'assessment of John Kumalo's personality' should not 'affect the way we see his views on society'; after all, he notes, 'people we dislike can be right while those we are fond of can talk nonsense'.[139] The emphasis on the difference between the logic of Paton's text and its perception and reconstruction by the reader, paying less attention to construed authorial intention, are clearly functions of contemporaneous movements in critical theory, and Ellis freely admits that, like many schoolteachers of the time, he was increasingly interested in ideas being promoted by the likes of Catherine Belsey.[140] The South African authorities would not allow that edition to be used in the country, but, as so often with apartheid-era censorship, not for the reasons one might have expected: Longman South Africa informed Ellis that it was his description of Paton's novel as representing entrenched discrimination against women in South Africa which was found especially objectionable.[141]

Just as Paton's novel was the target of much radical reappraisal in South Africa in the 1980s, so its suitability for teaching in British schools was also questioned. Teacher David Evans offered a critique in 1986, arguing that there was 'something suspicious' about a writer 'belonging to a power elite (however marginally) enjoining the powerless to eschew power', and something 'offensive' in his use of 'one of the powerless to convey the message of restraint'.[142] Just as Lewis Nkosi had done thirty years previously, Evans called the Reverend Kumalo an 'unrepresentative figure, even from the perspective of 1946–48', merely 'a white man's construct: too simple, too moral, too innocent'. Paton's novel appealed 'to the liberal-conservatism, the paternalism and the latent racism' of the British 'educational establishment', he charged: 'Revolutionary, autonomous blacks are not wanted in either Britain or South Africa, in fact or fiction. What is wanted is blacks who are cooperative, apologetic, servile and preferably a bit simple.'[143] As if responding to Ellis's Introduction, which he may well have been doing,

Evans declared that, 'whatever its author's intentions', *Cry, the Beloved Country* was a 'dated, deeply paternalistic and even reactionary book' which ought to be replaced by another 'which upsets, not reinforces, white half-way house compassion and milky complacency'. A better choice might be made from work by Nadine Gordimer, Athol Fugard, Alex La Guma, Bessie Head or any of the new black authors being published by Ravan Press, he suggested.[144]

Despite this criticism, *Cry, the Beloved Country* continued to be set for examinations. The 1986 edition proved moderately successful in Britain, until the introduction of the GCSE examinations (when, in Ellis's assessment, educational publishers began aiming at a mass market). The 'Study Text' series books 'were seen as too difficult for GCSE', while 'A' level boards do not prescribe editions.[145] Nonetheless, the market for Paton's novel did not dry up completely: Longman reprinted the 1966 typesetting again in 1991, in a new series, 'Longman Literature', with new introductory and explanatory material, an additional glossary, study programme with questions and a list of further reading – including several South African novels: *The Story of an African Farm*, Gordimer's *July's People*, Mbulelo Mzamane's *Children of Soweto* and Beverley Naidoo's *Journey to Johannesburg*. This edition, aimed primarily at British schools and English-speaking schools in Anglophone Africa and the Caribbean, has had sixteen impressions to date and is still in print.[146] Longman has also republished the text of Wear and Durham's 1953 simplified version – in 1996, and again as a Penguin Level Six Reader aimed at the international second-language English teaching market, in 1999. The firm is reluctant to provide information on sales figures, but the Reader is currently in its second impression: Pearson Educational has consolidated the Longman and Penguin imprints; it remains open to speculation whether it continues to publish this text merely because it has the rights to it.

Paton and the global mediascape

Not only has Paton's novel sold in large numbers in multiple trade, book club, school and college editions, as well as in serialised, abridged and simplified print versions, it has also long been a multimedia phenomenon. In the decade following its publication and early reception, that extended originary moment of February to September 1948, dramatic, musical and cinematic adaptations, a self-propelling momentum as a best-seller, abridgement in school and *Reader's Digest* editions, and consistent investment at school level kept Paton's novel in the global public imagination.[147] Within a month of publication in the USA, rights were being negotiated to adapt it for the stage and for film. Kurt Weill and Maxwell Anderson's Broadway musical *Lost in the Stars*, based on the novel, opened in October 1949 and had 273 performances. It was revived by the Boston Lyric Opera in 1992, and a filmed version, loosely adapted by Alfred Hayes, appeared in the American Film Theatre series in 1974.[148] There have been at least two filmed adaptations of *Cry, the Beloved Country*. The first, produced by the famous Korda brothers' London Film Corporation and directed by Zoltan Korda, was filmed in South Africa and at London's Shepperton Studios in 1951 and released in 1952. The second, directed by Darrell Roodt and produced by Anant Singh, was released by Miramax in 1995. [149] In addition to these musical and film adaptations, there was a British verse drama adaptation by Felicia Komai, first performed at St Martin-in-the-Fields in London in February 1954. Roy Sargeant produced a 'new' stage adaptation at the South African National Arts Festival in Grahamstown in 2003 (reviewed as 'art that can heal').[150] Each adaptation has, without fail, emphasised the novel's universal themes or exploited its resonances for foreign audiences (and even, increasingly, for a new generation in the 'new' South Africa, for whom its problematic 'liberalism' is historical).

Set in an unrecognisable South Africa, *Lost in the Stars* draws on stereotypical representations of African-American culture to depict both Johannesburg and Zululand, confirming the reading of Paton's work as speaking to American anxieties about race. Maxwell Anderson's book alters the South African historical contexts of the novel, too: the letter which summons Kumalo to Johannesburg (sent in the play by John Kumalo rather than Msimangu) is dated 9 August 1949, setting the action of the musical in its audience's immediate past, but at least three years later than in Paton's novel and, significantly, *after* the National Party victory in South Africa in 1948.[151] The reconciliation between James Jarvis and Stephen Kumalo also involves a greater change of heart than in the novel, as Jarvis is initially portrayed as being extremely racist (this was to be repeated in the 1951 film). [152] Among many changes in *dramatis personae*, the musical introduces a chorus with a 'Leader' and an 'Answerer' to comment on the play's action, in the manner of a Greek tragedy (and in the call-and-response form of much traditional African-American music), exemplifying the widespread perception of the novel's plot as allegorical and archetypal (and speaking to American audiences in particular). Like *Lost in the Stars,* Komai's dramatic adaptation made use of representative, chorus-like figures ('Black Man' and 'White Man'), and developed Kumalo's analogy of 'a man/ Sleeping in the grass', over whom 'is gathering/ The greatest storm of all his days', into a strategically repeated motif.[153] The verse attempts to capture the biblical cadences of Paton's supposedly translated Zulu idiom, and these figures and symbols invite a reading of racial injustice as a tragedy, enacted by vast, inhuman agents. Both *Lost in the Stars* and Komai's version exaggerate – and thereby foreground – the novel's amenability to be read as making the causes of the novel's tragic events seem 'the function of some Fate or divinity', obscuring 'the real reasons (and hence possible solutions) for the tragic incidents' (in the words of Stephen Watson's critique).[154]

Zoltan Korda had previously made imperial adventures like *The Four Feathers* (1939) and justifications of imperial rule like *Sanders of the River* (1935). Always more left-wing than his brother Alexander, he had long looked for a vehicle for a more nuanced representation of Africa, and felt he had found it in Paton's novel.[155] Despite casting mostly Americans in the lead roles (the young Sidney Poitier played Msimangu), Korda nonetheless took risks, jeopardising American distribution by casting the African-American actor Canada Lee, blacklisted in Hollywood for his communist sympathies, as Stephen Kumalo. American distributors further 'infuriated Korda', Peter Davis notes, by renaming the film *African Fury*, and so removing possible association with the novel and implying 'a totally different character for the film, changing it to the jungle genre'.[156] The film was not a commercial success, and Paton claimed that he received little more than the £1,000 for which his agent had sold the film rights.[157]

Others have written at greater length about both filmed adaptations. As Mark Beittel observes, both are clearly products of their times and intended audiences. The 1951 film draws on conventions of early documentary film and *cinema verité* (the shantytown scenes really were filmed in townships), and emphasises the universality of the film's (and novel's) themes by avoiding all references to dates, thus making its historical present deliberately vague: it casts 'the story in a symbolic mode as part of an indefinite present and emphasizes the struggle against evil and the hope for a better day'.[158] The 1995 version, appearing a year after the first democratic elections in South Africa, focused less on the symbolic hope of the first film, producing an account of injustice and so 'historici[sing] Paton's parable of good versus evil'.[159] Nelson Mandela's speech at the 1995 film's premiere in New York City endorsed that reading, calling the film a historical representation of 'the terrible past from which South Africa has just emerged', as well as a 'monument to' – or for – 'the future'.[160] Once again, emphasising the film's intention to appeal to a global audience, the leads were played by non-South Africans: James Earl Jones as Stephen Kumalo and Richard Harris as James Jarvis.

The history of the novel's global reception recently took a strange turn, as I intimated earlier: in late 2003, it was the second novel to be featured on Oprah Winfrey's revamped Book Club, 'Traveling with the Classics'. Winfrey's phenomenally successful Book Club made her, for a time, arguably 'the most powerful literary tastemaker' in American history; her choices for the first club made the best-seller list twenty-eight times in a row by the end of 1999.[161] She cast Paton's novel as both expressly the 'personal and political story of a nation' (especially the 'new' nation – Winfrey offered three readers a chance to visit the country and has herself adopted South African charities with remarkable dedication and vigour) – and, once again, as a novel with powerful universal resonances for a global audience.[162] The symbolism of its endorsement by a black media figure whose cachet transcends racial divisions in the USA is profoundly telling, too; such an endorsement could not, one feels, have come from a black South African media figure without considerable dissent from black intellectuals. Rita Barnard, an expatriate South African academic at the University of Pennsylvania, acted as the Book Club's online 'literary expert' for several months in late 2003, answering (mostly American) readers' questions about the novel, sketching an admirably nuanced picture of the novel's reception and continuing resonance by reminding readers that 'in South Africa, *Cry, the Beloved Country* is not as beloved as it is overseas. The novel has been vulnerable to criticism, especially on the basis of its liberal and paternalistic view of race relations.'[163] In an assessment of her engagement with the Book Club, Barnard suggests that the complex implications of Oprah's endorsement of *Cry, the Beloved Country* challenges notions of the 'political' in judgements of literary value and processes of reputation and reception. It is possible, she suggests polemically, that if interest in South African writing abroad was, in the past, 'fed and financed to the degree that it provided a vicarious sense of indignation, or moral *frisson*, in countries where politics seemed less urgent and dramatic' (or, as I have suggested, where it was easier to concentrate on problems far from home), future interest in the country's literary and cultural production may now depend 'on the degree that it provides images and narratives of suffering and its overcoming'.[164] *Cry, the Beloved Country* thus seems eminently well placed for an even longer afterlife.

Notes

1 Jacobson, 'Nostalgia', 830.

2 Callan, *Cry*, 17; Iannone, 'Tragic Liberalism', 442; see Alexander, *Paton*, 222.

3 Nixon, *Homelands*, 26.

4 Alan Paton Centre, Pietermaritzburg (APC), PC1/1/1/6–3, Paton to Juta. All unpublished Alan Paton correspondence quoted with permission, Mrs Anne Paton and the Alan Paton Centre.

5 See, for example, Nkosi, *Home and Exile*, 3; Nixon, *Homelands*, 26–7.

6 Paton, *Cry, the Beloved Country* (Scribner's 1948) and (Jonathan Cape, 1948), hereafter *Cry* (S) and (C). On the significance of the novel's success and the National Party's victory, see Paton's *Kontakion*, 82, and *Journey Continued*, 8; see also Van der Vlies, 'Alan Paton', 501–11.

7 Paton, *Cry, the Beloved Country* (Penguin, 2001), rear cover. Woods was editor of the *Daily Despatch* from 1965 to 1977, and famously a friend and supporter of Steve Biko.

8 Arac uses the term 'hypercanonization': *Idol and Target*, vii, 6.

9 See Barnard, 'Oprah's Paton', 94.

10 Alexander, *Paton*, 221.

11 APC, PC1/1/1/5, Dunn to Paton.

12 Scribner's, Advertisement.

13 Paton, *Cry* (S), dust-jacket cover blurb.
14 Sullivan, 'Fine Novel', 6.
15 Prescott, 'Books of the Times', 17.
16 Hansen, 'A Gentle Protest'.
17 Koch, 'Comfort in Desolation'; see also T. M. O., 'Without Fanfare'; Gardiner, 'On Saying "Boo!"', 662.
18 Gross, 'South Africa Presented'.
19 Locke, 'Dawn Patrol', 6, 7.
20 Quoted in Arac, *Idol*, 128.
21 Trilling, *The Liberal Imagination*, 220; see 205–22.
22 *Ibid.*, 214, 215.
23 Arac, *Idol*, vii, 7, and chapter 5; see Trilling, *The Liberal Imagination*, 104–17.
24 Nims, 'Grim View'.
25 Burns, 'Mirror to the South', 408–10.
26 See Paton, 'Negro in America Today' and 'Negro in the North'. *College English* noticed Paton's articles with the observation that 'he sees with a fresh eye and a sense of perspective almost impossible to a native American': Anon., 'News and Ideas', 192. Paton's photographer on this tour, Dan Weiner, later collaborated with him on a journey around South Africa which resulted in *South Africa in Transition* (1956). Paton's output of writing on race relations and related issues was prodigious: Alexander, *Paton*, 294–5, 493–8.
27 See 'Ebony Awards for 1948'; APC, PC1/1/1/5, Canby to Paton.
28 Cowling, 'The Beloved South African', 89.
29 Quoted in *ibid.*, 89.
30 Colleran, 'South African Theatre', 228; see Kruger, 'Apartheid on Display'.
31 APC, PC1/4/1/2, Paton to Howard; see Howard, *Jonathan Cape*, 214.
32 Alexander, *Paton*, 223. Alexander's biography of Plomer cites Paton as the source for the claim that Plomer was delighted by the success of Paton's novel, which he 'had highly recommended to Cape's when he first read it in manuscript': Alexander, *Plomer*, 292, 377; see Alexander, *Paton*, 463.
33 APC, PC1/1/1/5, Plomer, 'CRY, THE BELOVED COUNTRY', 1, 2.
34 *Ibid.*, 2.
35 APC, PC1/1/1/5, D.G. and L.L., 'Two Readers' Reports'. On Bunting, see Howard, *Jonathan Cape*, 178–83. Lamplugh also recommended the novel.
36 George, 'Evil City'.
37 Cape had been discouraged by the Ministry of Information from publishing Orwell's book lest it offend Russia, Britain's wartime ally. Secker and Warburg published it after the war: Howard, *Jonathan Cape*, 179.
38 In April 1948 Margot Barkham, an expatriate South African in New York City, reporting on the novel's American success, noted that 'Paton's London publisher' did not expect to have enough paper for publication until 1949: Barkham, 'South African's FIRST NOVEL', 77; see APC, PC1/1/1/5, Paton to Scribner, and Paton to Meyer.
39 Paton, *Cry* (S), v; (C), 5.
40 The fourth chapter of the second book in the American edition is thus Chapter 21, while in the British edition it is Book Two, Chapter 4. Chapters are cited hereafter as, e.g., 2:21/2:4, for *Cry* (S)/(C).
41 Paton, *Cry* (S), 257; see also (C), 239.

42 Street, 'Displaced Persons', 176.

43 Anon., 'Some New Novels', 3.

44 Herron, 'A Great Novel Comes Out of Africa'; Fausset, 'New Novels'.

45 Young, 'Out of Africa Something New'; see Hall, *Francis Brett Young*.

46 Paton, *Cry* (C), inside front cover flap of 1948 first edition and 1952 twentieth impression.

47 Allen, 'New Novels', 445, 446.

48 Bain, 'Four New Novels', 18.

49 Green, 'Grave and Sombre Words'. Comparison with social reformer–novelists like Trollope, Reade, and, pre-eminently, Dickens, was made by 'Castor', 'In Darkest Johannesburg', 581.

50 See Davenport and Saunders, *South Africa*, 360–1.

51 Green, 'Grave and Sombre Words'.

52 The 1977 Cape edition cites 5 reprints in 1948, 7 in 1949, 5 in 1950, one in 1951, 2 in 1952, one each in 1953, 1954, 1955, 2 again in 1957, and one a year in 1959, 1961, 1965, 1967, 1970 and 1977.

53 APC, PC1/4/1/1, Howard to Paton (1956), and Paton to Howard. In 1959, Penguin incorporated the note Paton wrote for Cape's 1959 edition. In 1988 the novel appeared in Penguin's Twentieth-Century Classics series, with Paton's note for the 1987 Collier Macmillan (New York) edition. It was repackaged for the Penguin Classics series at the turn of the new century.

54 APC, PC1/4/1/2, Poulton to Paton.

55 In 1976, the five-year extension of their licences earned Paton £6,000 for *Cry, the Beloved Country*, and £5,000 for the short story collection *Debbie Go Home* and his second novel, *Too Late the Phalarope*. Renewals in 1982 earned him £30,000 for *Cry, the Beloved Country*, in addition to a 12.5 per cent royalty (less Scribner's and Cape's shares). Further 5-year renewals, from 1987, earned £58,000, £55,000 of which for *Cry, the Beloved Country*: APC, PC1/4/1/4, Poulton to Paton, and Logan to Paton.

56 Aschman, 'Distinguished New South African Novel', 8.

57 Anon., 'New Books'.

58 Compare Scribner's, 'A Best-Seller Is Born!', and Central News Agency, 'A Best-Seller Is Born!'; see figs 4.1 and 4.2.

59 Anon., 'S.A. Novel Meets With High Praise'.

60 Anon., 'New Books'.

61 See Anon., 'Ein Buch', 4–5.

62 Anon., 'Alan Paton's Significant Scrutiny', 53, 55.

63 Anon., Review of *Cry, the Beloved Country*, 19.

64 S., Review of *Cry, the Beloved Country*.

65 *Ibid.*

66 Anon., 'New Books'.

67 Sachs, 'Books of the Month', 25.

68 *Ibid.* Lithuanian-born Sachs (1908–68) arrived in South Africa as a boy. He contributed widely to English-language newspapers and journals in the country: Herzberg, 'Dr. Joseph Sachs', 17.

69 S. C., '"Cry, the Beloved Country": Another View'; on *Torch* see Adhikari, *Not White Enough*, 96–116; and for my use of 'Coloured' see *ibid.* generally.

70 J. M., 'The Reviewer Reviewed', 5.

71 Paton, *Cry* (S), 262–3; (C), 244–5.

72 Paton, *Cry* (S), 43; (C), 45; (S), 39; (C), 41.

73 Paton, *Cry* (S), 45–6; (C), 47–8.

74 Nkosi, *Home and Exile*, 5.

75 Mphahlele, 'What the South African', 175; he repeated much the same analysis in *African Image*, 157–60.

76 Nakasa, 'Writing in South Africa', 38.

77 Nixon, *Homelands*, 26.

78 *Ibid.*, 261.

79 Carlin, '*Cry, the Beloved Country*', 10, 11.

80 For example, Young, 'Out of Africa', 3. Paton's language was imbued with cadences of the Authorised Version from childhood. Other influences include Steinbeck's *Grapes of Wrath*, Hamsun's *Growth of the Soil*, and Bunyan's *Pilgrim's Progress*. See Alexander, *Paton*, 198; Paton, *Towards the Mountain*, 267–72.

81 Anon., 'New Books'.

82 Coetzee, *White Writing*, 129; see 126–9, and compare with Carlin, '*Cry, the Beloved Country*', 10; see also Morphet, 'Stranger Fictions', 54–5.

83 Carlin, '*Cry, the Beloved Country*', 11.

84 *Ibid.*, 10

85 Bhabha, *Location of Culture*, 67.

86 Said, *Orientalism*, 10.

87 For more on *Drum*, see Chapman (ed.), 'More than Telling a Story'.

88 Anon., 'At Bloemfontein Africans Choose'; Anon., 'The Story of Bethal'; Xuma, 'Black Spots or White Spots?'; see Nixon, *Homelands*, 25–6. On the ANC and AAC, see Davenport and Saunders, *South Africa*, 327, 361–6, 383.

89 Anon., 'Opinion', *African Drum* 1.2, 1.

90 See fig. 4.3.

91 See Paton, 'Cry', *African Drum* 1.2 (April 1951), 5, 6; and compare *Cry* (S), 35–8; (C), 38–41.

92 Bhabha, *Location of Culture*, 112.

93 Ngiyeke, 'Mlung' Ungazikhohlisi', 11.

94 Paton, *Cry* (S), 25; (C), 30. The voicing of the humility and forbearance of Paton's black characters might also be read as (unconscious) subversive mimicry: Bhabha, *Location of Culture*, 36–7.

95 Anon., 'Opinion'.

96 Lindfors, 'Post-War Literature', 51, 52. 'While we were preaching tribal culture and folk-tales, they were clamouring to be let into the Western world', Anthony Sampson recalled: *Drum*, 21. The title on the contents page remained 'The African Drum', but from late 1951 the cover, and each page, referred to the journal as *Drum*.

97 The photographs are of Canada Lee, who played Stephen Kumalo, relaxing off set, and of Paton and Korda (in vol. 1.9, 30–1) and of the glamorous Ribbon Dhlamini, who played Gertrude Kumalo (in vol. 2.1, 31).

98 Modisane, 'The Dignity of Begging'. Sanders discusses Modisane's intention (which he described in *Blame Me On History*) to have the beggar in the story represent black South Africans in a society 'which has determined that black is the condition of being dependent on white charity': Sanders, *Complicities*, 110.

99 Compare *Cry* (S), 151–2; (C), 143, 145; and 'Cry', *African Drum* 1.6

(September 1951), 36.

100 See Paton, 'Cry', *African Drum* 1.7 (October 1951), 18.

101 Compare *Cry* (S), 220, 221, and *Cry* (C), 206, 207 with 'Cry', *African Drum* 2.2 (February 1952), 30. For a political essay which drew on Paton's novel as evidence for 'Native' South Africans singing *Nkosi sikelel' iAfrika* see Deutsch, 'The Growth of Nations', 189.

102 Compare *Cry* (S), 238, 242, and *Cry* (C), 222, 226 with 'Cry', *African Drum* 2.3 (March 1953), 31.

103 See Paton, 'Cry', *African Drum* 2.4 (April 1952), 20.

104 APC, PC1/1/1/5, Scribner to Paton; see Alexander, *Paton*, 230.

105 Radway, *Feeling for Books*, 279.

106 Sharp, *Condensing the Cold War*, vii–xiv; see 43–4, 165–7.

107 Sales figure are quoted in APC, PC1/4/1/1, Howard to Paton (1957).

108 Grigely, *Textualterity*, 2.

109 References to the text of the North American abridgement are to the 1956 Canadian volume; the British volume is *Condensed Books* (1958). Paton, *Cry, Condensed* (1956), 196 and (1958), 346.

110 For example, passages are omitted in Chapter Eighteen – *Cry* (S); or (C) 2:1 – in which James Jarvis is shown to know about poor agricultural practices and food shortages in the tribal reserves: *Cry* (S), 127; (C) 121, and compare *Cry, Condensed* (1956), 259; (1958), 416.

111 Including Msimangu's account of how John Kumalo and his followers call the Bantu Press the 'Bantu Repress', and the description of Stephen Kumalo's shock at conditions in Claremont. Compare *Cry* (S), 28; (C), 32 and *Cry, Condensed* (1956), 212; (1958), 263.

112 See Paton, *Cry* (S), 49–62; (C), 51–62 and *Cry, Condensed* (1956), 228; (1958), 378.

113 Compare Paton, *Cry* (S), 39; (C), 42 and *Cry, Condensed* (1956), 220; (1958), 372.

114 Compare Paton, *Cry* (S), 180–1; (C), 169–70 and *Cry, Condensed* (1956), 291; (1958), 452.

115 Paton, *Cry* (S), 264; (C), 245; see *Cry* (S), 58; (C), 58; (S), 220; (C), 206.

116 Compare Paton, *Cry* (S), 271; (C), 252; *Cry, Condensed* (1956), 334; (1958), 499.

117 The passages omitted are from 1:16, 1:15, 2:29/2:12, 3:36/3:7 respectively.

118 Ellison, 'Art of Fiction', 212, 223–4.

119 Rivers, '*Cry, the Beloved Country*', 51.

120 Collins, 'Broken Tribe', 379.

121 *Ibid.*, 380, 385.

122 APC, PC1/4/2/1, Scribner (Jnr) to Paton (1961); and see Scribner (Jnr) to Paton (1959).

123 Baker, 'Paton's Beloved Country', 56, 60.

124 Baker (ed.), *Paton's* Cry, the Beloved Country. Other titles in the series included volumes on Hemingway and editions of *Julius Caesar*, James's *Daisy Miller*, and Wharton's *Ethan Frome*. The text of the novel appears on pages 7–132 (with pagination from the Scribner's first edition in parentheses). See Huddleston, *Naught for Your Comfort*; Steward, *You Are Wrong*.

125 Baker, Introduction, 1.

126 *Ibid.*

127 Bright. 'The Bridge Series', v.

128 *Ibid.*, vi.

129 Paton, *Cry* (1953), 3.

130 Blacksell, Introduction, 5, 6.

131 The omissions are too numerous to cite here, but for one example, compare the treatment of the original text's introduction of Absalom's pregnant girl-friend: see Paton, *Cry* (C), 65, 66 and this 1962 abridgement, 47.

132 Blacksell, Introduction, 6.

133 Clark, Introduction, 255.

134 *Ibid.*, 260.

135 *Ibid.*, 265.

136 See Evans, *Novel as Political Tract*, 1, 12. Not all new examining bodies have maintained their archives, and it has proved impossible to trace precisely when and where *Cry, the Beloved Country* was prescribed and examined, or to obtain copies of all relevant examination questions. Edexcel, whose examination papers are used by many schools in the south of Britain, has not prescribed *Cry, the Beloved Country* for some years (Davies to Van der Vlies, private correspondence). The Cambridge Local Examinations Syndicate archive confirms that the novel was set for British CSE examinations, but the CSE examining boards which merged with UCLES – the southern regional and west midlands boards – passed on very few records, and UCLES holds little examination material (Emerson to Van der Vlies, private correspondence). Jonathan Cape told Paton that the 1966 Longman edition had sold well 'and never been out of print': APC, PC1/4/1/4, Mossop to Paton.

137 Ellis to Van der Vlies, private correspondence, and Ellis, Interview.

138 Ellis, Interview. Paton approved this material in due course: APC, PC1/4/1/4, Paton to Mossop (January and July 1985).

139 Ellis, Introduction, xx.

140 Ellis, Interview.

141 *Ibid.*

142 Evans, *Novel as Political Tract*, 6.

143 *Ibid.*, 11.

144 *Ibid.*, 11, 13.

145 Ellis to Van der Vlies, private correspondence.

146 Timothy to Van der Vlies, private correspondence.

147 The novel has also been translated widely. Norwegian, Danish, Swedish, Dutch, Finnish, Czech and French translation were all first contracted in 1948, Portuguese and Italian in 1949, Japanese and Hebrew in 1950, and subsequently German (1951), Icelandic (1955), isiZulu (1957), Malayan (1959), Ovambo (1974), Spanish (1976; significantly, after Franco), Greek (1983), and Tsonga (1998). There have subsequently been new translations in some of these languages.

148 Alexander, *Paton*, 466; Paton, *Journey Continued*, 20, 23–4; Anderson, *Lost in the Stars*; Matlaw, 'Alan Paton's', 272. Paton, unimpressed with the Broadway production, was particularly upset by its tone of religious scepticism: Paton, *Journey Continued*, 20, 23–4.

149 Alexander, *Paton*, 221–2, 260–4, 266, 268; Beittel, '"What Sort of Memorial?"'.

150 Sargeant's production was directed by Heinrich Reisenhofer: Bothma, '"Cry'

op die Verhoog' (online).
151 Anderson, *Lost in the Stars*, 11.
152 See *ibid.*, 18–20, 92–4.
153 Komai, *Cry*, 45, 65; see 6. Compare Paton, *Cry* (S), 105; (C), 101.
154 Watson, 'Failure of Liberal Vision', 32, 33; see also Parker, 'The South African Novel', 8.
155 Beittel, '"What Sort of Memorial?"', 73–4; Davis, *In Darkest Hollywood*, 39–42.
156 Davis, *In Darkest Hollywood*, 44.
157 Paton, *Journey Continued*, 54; see 17–19, 41–9, 53–5.
158 Beittel, '"What Sort of Memorial?"', 72.
159 *Ibid.*, 84.
160 Mandela, 'Remarks at the Miramax Films World Premiere' (online).
161 English, *Culture of Prestige*, 34.
162 Winfrey, Book Club e-mail; see Barnard, 'Oprah's Paton', 94–8.
163 Barnard, online answer.
164 Barnard, 'Oprah's Paton', 101.

5

Alex La Guma's marginal aesthetics and the institutions of protest

A short book review in Cape Town's *Cape Times*, on 4 August 1962, high-lighted the absurd consequences of the banning of political opponents of the South African Government. Reporting the arrival of a book from Nigeria which 'everyone was scared to touch', it noted that the reviewer could not 'give it away, sell it, or leave it in a bus or train or even on a park bench without technically breaking the law' by 'disseminating' the work of a banned person; the newspaper could print little about the book besides its publisher and place of publication, a description of its cover and that it had '90 pages and 19 chapters'.[1] Its epigraph, however, which *could* be quoted (because not the words of the book's proscribed author), hinted cheekily at the title:

> I am thy father's spirit;
> Doom'd for a certain time to walk the night,
> And for the day confined to fast in fires,
> Till thy foul crimes done in my days of nature
> Are burned and purged away. WILLIAM SHAKESPEARE: *Hamlet*, Act I,
>   Scene V.[2]

The book was Alex La Guma's *A Walk in the Night*, a novella set in the squalor of District Six, the mixed-race slum in central Cape Town – soon to be demolished by the apartheid Government – whose inhabitants are likened by one of the characters (the alcoholic actor, Doughty) to 'Hamlet's father's ghost'; Doughty tells Mikey Adonis, who will later kill him in a moment of misdirected rage, that they are all 'doomed to walk the night'.[3]

Another Cape Town newspaper, *New Age*, did defiantly print the title, declaring the book 'a great beginning to Alex La Guma's literary career', and 'one of the most significant contributions to South African literature in recent years'. Despite being 'prevented from circulating in South Africa', *New Age* predicted, it would 'undoubtedly make its mark abroad'.[4] That it did, along with La Guma's subsequent novels, although none was published by northern-hemisphere *literary* or mainstream trade presses, hitherto the major sites of metropolitan cultural validation of Anglophone South African writing. La Guma's publishers were, in many differing senses, 'marginal': Mbari, a cultural club in Ibadan, Nigeria, published *A Walk in the Night*; *And a Threefold Cord* (1964) and *The Stone Country* (1967) were published by a small firm in East Berlin. *A Walk in the Night* was republished, with selected short stories, by Heinemann Educational Books and included in the firm's influential 'African Writers Series', aimed chiefly at an educational market in Africa, in 1968. *In the Fog of the Seasons' End* (1972) and *Time of the Butcherbird* (1979) appeared in the same series, which also reprinted *The Stone Country* in 1974. A survey at the end of the 1980s revealed that of African authors whose novels were taught in literature courses in Anglophone African universities only Ngũgĩ wa Thiong'o, Chinua Achebe and Ayi Kwei Armah were more popular than La Guma.[5] However, almost all South Africans were prevented from reading this work because, highly placed in the liberation Congress movement, La Guma was regarded as a threat to state security until the 1990s. His erstwhile comrade South African Constitutional Court Justice Albie Sachs recalls that La Guma's books 'just weren't around, for the universities, for schools – Alex wasn't around'.[6]

Born in District Six on 20 February 1925, La Guma became involved in politics early. The son of a prominent trade unionist, he joined the Communist Party in 1948, was a founder member of the South African Coloured Political Organisation in 1954, and was active in planning the 1955 Congress of the People at Kliptown, at which the Freedom Charter was adopted. A defendant in the notorious mass treason trial (1956–60), after his acquittal he was regularly arrested and detained without trial, and finally banned in August 1961.[7] La Guma had worked on a series of anti-government newspapers since 1956, but his career ended with the banning order, which, among other things, prevented his quotation or publication. In December 1962, he was one of the first to be placed under indefinite, twenty-four-hour, house arrest, under the terms of the Sabotage Act. He was detained again in October 1963, spending five months in prison. Finally, in September 1966, he was allowed to leave the country with his family on what was euphemistically called an exit permit; he would never visit South Africa again. La Guma chaired the London branch of the African National Congress (ANC) between 1970 and 1978, when he and his wife Blanche moved to Cuba as the ANC's representatives in Latin America. He died there, of a heart attack, on 11 October 1985.[8]

In an address, in 1971, to the Afro-Asian Writers' Organisation (of which he was secretary general after 1979), La Guma explained that manuscripts in South Africa which did not 'conform to the standards of the racist publishing houses, or the Bantu Education Authorities, the Publications and Entertainments Board, or the Minister of Justice' languished on dusty shelves, while '[g]enuine authors who aspire to see their work in print have had to leave the country and write in exile'.[9] His own writing was, of necessity, part of this tradition: proto-postcolonial rather than post-independence; looking forward to a liberated South Africa, but tinged always with a simmering frustration; marked in its material forms by the politics of the circuits through which it was forced to move, each site of publication and each situated act of critical judgement implicating it in contending regimes of value. Variously implicated in cultural debates about pan-Africanism and the Cold War, negotiating tensions between expectations of social-realist protest and the demands of Western readers and publishers (driven often by economic rather than political, and by differently construed aesthetic, imperatives), La Guma's fiction becomes both a focus and a *locus* of intense debate about ideology and aesthetics. The fates of *A Walk in the Night* demonstrate these predicaments of an exilic 'South African' textual condition; they are canvassed here, comprehensively, for the first time.

African, South African, socialist, realist: La Guma in Nigeria and East Berlin

The Ibadan-based Mbari Club and its publishing arm, Mbari Press, was run by Ulli Beier, an expatriate German who arrived in Nigeria in 1950 to teach English. In 1957, he founded *Black Orpheus*, a significant early journal dedicated to publishing writing by Africans and African diasporans, which he called '"propaganda" ... to educate English-speaking Africans about the rest of the black world', and 'to inspire and encourage young writers' during a period 'still dominated by colonialist chauvinism'.[10] *Black Orpheus* published several of La Guma's short stories, as well as work by exiled South Africans Dennis Brutus, Arthur Maimane and Bloke Modisane. La Guma's wife Blanche originally posted the typescript of *A Walk in the Night* to Mbari in late 1959 or early 1960, but the South African authorities refused to allow a parcel associated with a known communist to leave the country, and it was returned to her. It was ultimately smuggled out of South Africa by Beier himself, who met La Guma surreptitiously in Cape Town while on an African tour later in 1960.[11]

Beier's trip was funded by the Rockefeller Foundation, and Mbari, in turn, by the Ministry of Education of Western Nigeria and the Farfield Foundation, the 'parent organisation' of a Paris-based outfit called the Congress for Cultural Freedom, which itself raised money for Mbari from the Merill Foundation in New York. Es'kia Mphahlele had recently begun to serve as a roving African representative for the Congress, and was recruited on to Mbari's board by Beier and his impressive committee of Nigerian writers – including Wole Soyinka and Christopher Okigbo. Completing the chain, Farfield was covertly funded by the American Central Intelligence Agency (CIA), although it appears not to have exerted pressure on Mbari's editorial policy, the funding rather supporting a

policy of encouraging the development of an intellectual elite to act as a
stabilising force in newly independent African states which the United
States feared were susceptible to Soviet influence.[12] La Guma's first book
was thus, by virtue of its publication by Mbari, implicated in a more
complicated patronage structure than he might have imagined. It is ironic,
too, that La Guma was a committed Marxist, and perhaps not insignificant that Mphahlele, who insisted that Mbari's editorial policy was to
'publish good African writing which, for commercial and "aesthetic"
reasons would not be taken by big publishing houses', sought (albeit
twenty years later) to downplay La Guma's ideological commitment – to
insist on his literariness over his political engagement.[13]

The Mbari edition of *A Walk in the Night* comprised ninety pages, in a
large format (22cm x 14cm), with a blue, white and black paper cover
depicting a jauntily drawn street by night, deserted but for a single dark
figure, a police van and a black cat stalking along a wrought-iron
railing.[14] Mbari planned to distribute the book in Africa, the United
States and Britain, but lacked a robust distribution network. Soyinka's
review of the novel in the Lagos *Sunday Post*, while congratulating it for
'turning out a volume … so satisfactory in every respect', suggested that
it was 'a disgraceful matter that the bigger bookshops and stores in
Nigeria still [fought] shy of accepting books published in Nigeria', and
partially blamed Mbari, suggesting that 'it should be the function of a
club of this kind to make positive drives to sell both their publications and
other worthwhile Nigerian publications on the open market'.[15] When
Heinemann Educational Books approached Mbari in July 1963 about
republishing the novel, 600 of the 2,000 copies printed remained
unsold.[16]

Despite its small print run and unsatisfactory distribution, the novel
was disseminated through a network of black intellectuals and writers,
some in exile in Europe, and warmly received at a conference on African
writing held in 1962 at Makerere University College, Kampala.[17] Initially
reviewed almost exclusively in Africa, the few reviews in American or
British sites were written by expatriate academics working in Africa.
Anthony Astrachan's review in *Black Orpheus*, in February 1964,
described it as making 'refreshing reading' after what he called critics'
tired, 'revolving-door discussions' about what constituted 'African literature'.[18] Contrasting it with two novels about the Coloured community in
Cape Town, both by white writers (David Lytton's *The Goddam White
Man* and Eugene O'Donnell's *The Night Cometh*), Astrachan argued that
A Walk in the Night did not share their faults of self-consciousness or
stilted plot: La Guma 'apparently did not worry about whether he was
creating literature, and so he has done it'.[19] This notion of *the literary* as
an achieved state, the product of genius rather than studied technique,
betrays an interestingly ambiguous manoeuvre on the part of the reviewer: Astrachan does not feel the need to apologise for the political

5.1 Mbari's edition of La Guma's *A Walk in the Night*, 1962

imperative of La Guma's novel, but, anticipating some Western critics' perceptions of much African writing as somehow *not* 'literary', construes La Guma's apparent unconcern about Western aesthetics positively – only because the resulting work *is* able to be judged successful in terms of the aesthetics the author is supposed to have disdained. Soyinka's *Lagos Post* review evidenced a similar anxiety about the assumptions with which much African writing was habitually read in the West. Praising *A Walk in the Night* for having achieved what other, much longer novels by African writers were 'still merely groping towards', a sensitivity of description supporting but not existing solely to convey a political message, Soyinka enthused that La Guma's work was like 'an ink sketch', and the novel's tremendous detail 'valid' because it did 'not obtrude'. Sensitive to charges that politically engaged African writing was propaganda, Soyinka noted that 'the squalor' La Guma depicted, and 'the engineered purposelessness' of his characters' lives, became 'almost a concrete factor in themselves', as 'no vitriol-spitting propaganda' could.[20]

Two other reviews published in Africa seemed oblivious to the debates about committed literature. One, Joseph Muwanga's review in *Transition*, sought to place *A Walk in the Night* as specifically, even authoritatively, South African, deserving wide circulation and a 'place on the shelves along with Alan Paton's *Cry, the Beloved Country* and Doris Lessing's *Five*'.[21] La Guma's perhaps unexpected association with those authors suggests that his work was regarded as a similarly significant statement on Southern African conditions. Robert July's review, in the same issue of *Black Orpheus* as Astrachan's essay, sought to cast the novella as a socio-anthropological document with universal – or at least pan-African – relevance. July, assistant director for the Humanities at the Rockefeller Foundation, considered *A Walk in the Night* alongside three West African novels: Cyprian Ekwensi's *Jagua Nana*, Onuora Nzekwu's *Blade Among Boys* and Cheikh Amidou Kane's *L'Aventure ambigue*. Interested in the character *types* portrayed, and in the *generality* of the location (rather than the novels' politics or specific regional contexts), July was concerned to read for insights into 'African personality', believing that literature offered more perceptive insights into psychology than 'more analytical methods'. While La Guma's characters were 'authentic Africans', July suggested, they belonged 'to the new Africa of the industrial city', and 'none of the ways of tribal Africa show[ed] through'. However, here July erroneously universalises a spurious pan-African identity: being mostly Coloured, Malay and white, they had no strictly *tribal* 'ways' to abandon.[22] July also attempts more global comparisons, noting of La Guma's District Six: 'The conditions we see ... could fit with equal authority a city slum in Europe or America'; La Guma's setting might have been in 'Chicago, St Louis, [or] New York'.[23]

These early reviews illustrate the speed with which La Guma's reputation as an eminent South African, and his critical construction as a pan-African writer, took shape *in* Africa, although frequently mediated (or even directed) by non-African critics. This was no doubt because of Mbari's restricted distribution network, but also comments on the British and the American critical establishment's perception of African writing. The first reviews in non-African periodicals, although by critics with African connections, spoke to the unease in Western humanist critical discourse with the literary status of social documentary protest. Martin Banham worked at University College, Ibadan, and was almost certainly in contact with Beier and the Mbari Club. His review in the American journal *Books Abroad* praised *A Walk in the Night* as 'one of the most exciting books to emerge from Africa in recent years'; it was 'protest writing', but 'way above mere propaganda'.[24]

Lewis Nkosi, exiled critic and writer, was perhaps the most vocal black South African critic of what he saw as the aesthetic poverty of *protest* writing. Despite 'the best will in the world', he argued famously, it was not possible to detect in the fiction of many black writers 'any significant and complex talent which responds with both the vigour of the imagination and sufficient technical resources to the problems posed by conditions in South Africa'.[25] Because what was most frequently produced was 'the journalistic fact parading outrageously as imaginative literature', he wondered provocatively whether it might be prudent to 'renounce literature temporarily' in order to 'solve the political problem first rather than continue to grind out third-rate novels'.[26] Nkosi felt slightly differently about La Guma's writing: the second review in a non-African site (but by an African writer) was his assessment of *A Walk in the Night* in the British *New Statesman*, in January 1965. He wrote that, although apartheid's 'monstrous workings' precluded any other 'background or tradition', La Guma had managed to show 'real people waging a bloody contest with the forces of oppression'.[27]

It appears that La Guma, or those acting on his behalf, attempted to have *A Walk in the Night* republished elsewhere soon after it appeared in Nigeria. Ronald Segal, erstwhile editor of the radical *Africa South* journal, then in exile in London and engaged, with Ruth First, in selecting and publishing African titles for Penguin, passed the Mbari edition to Tom Maschler at Jonathan Cape, who replied to La Guma on 29 October that he thought the book too brief and 'too slight' to be successful in Britain, but added that Cape's readers admired the prose and that the firm would be interested in considering 'a longer book' in future.[28] It is true that, at ninety pages, the novella was possibly unusually short for a Cape book, but having published Alan Paton and Phyllis Altman, among others, and with William Plomer having been a principal reader, Cape might have been thought likely to be sympathetic to South African writing.

While publication by Mbari in Nigeria allied La Guma's work with an anti-colonial, post-independence, pan-Africanist agenda, and also involved it indirectly in a complex system of American patronage, another firm with which he tried to republish *A Walk in the Night* had very different ideological designs on its texts. La Guma sent a copy of the novella to Seven Seas Press, in East Berlin, in mid-1962. Established in 1958 by Gertrude Gelbin, an American woman married to the German author Stefan Heym, it sought to 'bring English literature to German readers' and to 'keep alive the works of American and other English-speaking "progressive" authors' neglected, or censored, in their own countries, favouring work demonstrating 'anti-Fascist, anti-racist and anti-war propaganda themes', but which also possessed 'considerable literary merit'.[29] Seven Seas published several South African titles, including Mphahlele's memoir *Down Second Avenue* and fiction by Jack Cope, Harry Bloom and Richard Rive, but was unwilling to consider republishing *A Walk in the Night* while Mbari retained distribution rights for the USA and Britain, two of the Berlin firm's biggest markets.[30] It did, however, publish La Guma's next two novels, *And a Threefold Cord* and *The Stone Country*, situating his writing in an expressly political context, with each volume's paratextual material clearly participating in this construction. *And a Threefold Cord*'s cover depicts a dilapidated shack, a blurb on the first page emphasises La Guma's authority to depict such suffering, a biographical note lists his arrests and detentions, and a Foreword by exiled South African journalist and politician Brian Bunting argues that only art which reflects social conditions and injustices could 'have any significance' in conditions like those in South Africa.[31] *The Stone Country* appeared with similar paratexts: the rear cover echoes Bunting's assertion that there could be no 'art for art's sake' in a book reflecting 'the truth about apartheid', and stresses La Guma's work's engagement with immediate political concerns.[32] Seven Seas Press was nonetheless aware of the need to balance emphasis on commitment as a primary valorising characteristic with an argument that what they were publishing really was also *literature*. An anthology entitled *Come Back, Africa!*, published in 1968, which featured La Guma's short story 'A Glass of Wine' (first published in *Black Orpheus* in 1960), included a substantial introductory essay which made particular mention of his 'literariness', suggesting that representing the 'harsh reality' of conditions in Africa required 'a commitment which must be broad and humanitarian and not limited to immediate protest and political objectives', and that La Guma, in particular, was equal to this task. It singled out *A Walk in the Night* as a 'powerfully realistic novella' which attempted 'to add another dimension to African literature' by exploring the psychology of *both* black *and* white characters.[33]

Educating Africa: La Guma and the 'African Writers Series'

British publishers had long regarded East and West Africa as a market for books, rather than a site for publication or a source of publishable writing in English. This changed after the publication of Nigerian author Chinua Achebe's groundbreaking *Things Fall Apart* by William Heinemann in London in 1958. Soon after, Alan Hill, who had started Heinemann's educational publishing section in 1946 (and would run it as Heinemann Educational Books after its separation from the parent firm in 1961), discovering that few copies had reached Nigeria, saw a need for a reasonably priced paperback series of African writing with wide distribution in Africa. Assisted by Van Milne, he launched the 'African Writers Series' (AWS) in 1960, to publish writing *from* Africa rather than, as had hitherto been the case for British firms, to export writing *to* the Continent.[34] Achebe acted for some time as editorial advisor to the series, and, in March 1963, he sent a copy of *A Walk in the Night* to the overseas director, Keith Sambrook, who responded enthusiastically and approached Beier about taking over Mbari's type and cover.[35] It was not to be a straightforward operation, however. The National Press of Nigeria had dumped the type, and Mbari wanted to sell its 600 remaining copies first.[36] Sambrook was determined to acquire what he regarded as 'probably one of the best short novels by an African writer', and told Mbari he could wait until October 1964 for terms to be agreed.[37]

Sambrook was confident that his firm's distribution network – which sold primarily to schools, universities and government agencies in East and West Africa – could achieve higher sales than Mbari, offering the AWS edition for sale at less than Mbari's 8s. The primary market envisaged for the book was still an African one, but, by mid-1964, concerned that the general African market for the book was already taken by Mbari and that *A Walk in the Night* might be too short to republish on its own, Sambrook began exploring the possibility of an expanded volume. Eventually, in September 1966, as La Guma headed into exile in Britain, a collection including several short stories alongside *A Walk in the Night* was finally ready for publication.[38] Conventional wisdom dictated that only hardback publication attracted reviews in London newspapers, so Heinemann Educational sought a publisher for such an edition to precede the planned AWS volume.[39] As early as April 1964, an approach was made to Macmillan, which had expressed interest in La Guma on the strength of his stories in *Quartet*, a collection edited by Richard Rive and published by Crown in New York in 1963.[40] Macmillan's David Machin replied, however, that although 'very interested' in an author whose 'writing is so often exactly right', he thought the novel too short, and suspected 'a lot of the market [had been] scooped already by the African publication', but indicated that Macmillan might be interested in a future 'full-length novel'.[41] David Farrer at Secker & Warburg was approached, but was also unwilling to take the book.[42] It was certainly not true that no South African writing was being published by mainstream British and American publishers: Victor Gollancz published Nadine Gordimer, who had a solid reputation by the late 1960s, and Secker & Warburg would publish Coetzee's *In the Heart of the Country* (1977) and *Waiting for the Barbarians* (1980). It is arguable, however, that sophisticated 'white writing' – in the sense used by Coetzee to refer to literature owing formal and metaphysical allegiance to Europe – conformed more to the expectations of readers and reviewers in Britain and the USA, and it became increasingly difficult to persuade mainstream publishers to issue hardbacks in advance of AWS paperback editions.[43] Having attempted unsuccessfully to find a heavyweight publisher with 'literary' credentials to bring La Guma's work, in hardback, to the attention of critics and readers in London, Heinemann Educational decided to publish the British hardback itself, in July 1967. Ten thousand sheets were printed, from which 3 editions were bound: 1,500 hardback (crown octavo) to sell for 18s; 7,500 in paperback priced at 6s; and 1,000 copies for the American edition were sold to Northwestern University Press for 2s 10d each.[44] William Heinemann undertook to manage the hardback's marketing, but the marketing team was not enthusiastic about selling African literature; sales were poor, and Heinemann Educational did not attempt to enlist its assistance in promoting La Guma again.[45]

The publicity questionnaire which La Guma completed in advance of publication illuminates his sense of how *A Walk in the Night* might be received. Asked to describe the work, he stressed its novelty as an engagement with 'the life of the Coloured (mixed-blood) people of South Africa'.[46] The explanation anticipates uncertainty about the term in Britain and (especially) North America, where 'coloured' more commonly denoted 'African-American', and was a contested term by the 1960s. It also draws attention to La Guma's sense of his own commitment to representing the 'true life experiences' of a 'community of $1^1/_2$ million people within the structure of apartheid South Africa'.[47] He always identified himself as Coloured, and despite risking a validation of racial classification propagated by apartheid, he clearly believed that a writer had a duty to let the 'world know what [was] happening' in whichever community he knew most about, 'even within a framework of racial separateness'.[48] While disappointed that his work could not be read, legally, in South Africa, La Guma recognised that it served to educate an international audience.[49] Despite his wishes, however, the blurb on the hardback dustjacket made little mention of a specifically 'Coloured' experience. The word appears once, but in a context which echoes racial stereotypes and colonial paternalism: 'The main story is about Michael Adonis, a Coloured *boy*, unjustly thrown out of his job.'[50] Nonetheless, one of the book's first mentions in the British press, in the 'Diary' column in *The Times* on 31 August 1967, made much of it being the first presentation of the 'Coloured Voice'. 'Like so many countries where personal freedom is in short supply', the reviewer remarked, South Africa had 'maintained a brisk turnover in literary exports', although almost all writing presented the country from the perspective of the 'liberal white man' and, very occa-

5.2   The AWS edition of *A Walk in the Night and Other Stories*, 1968

sionally, 'the African'. La Guma was supplementing a lack by writing about 'the coloured man in between'.[51] This reading casts La Guma's work as specifically South African, but also as social documentary of a definitively marginal character.

After the publication of *A Walk in the Night and Other Stories*, James Currey (who had taken over the AWS in 1964), eager to see more of La Guma's work in the series, pressed the author for another novel.[52] La Guma sent the manuscript of his fourth, *In the Fog of the Seasons' End*, which he completed in South Africa before his departure in 1966, and Heinemann set about attempting to find a London publisher prepared to handle the hardcover edition. Secker & Warburg's managing director Tom Rosenthal replied that he and two colleagues had read the manuscript but that, while it would fit into the AWS, Secker would be unable to publish it. The 'appreciable South African sale' it might have enjoyed was clearly denied it (La Guma being banned), Rosenthal noted, and, he continued,

> it is perfectly competent, but politically not sufficiently startling to do any more than preach to the converted, and, from the literary point of view, without any of the high spots that make one think that the sheer quality of the book is so over riding as to make people want it in hard cover, at hard cover price.[53]

Rosenthal appears to judge La Guma's writing mediocre as *literature*, and mediocre as *protest*: it had neither literary nor political novelty. Heinemann proceeded with its own hardback edition in October 1972. As Adrian Roscoe noted in the *Listener* in 1978, the situation in South Africa was seldom on the front pages of newspapers in Britain during the 1970s, and had come to seem less urgent than more spectacular Cold War fronts. It was less likely to provide material for best-selling fiction because it had come to seem 'irrelevant to the great global debate between East and West'.[54] Rosenthal was more direct when sent the Seven Seas edition of *The Stone Country* in 1973: 'Basically we just don't think it is good enough in literary terms to stand on its own feet over here, no matter how passionately one might agree with the sentiments.'[55] This time Heinemann decided against a hardcover edition, and published an AWS paperback edition as soon as rights had been negotiated with Seven Seas, in 1974.[56] La Guma's final published novel, *Time of the Butcherbird*, appeared only in the AWS.

The influence of various systems of patronage which gave African writing access to print has always been ambivalent. That this continued to be the case for the 'first generation of post-independence Africa writers', as Gareth Griffiths suggests, 'may seem less surprising in the light of this longer history of intrusive control'.[57] The role of Western publishers in enabling African authors was highly contentious. The issue of what attitude to take towards writers' political activities, for example, confronted Heinemann Educational soon after the launch of the AWS. Alan Hill claimed that the firm was always clear: 'we are not interested in an author's politics or creed, but only in the quality of his writing'.[58] Gail Low observes, however, that it was 'clear from the outset ... that Hill was very sure' that the series was one of '*educational* books' and not 'strictly *literary* material'; marketability counted most.[59] James Currey has always been concerned to stress the tension between literariness and more commercial imperatives, however. He observed in 2003 that the AWS was 'a general *literary* series of original contemporary work', despite being 'published by an educational company', and that this brought occasional problems: 'The education industry wants to know where it is.'[60] The problem of publishing in an environment in which there 'was no canon of established texts by African writers', in Currey's words, made for difficult choices, and the inevitable charges of bad ones: South African writer Bloke Modisane, reporting on the African Writers' Conference at Makerere in Kampala in 1962, drew attention to a particularly heated session during which writers protested 'against the publishing of bad African literature'.[61] Adewale Maja-Pearce, a consultant and editor of the AWS from the mid-1980s, concedes that early success came at the price of 'a number of books of doubtful literary merit', because 'African writers had hitherto been judged by standards which would never have been applied to their European counterparts'.[62]

Despite these criticisms, La Guma's inclusion in the AWS undoubtedly made his work more readily available to an international audience, although none of his books sold more than 20,000 copies.[63] An indication of early sales figures for *A Walk in the Night* is given in a letter from Currey to La Guma in 1970. The cased (hardback) edition sold 1,450 copies in 1967, 142 in 1968, and 131 in 1969. The AWS paperback sold 908 copies in 1968, and 4,355 copies the following year.[64] Launched in a new AWS format in 1985, by July 1990 its 'home' sales reached 2,598 and export sales 3,586 copies.[65] By July 1994, 'home' sales had increased to 6,834 copies, reflecting a growing awareness of La Guma's work in Britain both as South Africa's negotiated political settlement played itself out in the British media and as La Guma's work became more widely studied in universities. It also, undoubtedly, had to do with unfavourable exchange rates in African countries: exports sales remained relatively static at 3,633 copies.[66] These are not bad figures, but La Guma could never approach Achebe's success; by the early 1990s, *Things Fall Apart* had sold in excess of three million copies in its Heinemann editions alone.[67] By mid-1996, AWS editions of *In the Fog of the Seasons' End*, *Time of the Butcherbird* and *A Walk in the Night* were out of print, and the rights reverted to Blanche La Guma, ten years after her husband's death.[68]

The AWS had come by then to be seen as a canon of pro- and post-independence African writing, for sale to Africa and a small niche readership in Britain.[69] The significance of La Guma's work appearing in an educational imprint is not to be underestimated: it made it on to the list of a British publisher, but that was still a marginal list relative to the output of large publishers of popular and literary fiction. Furthermore, while Currey describes it as being 'published by an educational publisher and used in Africa for educational purposes, at university as well as at school level', it also came to be regarded more ambiguously.[70] Bessie Head, writing to Currey in 1978 in response to his enthusiasm about the success of the series, noted that it was 'more than a prestigious venture', being regarded by some 'as a collector's item; they buy up each new edition, not so much through love for the writers but to have the whole collection. Something might be wrong here, but that's the position.'[71]

Surveying its first three decades, Odia Ofeimun offered a cautious critique of the series, noting that its influence on the course of African literature had been so strong that many African intellectuals had begun to regard it as a 'special cornering of the turf', part of a neo-colonial infrastructure which had limited indigenous potential.[72] It bore an *educational* patina in the former colonies, and presumed to present a canon of African writing effectively authorised in, and by, the former imperial centre. Graham Huggan suggests that the series was a 'valuable promoter of cross-cultural understanding', but also an 'ironic purveyor of exoticist modes of cultural representation'; a well-intentioned undertaking, it nonetheless aided the 'continuing exoticisation of Africa through misdirected anthropological images'.[73]

'*Bona fide* literature': protest and apartheid reading

Copies of the Mbari edition of *A Walk in the Night* made their way from Nigeria to South Africa shortly after publication in 1962. Beier managed have some smuggled to the Vanguard bookshop in Johannesburg, which sold copies of *Black Orpheus* under the counter, and others were posted to radical or sympathetic Cape Town newspapers, including the *Cape Times*, *New Age* and *Spark*.[74] Fifteen copies sent to La Guma himself were seized by Customs and Excise officials at the Cape Town docks, in November 1962, and the process of formal consideration by the censors initiated.[75] The reader appointed to consider the novella under the terms of the Censorship Act (1930, as amended) provided a plot synopsis and a list of 'indecent, obscene, or objectionable' material in the text. He noted a bribe offered to Raalt (the police constable) but omitted mention of Raalt's racist remarks, although he did concede that Willieboy's death in the police van was a result of the policeman's indifference. He listed blasphemous passages, 'anti-white propaganda' and insults with a racial content (especially about 'Coloureds').[76] These last two categories, in particular, furnished references cited by the Board of Censors in its recommendation to the Minister of Home Affairs, on 3 December 1962, that *A Walk in the Night*, because likely to arouse anti-white sentiments, be banned.[77] The prohibition on the novel's importation and distribution was endorsed in January 1963.[78]

A couple of weeks after the notice confirming the ban appeared in the *Government Gazette*, an editorial in *Spark* protested the imminent passing into law of the new Publications and Entertainments bill (Act 26 of 1963). Fifteen thousand items were already banned under the Customs Act, *Spark* noted, including 'Alex La Guma's novel "A Walk in the Night"', despite its being 'acclaimed both in this country and abroad as a work of merit'.[79] The bill passed, and the new Act replaced the Board of Censors with a more euphemistically titled Publications Control Board, empowered to declare material undesirable on grounds of indecency or obscenity, blasphemy, the likelihood of offence being caused to the religious convictions of any faith community, ridicule for any racial group or likely prejudice to state security. The 'standard' by which works were judged, although officially that of the average South African, was in practice the Calvinist Afrikaner establishment. Works submitted for consideration were scrutinised by committees of readers appointed from lists approved by the Minister of Home Affairs, and appeals against decisions were to be made through the courts.[80] While it was already clear that nothing La Guma published abroad could legally be read in South Africa, apartheid bureaucrats clung fervently to the performance of a spurious kind of due process, and insisted on submitting each new book to a committee of readers. So it was that *And a Threefold Cord* and *The Stone Country* were considered, and banned. Interestingly, the reader appointed to consider the latter, Professor A. H. Murray (notorious even among his colleagues for his conservatism), objected more to *The Stone Country*'s paratextual material – especially the Dedication, author's biography and the Preface – than to its plot.[81] The report did mention that La Guma was 'still on the banned list', but merely included that information in a list of cumulatively sufficient conditions for prohibition.[82]

In 1974, a new Publications Act (42 of 1974) retained the 1963 Act's categories of undesirability, but introduced Publications Committees to make recommendations to a director of publications, and abolished the process of appeal through the courts, introducing instead a Publications Appeal Board of thirteen members, appointed by the country's President.[83] Crucially, all previous decisions to ban work had to be reviewed, and the reviews undertaken on La Guma's texts reveal growing tensions in the censors' construal of 'literariness'. An application to review the ban on *A Walk in the Night* was brought in September 1976 by Mrs E. Steytler, better known as the prolific and acclaimed Afrikaans novelist Elsa Joubert, and although the subsequent review confirmed the ban, some objections – specifically indecency, obscenity and harm 'to public morals' – were withdrawn, and some literary merit detected.[84] The reviewing reader concluded:

> The story is well written, the literary style not unlike T.S. Eliot's in his *Wastelands* [*sic*]. The author captures the sordid, rancid atmosphere and the stench of District Six; the squalor and degradation; the dehumanising effect of

the area upon those who inhabit it. The Police are portrayed in an unfavourable light; as arrogant bullies, aggressors, extortioners – men with a callous contempt and disregard for those to whom they should minister.[85]

Because of this 'literary' merit, and the veracity of some of its admittedly troubling representations, consideration might have been given to lifting the ban in 'normal times', the reader concluded, had the 'present political and racial climate' not precluded this; the Soweto student riots had erupted only six months previously.[86] A review of *And a Threefold Cord* confirmed the ban on that book, too.[87] Both acts of re-reading were disingenuous: La Guma's writing could not be disseminated because he was still a banned person, and had it not been banned by the censors, it could and would have been proscribed under several other restrictive Acts of Parliament.[88]

Nonetheless, there does appear to have been a slight relaxation in the terms by which 'literariness' was considered a potentially mitigating condition by the apartheid censors. In 1979, a decision on an appeal against the banning of André P. Brink's *'n Droë Wit Seisoen* made this relaxation – or, rather, reconfiguration – explicit, substituting the standard of the *reasonable reader* for that of the *average person* as the test in deciding undesirability. This was later refined to the *probable* or *likely* reader, and work considered 'literary' was considerably less likely to be banned because of its restricted *likely* audience.[89] As Peter McDonald notes, many of the readers on Publications Committees shared this idea of a 'category of the literary', understood in a 'quasi-sociological' and also a formal sense – in other words, writing without mass appeal and writing with 'formal or rhetorical complexity, subtlety, or obscurity', whose 'aesthetic qualities functioned as a kind of protective covering that rendered any potentially undesirable sexual' or political 'content innocuous'.[90]

However, this comparatively more lenient attitude did not always influence the readers on the Publications Committees who actually made the recommendations about banning, as became clear in August 1979, when the director of publications appealed against a Publications Committee's decision to ban Nadine Gordimer's seventh novel, *Burger's Daughter*.[91] This had been published by Jonathan Cape in London in June 1979, embargoed on its importation into South Africa later that month and banned on 11 July. The Publications Committee charged with considering it reached the conclusion that the novel's literary merits did *not* outweigh its criticism of the South African regime – one member even suggested that it possessed no qualities which could 'save it as a work of art'.[92] The appeal lodged by the director of publications was considered in October 1979 by two appointed 'experts', both, significantly, university teachers of literature: P. J. H. Titlestad, a professor of English Literature at the University of Pretoria, argued that the Publications Committee had misread Gordimer's novel.[93] Rialette Wiehahn suggested that the novel's 'literary devices' ensured that it avoided the 'oversimplification ... inherent in propaganda', but which had 'no place whatever in serious literature'; it was 'bona fide literature'. [94] The Appeal Board was less interested in such questions, but was grateful to the experts for suggesting the audience which a 'literary' work could expect: a limited readership not likely to be worked into a state of insurrectionary fervour by a difficult novel. In the present case, these were judged 'extenuating circumstances in considering possible prejudice to safety of the state', and the decision of the Publications Board to ban Gordimer's novel was overturned. [95]

It seems indisputable that the director of publications could, and did, choose particularly constituted panels of readers to consider individual texts; it is striking that such 'unusually sophisticated' and apparently 'sympathetic' readers were deliberately chosen (for example) for J. M. Coetzee's work. [96] It is also clear that they were not, at least initially, chosen to read La Guma's. Gordimer discerned this strategic manoeuvring, calling the Board's decision in the *Burger's Daughter* case an attempt to buy off with 'special treatment' those (white) opponents of censorship with international reputations: 'No ban on any black writer's work [was] likely to be challenged by the Director's own application to the Appeal Board', she suggested. [97] The Board did, in fact, rule the following year that Sipho Sepamla's *A Ride on the Whirlwind*, while not successful 'as a work of art or great literature', had sufficient 'literary pretension' to limit its readership, but the appeal was *not* brought by the Directorate. [98] It appears, too, from the censors' consideration of La Guma's fifth and final novel, *Time of the Butcherbird*, in early 1980, that the apparent relaxations in evaluative criteria made little difference to the reading of La Guma's work by state institutions in South Africa. In this case, the novel was banned, but not without some disagreement among the Publication Committee's three members. [99] One argued that the novel's literary merit might excuse its coarse and undesirable language, but did not mitigate its potential threat to race relations in its presentation of some white characters' extreme contempt for blacks. [100] A third reader, and one of the first *literary* experts to consider La Guma's work, children's author and retired academic R. E. Lighton (who also read Coetzee's *Waiting for the Barbarians* in the same year), dissented, arguing that the novel *did* have 'literary merit', and the likely 'intelligent reader' would take the potentially subversive material 'in his stride'. [101] Even so, the novel was banned. [102]

Left-wing South African publishers were nonetheless determined, if at all possible, to secure La Guma's publication in South Africa, taking advantage of this apparent receptivity to *literariness*. In March 1982, David Philip, a famously courageous and progressive Cape Town publisher, wrote to the Directorate of Publications to ask for a review of *A Walk in the Night*, which Philip hoped to republish in a new Southern African series. [103] Surprisingly, the Publications Committee charged with the review found it 'not undesirable', but for an unexpected reason – and ultimately to no avail.[104] One reader, J. A. Scholtz, thought the work unlikely to be dangerous not because it was 'literary', but because it was not: banning it would give undue prominence to a publication unworthy of further attention.[105] A second report, by the Committee's chair, suggested intriguingly that the potentially objectionable elements of the work were rendered ineffectual not because the work was not literary (as Scholtz argued), but because it was the work of a 'Coloured' writer: the reader clearly had in mind the derogatory language used about some characters in the novel, reading it as being neutralised by the fact that La Guma was himself 'Coloured'.[106]

The recommendation that the novel was 'not undesirable', as one might imagine, set the proverbial cat among the bureaucratic pigeons. Members of the Directorate were ambivalent, at best, about the outcome, and one scrawled a comment on the final report, on 16 June 1982 (a psychologically significant date, the anniversary of the start of the Soweto student uprising in 1976): 'For me the fact that Alex La Guma is a listed person is a sufficient aggravating factor to ban the book again.'[107] Next to this, another wrote on the following day that, in line with recent guidelines issued by the Appeal Board, this fact was irrelevant.[108] The first reiterated his concerns, however, and the censorship records preserve several pages of notes recording a series of phone calls made on 21 June, establishing that La Guma was still a listed person, and that his work could thus not be published, even if found 'not undesirable'. A rushed, unsigned memorandum to the clerk of the Publications Appeal Board on the same day gave notice that the Directorate would appeal against the decision of the Publications Committee (in effect, to reinstate the ban, or cancel the unbanning). It seemed as if the *Burger's Daughter* episode was to repeat itself, in reverse, but the memorandum was cancelled, and the notice of suspension of the ban on *A Walk in the Night*, which appeared in the *Government Gazette*, simply reversed in a subsequent issue.[109] Legislated marginalisation trumped any pretence of considering literary merit or likely readership as mitigating factors. Nothing confirms quite so completely the superficiality of the veneer of due judicial process which the State attempted to give its censorship apparatus.

David Philip persevered, attempting, without success, to negotiate with the Department of Justice about the publication of a banned person. The firm sent copies of *A Walk in the Night*, *And a Threefold Cord*, *The Stone Country* and *Quartet* (Rive's anthology, containing four short stories by La Guma) to the Department's director in July 1982, pleading for permission to publish work which the Directorate of Publications no longer appeared to consider objectionable *per se*.[110] The letter argued that La Guma's work contained no trace of 'communist or subversive elements', and that, if permission was granted, would be republished in a series which sought to promote 'good writing by South Africans' – particularly work which had 'been out of print for a long time or [had] never been issued in this country'. The firm was at pains to distance itself from the formats in which the censors had previously encountered the works: 'We will stress the literary merits of the works. The "political" stance that the Heinemann Series adopts will be absent.'[111] This attempt on the part of a liberal, English-language publishing house in South Africa to renegotiate La Guma's identity as a serious national–literary figure, and its invocation of the AWS as a purveyor of a radical, political, pan-Africanist ideology, is noteworthy.

The attempt to appeal to a nationalist sensibility was, however, futile: La Guma's work remained proscribed until after his death, when successful appeals were submitted by, among others, the National Library in Cape Town. David Philip was finally able to publish *A Walk in the Night and Other Stories* in its 'Africasouth' series, in 1991.[112] Being considered 'bona fide literature' was clearly not an individually sufficient condition for avoiding censorship, whatever the fates of, for example, Coetzee's and (some of) Gordimer's novels might suggest. Had Coetzee or Gordimer been listed communists, it is clear that their *literariness* would not have saved their books from the censors. This is not necessarily to suggest that La Guma's work was of the same order of *literariness* as Coetzee's; to effect any kind of comparative judgement would be to enter into a different kind of argument altogether. It is clear, however, that Coetzee himself regarded La Guma as self-consciously *literary* – although, intriguingly and potentially instructively, not as necessarily positively or disinterestedly so, as I presently show.

Institutions of literariness

One of the most influential readings of La Guma's protest message is that offered by Coetzee in a 1974 essay entitled 'Man's Fate in the Novels of Alex La Guma', which develops an analogy between tragedy and La Guma's representation of oppression. If the power of tragedy exists in the transformation of defeat into victory through a catharsis (prompted by identification with a defeated tragic hero), Coetzee argues, then the naturalistic novel offered post-Darwinian biological and Marxist historical-materialist determinants in place of the inscrutable fate authored by the gods in Greek tragedy. Coetzee suggests that, in *A Walk in the Night*, Willieboy's death at the hands of the police and Michael Adonis's impending and inevitable fall into a life of crime appear to the characters themselves to be fate dictated by an inscrutable power; the reader's equation of this ill-understood fate with the apartheid State makes of the novel, as a latter-day tragedy, an implicit critique of a political system.[113] La Guma could not portray characters with a radical awareness of the political situation because that would have been an unfaithful representation of the actual situation, Coetzee suggests. Rather, he locates the potential for change 'in his reader's synthesizing intelligence'.[114]

Coetzee's essay was actually a revised and much expanded version of a shorter piece, 'Alex La Guma and the Responsibilities of the South African Writer', published, in 1971, in a small journal dedicated to African literature and culture. Lewis Nkosi had suggested that black writers had learnt nothing from Western experimentalism, that they were 'crudely attempting to solve problems to which European practitioners ... [had] responded with greater subtlety, technical originality and sustained vigour'; Coetzee countered that this idea of a necessary 'homage' involved 'a rather simple-minded view of an absolute', and mythical, '"technique"'.[115] He agreed implicitly with Nkosi's criticism of literature which merely chronicled the lives of people crushed by forces beyond their comprehension or control.[116] He also agreed with Nkosi about the literary merits of La Guma's work, but on different grounds. While Coetzee agreed with the Marxist critique of European naturalism as having conceded victory to the forces which had brought about the social fragmentation it so painstakingly depicted, he argued that La Guma's work (specifically *A Walk in the Night*) – in its presentation of characters (Joe, Greene, Frankie Lorenzo) who begin but fail to apprehend modes of resistance – offers a Marxist–materialist, ideological 'critique of the Colo[u]red proletariat', which makes the author 'not a naturalist but a critical realist'.[117]

By 1974, Coetzee was arguing that La Guma's was *not* Lukácsian critical realism, because the novels display a stasis: the characters only imperfectly perceive the ideological nature of their reality, and take only tentative steps to challenge their oppressors. This stasis, he argued, belonged to the naturalistic novel.[118] In an assessment which reads unevenly as both apologia and critique (and reveals the influence of Roland Barthes), Coetzee argued that La Guma's fastidious attention to detail was a straining after excessive literariness, an inheritance of 'the worst excesses of realism'.[119] He repeated the charge of a 'tendency to lyrical inflation' in La Guma's descriptions of place, in his 1986 essay 'Into the Dark Chamber'.[120] The many passages in which La Guma emphasises the sordid environs inhabited by his characters seemed excessively literary to Coetzee. They appeared similarly to Nkosi, who, in his own copy of the Mbari edition, highlighted some of the same passages as Coetzee cited in his 1974 essay.[121]

Validations of his literariness, like those by Coetzee and Nkosi, were themselves acts of self-interested positioning. Both of those writers were, at the time of their interventions, attempting to justify the value of their own cultural labour, abroad. Coetzee's particular investment in making the case for La Guma is revealed in his admission, in an interview with David Attwell, that his work on La Guma dates from the late 1960s, when, as a young academic in the United States (at SUNY, Buffalo), he was resigning himself to the idea that establishing a career in the USA might necessitate his becoming an Africanist. His work on La Guma, he suggests, represented an attempt to 'find an imaginative (an imaginary) place' for himself 'in the Third World and its narratives of itself'; he had 'dipped [his] toe in the waters of Marxism by writing in what was intended to be a positive spirit about the novels of a native South African Marxist'.[122] Coetzee continues:

> Rereading the La Guma essay today, I detect something in it that may be invisible to you: a tension between asserting the particularity of South African literature, and asserting the amenability of South African writing to European standards of judgment; or, in more immediate terms, a tension between wanting to validate the profession of Africanist and wanting to create a space in African studies for a person with my rather European tastes.[123]

These comments are intriguing both because they illustrate the manner in which La Guma's work was subject to assessment by explicitly and confessedly Western, and also very *interested*, conceptions of literariness – and, in Coetzee's case, by a writer who tried, during the worst of the emergency in South Africa, to stake a claim for literature's absolute difference from the discourses of history, or their pressures.[124]

For Albie Sachs, La Guma's major achievement was that, despite being 'an intensely political person, totally engaged with the political struggle', his writing was 'non-directed, sensitive, filled with gentle irony, evocative of the actual emotions and thoughts and incomprehensions of a great variety of ordinary people'; it established the space for writing not driven by direct political preaching and 'prepared us for freedom, prepared us for a much more open, generous society than we otherwise might have ended up with'.[125] This formulation echoes Sachs's influential position paper 'Preparing Ourselves for Freedom' (1989), which urged a change in the discourse of liberation and signalled what Graham Pechey calls the 'late conversion' of the ANC 'to a non-instrumental view of the function of art under (and beyond) apartheid'.[126] 'It is as though our rulers stalk every page and haunt every picture; everything is obsessed by the oppressors and the trauma they have imposed', Sachs argued.[127]

Njabulo Ndebele diagnosed the same failing and advocated a similar response, a 'rediscovery of the ordinary', a refusal to represent the excessive violence, the absurdist spectacle of apartheid which merely reflected, and so tacitly reinforced, state hegemony. Ndebele suggested, too, that debates about the aesthetic value of protest were futile. The writing 'validates itself in terms of its own ... emergent, complex system of aesthetics', he argued, its 'aesthetic validity' lying in its 'readers' recognition of the ... rendering of a familiar oppressive reality'.[128] The problem with this assessment, of course, is that such readers were often denied access to such writing – as in La Guma's case.

La Guma's writing, however *literary* it was judged by any body of readers, could not be bracketed off from the political: it could not exist in a different order of discourse. So, while some of those enlisted to read and assess his writing on behalf of the censorship juggernaut felt ambivalent about recommending the banning of writing which they judged *literary* (according to 'European standards of judgement', in Coetzee's words), his being listed as a danger to the security of the apartheid State effectively prevented La Guma's writing from being freely available in South Africa until the 1990s. Jonathan Arac observes that La Guma's was 'more part of a world literature than that of any particular nation', even if in his writing he was 'struggling toward a nationhood'.[129] Because his reputation is essentially that of an exiled writer, however, the publication–reception history of his work is necessarily that of a literature in exile, a literature existing in an uneasy relationship to any claims on it by a national literary history. Publishers accepted or rejected his work depending on their respective investments in judgements about whether it was 'South African' or 'African', and what writing so construed should *do*: represent African conditions to African readers; represent conditions of oppression (whether or not specifically *South* African, or even African) to a concerned international readership; or be amenable to universalist, literary-critical judgement, and (more importantly) be saleable in the West. Because its fate is, arguably, representative of much black South African writing, and because it has been argued not to be thus representative, La Guma's oeuvre provides both an exemplary and an aberrant case study of the disputed nature of writing by a South African writer, which might or might not be 'South African' and might or might not be 'literature'. The fates of his works attest to the complicated lives of books in (proto-) post-colonial societies, in which the vagaries of meaning, and the contingency of *literariness* itself, are constantly contested, but in which the political, almost inevitably, triumphs.

Notes

1 Cape Times Reporter, 'La Guma Novel Too Hot to Hold'.

2 La Guma, *Walk* (1962), iv.

3 *Ibid.*, 24.

4 B.P.B., 'Alex La Guma's First Novel'.

5 Booker, *African Novel in English*, 169.

6 Sachs, Interview.

7 The Internal Security Act (44 of 1950) allowed for the prohibition of the publication or dissemination of utterances and writing by members of organisations banned under the 1950 Suppression of Communism Act, of anyone banned from attending gatherings and of those who had left the country and who, in the opinion of the Minister of Justice, were engaged in agitation against the state from abroad: Dugard, 'Censorship in South Africa', 67.

8 For biographical information see: Abrahams, *Alex La Guma*, xi–xv; Adhikari, Introduction; Blanche La Guma, 'Alex La Guma'; Blanche La

Guma, Interview; Van der Vlies, 'Alex La Guma'.

9 La Guma, 'Address by Lotus Award Winner', 196.

10 Benson, 'Border Operators', 435; see 432, 440; see also Benson, *Modern Cultural Awakening*; Killam and Rowe (eds), *Companion*, 159–60.

11 Blanche La Guma, 'Alex La Guma', 12; and Blanche La Guma, Interview; Beier to Van der Vlies, private correspondence.

12 See Benson, *Modern Cultural Awakening*, 34–6; Benson, 'Border Operators', 442; Mphahlele, *Afrika My Music*, 33; Killam and Rowe (eds), *Companion*, 159; James, 'The Protest Tradition', 110.

13 Mphahlele, 'Mbari – 1st Anniversary'. He wrote of La Guma in 1984: 'There's nothing in Alex of the radical posturing we have come to associate with marxists [*sic*] who enter every debate with the rhetoric that is a routine attack on capitalism … ': Mphahlele, *Afrika My Music*, 128.

14 La Guma received 10 per cent of the sale price of each copy, plus a £50 advance: Robben Island Mayibuye Archive, Belville (Mayibuye), MCH118/1/B.1, Hendrickse to La Guma; see fig. 5.1.

15 Soyinka, 'The Fight for Human Existence'.

16 Heinemann Educational Books Archive (HEB), 3/8, Hendrickse to Sambrook (1963). All HEB material with permission, Harcourt Education.

17 Modisane, 'African Writers' Summit', 5.

18 Astrachan, 'The Names Are Fictitious', 59.

19 *Ibid.*

20 Soyinka, 'The Fight for Human Existence'. The following year, in an essay in *The American Scholar*, Soyinka claimed La Guma's 'hurtful realism' as an example of the individual art from which a positive image of the African as human was emerging: Soyinka, 'From a Common Backcloth', 13.

21 Joseph Muwanga in *Transition*, quoted in Zell, *A New Reader's Guide*, 211.

22 July, 'African Personality', 35, 36.

23 *Ibid.*, 33.

24 Banham, 'South Africa'.

25 Nkosi, 'Fiction by Black South Africans', 211.

26 *Ibid.*, 212; see also Nkosi, 'African Fiction: Part One', 6; Lindfors, 'Post-War Literature', 51.

27 See Nkosi, 'Annals of Apartheid', 164, 165; among the texts reviewed in this essay were Richard Rive's *Emergency* and *Quartet*, the latter including La Guma stories.

28 Mayibuye, MCH118/1/B.1, Maschler to La Guma.

29 Frankel, 'Seven Seas East of the Wall', 32; see Tate, 'Stefan Heym'.

30 Mayibuye, MCH118/1/B.1, Pankey to La Guma. Pankey, also an American, was Gelbin's deputy editor. See lists of books in La Guma's *And a Threefold Cord*, 174–5, and *The Stone Country*, 170–1.

31 Bunting, Foreword, 16, 9; see also La Guma, *And a Threefold Cord*, 1 ('Briefly, About the Book'), 8 (epigraph), 176 ('Briefly, About the Author'). Bunting edited the anti-government newspaper *Guardian*, after 1948, and worked on several of its successors, including *Advance*, *New Age* and *Spark*. He was elected to Parliament as the white representative of blacks in the Cape Province, despite government attempts to disqualify him, but was expelled in 1953 under the Suppression of Communism Act. Subsequently banned and prevented from working as a journalist, he was forced into exile in London,

in 1963, and later published a scathing exposé of the apartheid regime: *The Rise of the South African Reich.*

32 La Guma, *Stone Country*, cover; see Bunting, Foreword, 9.

33 Shore, 'A Note', 26, 29. Other writers represented in the volume were Modisane, Mphahlele, Nkosi, Rive and, intriguingly, Paton.

34 Hill, *In Pursuit of Publishing*, 122–6, 168–71, 144. On the series, see also Killam and Rowe (eds), *Companion*, 4–6; Currey, 'Chinua Achebe'; Low, 'In Pursuit of Publishing'.

35 HEB, 3/8, Achebe to Sambrook.

36 *Ibid.*, Sambrook to Achebe, Sambrook to Beier (1963), Hendrickse to Sambrook (1963).

37 He offered Mbari royalties on 5s: HEB, 3/8, Sambrook to Hendrickse.

38 *Ibid.*, Sambrook to Beier (1964); Hendrickse to Sambrook (1964); Verity to Beier; Gelbin to Verity.

39 Killam and Rowe (eds), *Companion*, 5; Currey, Interview.

40 HEB, 3/8, Verity to Machin; Sambrook, Interview. See Rive (ed.), *Quartet*.

41 HEB, 3/8, Machin to Sambrook. Reproduced with permission of Palgrave Macmillan.

42 *Ibid.*, Verity to Farrer.

43 Coetzee, *White Writing*, 11; see Ehmeir, 'Publishing South African Literature'; Low, 'Finding the Centre?', 23–4.

44 HEB, 3/8, Putnam to Birley.

45 Sambrook, Interview.

46 HEB, 3/8, La Guma, publicity questionnaire.

47 *Ibid.*

48 La Guma, Interview with Robert Serumaga, 93; on La Guma's Coloured identity see Adhikari, *Not White Enough*, 116–30.

49 La Guma, 'The Real Picture', 22.

50 La Guma, *Walk* (1967), dust-jacket/back cover; my emphasis.

51 P.H.S., 'Now the Coloured Voice'.

52 HEB, 18/3, Currey to La Guma; HEB, 3/8, Currey to La Guma (1972).

53 *Ibid.*, Rosenthal to Sambrook.

54 Roscoe, 'Writers in South Africa', 533. A year previously, Roscoe had defended La Guma's 'special artistic qualities', arguing that his reputation had 'suffered too long from the misleading logic of the view that because South African conditions are inimical to the growth of good writing, none has in fact appeared': Roscoe, *Uhuru's Fire*, 233.

55 HEB, 12/8, Rosenthal to Currey.

56 *Ibid.*, Leresche to Currey; Currey to La Guma; Currey to Leresche.

57 Griffiths, *African Literatures*, 80.

58 Hill, *In Pursuit of Publishing*, 128.

59 Low, 'In Pursuit of Publishing', 34.

60 Currey, 'Chinua Achebe', 576; my emphasis.

61 There were, he continues, 'broad – and unfortunate – hints that Amos Tutuola would probably not have been published if his manuscript had been read by an African reader': Modisane, 'African Writers' Summit', 5. Tutuola's *The Palm-Wine Drinkard*, published by Grove in New York and Faber & Faber in London in 1952, became widely viewed by academics in the West as the harbinger of a new, supposedly authentic African voice. To the irritation of

many African writers who felt the need to engage with contemporary socio-political issues, this model drew heavily on traditional folktales and modes of storytelling: Larson, *Ordeal*, 1–25.

62 Maja-Pearce, 'Publishing African Literature', 127.

63 According to royalty statements from Heinemann Educational and correspondence with the Sayle Agency, *In the Fog of the Seasons' End* had, by 1994, sold 2,511 copies in the AWS B-format edition (first published in 1992); in 20 years, the original AWS edition (no. 110, 1972) sold 14,275 copies (it was reprinted 10 times; the figure was 11,484 by mid-1990). *Time of the Butcherbird* was out of print in the original 1979 AWS edition (no. 212) by 1991; it had sold 6,233 copies by mid-1990. In its new AWS B-format, *Time of the Butcherbird* sold 7,236 copies in Britain and 3,243 export copies: Blanche La Guma collection.

64 HEB, 3/8, Currey to La Guma (1970).

65 It was reprinted in the original format in 1970, 1972, 1974, 1977, 1979 and 1980.

66 Blanche La Guma collection, royalty statements, 1978–90.

67 Maja-Pearce, 'Publishing African Literature', 126.

68 Blanche La Guma collection, La Guma to Calder.

69 Michael Wade suggests that, with *A Walk in the Night*'s republication in the AWS in 1967, it was '[taken] into the London-based canon of "African writers"': Wade, 'Art and Morality', 164. See Low, 'In Pursuit of Publishing', 35.

70 Unwin and Currey, 'The African Writers' Series', 6; see Currey, 'Chinua Achebe', 576, 578.

71 Head to Rubinstein, 10 December 1976, quoted in Leistikow, 'Marketing Bessie Head', 21; see Currey, 'Publishing Bessie Head', 23.

72 Ofeimun, 'Challenges to the AWS', 56; see Iloegbunam, 'The Write Stuff', on the AWS relaunch. Becky Clarke, at the time the submissions editor for the AWS, assessed its legacy in Clarke, 'The African Writers Series'.

73 Huggan, *Postcolonial Exotic*, xi, 50; see also 52.

74 Beier to Van der Vlies, personal correspondence. The review in the *Cape Times* noted that it was 'almost impossible to say anything about the book without contravening the General Law Amendment Act'; see note 1 above. *New Age* (1954–62) and *Spark* (1962–63) were the final two incarnations of the *Guardian*, South Africa's most influential and important radical newspaper; *Spark* was permanently shut down by the government in March 1963: Zug, 'Far from Dead'.

75 Mayibuye, MCH118/1/B.1, Jordaan to La Guma.

76 Joubert noted, specifically, intermingling between prostitutes and sailors, blasphemy (all exclamations 'Jesus' or 'Jesus Christ'), anti-white sentiments (for example, 'mucking boer' and references to lynchings in the American South), statements insulting 'Coloureds' (the pejorative 'effing *hotnot* bastards', 'bushman bastards', 'hottentots'): Publications Control Board (PCB), Joubert, 'Report of Reader', 22 November 1962. I am indebted to Peter D. McDonald for assistance in accessing censors' reports.

77 'Hierdie verhaal van roof en geweld in Distrik Ses is bereken om 'n gevoel van haat teen die blanke op te wek' ('This story of robbery and violence in District Six is intended to arouse a feeling of hatred towards whites'): PCB, Chair, Board of Censors to Secretary of Home Affairs.

78 PCB, Department of Home Affairs to Chair, Board of Censors.
79 Anon., 'The Censorship Threat'.
80 The categories were defined under section 26(2) of the Publications and Entertainment Act (No. 26 of 1963): Merrett, *A Culture of Censorship*, 60–4; De Lange, *The Muzzled Muse*, 13–29.
81 PCB, 1/70, vol. 2, Murray, Report.
82 *Ibid.*
83 Merrett, *A Culture of Censorship*, 79–90.
84 PCB, P76/11/146, Steytler to Directorate of Publications; Directorate of Publications to Steytler.
85 PCB, P76/11/146, Wiggett, Reader's Report.
86 Wiggett suggested that the ban should be retained 'in the interests of good race relations, and because of the criticism of the Police and Police methods': *ibid.*
87 PCB, P76/9/166, Du Plooy, Application for a Review; Jansen, 'Reader's/Expert's Report'.
88 Numerous other Acts of Parliament – the Official Secrets Act, Defence Act, General Law Amendment Acts of 1962, 1963 and 1969, Criminal Procedure Act of 1955 and 1965, and Terrorism Act of 1967 – restricted publication in some way: Anon., 'Censorship in South Africa', 60.
89 Silver, *Guide to Political Censorship*, 1, 63; De Lange, *The Muzzled Muse*, 8–9, 131. Brink's novel was translated as *A Dry White Season* (1979), and later filmed.
90 McDonald, 'The Writer, the Critic and the Censor', 291, 292.
91 The director of publications lodged an appeal to the Publications Appeals Board against the decision of his Publications Committee to ban the novel, on 1 August 1979: Gordimer, 'What Happened to Burger's Daughter'.
92 Anon., 'Translation of the Minority Report'.
93 Titlestad, 'Chairman's Report', 40.
94 Wiehahn, 'Memo on "Burger's Daughter"', 49, 48.
95 Van Rooyen, 'Summary and Decision', 36.
96 McDonald, 'The Writer, the Critic and the Censor', 287, 300.
97 Gordimer, 'What Happened to Burger's Daughter', 2.
98 Quoted in Silver, *Political Censorship*, 97; see 201. The appeal was heard after the banning of the novel published in Johannesburg by Ad Donker in 1981; it was republished in 1984 in the AWS.
99 PCB, P80/1/148, Jansen, Reader's Report and Chairman's Report.
100 Like Jansen, T. Hicks thought it undesirable in terms of section (47)(2) (d) and (e). It had 'literary merits', but they did not outweigh 'the other drawbacks' (translations mine): PCB, P80/1/148, Hicks, 'Reader's Report'.
101 *Ibid.*, Lighton, 'Reader's Report'.
102 *Ibid.*, Anon., Schedule.
103 PCB, P82/3/59, Price to Director of Publications.
104 *Ibid.*, Biermann, 'Chairman's Report'.
105 *Ibid.*, Scholtz, Review.
106 *Ibid.*, Biermann, 'Reader's Report'.
107 *Ibid.*, anonymous comments scrawled on Biermann, 'Chairman's Report'. The original Afrikaans reads: 'Vir my is die feit dat Alex La Guma 'n gelyste persoon is, 'n genoegsame verswarende faktor om die boek weer to verbied'.

108 *Ibid.*

109 *Ibid.*, Directorate of Publications, Notification of Appeal.

110 *Ibid.*, Director of Publications to Price; Price to Director, Department of Justice. Price's correspondence cites PCB files for *Quartet* (P82/3/58) and *The Stone Country* (P80/3/60), indicating that similar reviews had found them no longer undesirable. They remained embargoed, however.

111 PCB, P82/3/59, Price to Director, Department of Justice, 26 July 1982. The Publications Appeal Board directed in the same year that the motives and status of writer, publisher, distributor, or series could not be taken into account in determining undesirability: Silver, *Political Censorship*, 25, 31.

112 La Guma, *A Walk in the Night* (1991); see Hofmeyr, 'Setting Free the Books'. Reviews of *And a Threefold Cord* (PCB, P86/7/121), *In the Fog of the Seasons' End* (P86/7/120), and *Time of the Butcherbird* (P86/10/51) saw these novels unbanned in 1986. There was some confusion about *The Stone Country* and *A Walk in the Night*, the latter being unbanned only in 1991 (P88/02/59).

113 Coetzee, *Doubling the Point*, 346–8.

114 *Ibid.*, 352.

115 Nkosi, 'Fiction by Black South Africans', 211; Coetzee, 'Alex La Guma and the Responsibilities', 6.

116 Coetzee, 'Alex La Guma and the Responsibilities', 8.

117 *Ibid.*, 10.

118 Coetzee, *Doubling the Point*, 352. Abdul JanMohamed continued to maintain that La Guma's work constituted Lukácsian critical realism, defined as writing 'which manifests in its detail and structure an ontological, dialectical conflict between self-as-an-individual and self-as-a-social-being': Jan Mohamed, 'Alex La Guma', 287.

119 Coetzee, *Doubling the Point*, 358. Barthes suggested that '[r]ealism is far from being neutral, it is on the contrary loaded with the most spectacular signs of fabrication': Barthes, *Writing Degree Zero*, 67–8. For a slightly different account of Coetzee's engagement with La Guma, see Attwell, *J. M. Coetzee*, 12.

120 Coetzee, *Doubling the Point*, 365.

121 Nkosi marked passages like: '"Okay," Michael Adonis answered [...] cockles of your heart'; see La Guma, *Walk* (1962), 22–3; (1968), 24–6. Coetzee quotes part of the same section (from the Heinemann edition): 'The room was as hot and airless as a newly-opened tomb [...] an accumulation of empty wine bottles stood like packed skittles': Coetzee, *Doubling the Point*, 358–9; Nkosi's copy courtesy of Hugh Macmillan, Oxford.

122 Coetzee, *Doubling the Point*, 338.

123 *Ibid.*, 336. Attwell had suggested to Coetzee that it was 'curious' that while, by 1987 (in his address to the *Weekly Mail* book week in Cape Town) he was 'arguing for the distinctiveness of fictionality as against history', in 1974 he had 'followed La Guma – a South African Marxist producing social realism – down a path marked out by Hegel, Marx, Lukàcs, and Sartre' (335).

124 McDonald, 'The Writer, the Critic and the Censor', 296; and see Coetzee, 'The Novel Today' (the text of the *Weekly Mail* address referred to by Attwell, note 123).

125 Sachs, Interview.

126 Pechey, Introduction, 4.
127 Sachs, 'Preparing Ourselves for Freedom', 240–1.
128 Ndebele, *South African Literature and Culture*, 47, 47–8; see also Mphahlele, 'Writers and Commitment'.
129 Arac, Introduction, 4.

6

Farming stories (II): J. M. Coetzee and the (heart of a) country

Thwarted pluralism: reframing the bi-textual, bilingual, anti-pastoral

J. M. Coetzee's second novel, *In the Heart of the Country*, is a formal and thematic critique of the pastoral novel, specifically the genre's twentieth-century Afrikaans-language embodiment in the *plaasroman* ('farm novel', about which Coetzee has written perceptively in *White Writing*); it is also a deconstruction of, and in part a homage to, the anti-pastoralism of Schreiner's *The Story of an African Farm*.[1] Coetzee has himself offered the description 'Cervantean pastoral or antipastoral', a highly self-conscious deconstruction of a genre, enacted by a character in the text itself.[2] The novel consists of 266 numbered sections, all apparently narrated either as a record or, at least in part, a fantasy, by Magda, a farmer's daughter in the Karoo. She complains that the 'pastoral has become one of those stifling stories', a family melodrama, and later contends that she has no taste for providing a mere account of farm life: 'Lyric is my medium, not chronicle.'[3] She is, Dominic Head observes, 'contained within a generic structure that defeats her, and which obliges her to have recourse to the wrong kind of love, the passion of an unregenerated pastoral'.[4] Elsewhere, in his 1987 Jerusalem Prize acceptance speech, Coetzee discusses white South Africans' 'failure of love', a love of the land but not of its people, which produced what he calls 'a less than fully human literature, unnaturally preoccupied with power and the torsions of power, unable to move from elementary relations of contestation, domination, and subjugation to the vast and complex human world that lies beyond them'.[5] Magda wrestles with just those preoccupations, all the time wondering about her own *textual* condition: is she 'a body propelled along a track by sinews and bony levers', she wonders, or 'a monologue moving through time, approximately five feet above the ground, if the ground does not turn out to be just another word'?[6]

Highlighting realism's artifice, but deconstructing, too, the political, religious and racial ideologies for which Magda reluctantly stands, the novel's recurrent concern is with *signification* – the mediation by language of representation. Barthes's *S/Z* informs Magda's view of language, Stephen Watson observes: both understand that realism is effected by the naturalisation of linguistic codes and conventions which, when revealed, threaten to undermine long-held assumptions.[7] In the South African edition of the novel, published by Ravan Press in 1978, those codes and conventions are particularly starkly revealed. Offered for sale only in South Africa, it contained long passages of dialogue, in Afrikaans, which had already appeared in translation, in an 'English version prepared by the author', in British and American editions, published respectively by Secker & Warburg, and Harper & Row (as *From the Heart of the Country: A Novel*), in 1977.[8] While the textual variations have been remarked on in the growing body of academic work on Coetzee, this is usually in passing, despite the fact that the multiple texts, their potential differences in meaning and their reception have important implications for studies both of Coetzee and of the institutions and the category of a 'South African' literature.[9]

More than almost any other 'South African'– or South African by birth – writer, Coetzee has repeatedly and self-consciously put under erasure the category of a national literature. In 1978, he declared himself 'suspicious of lines of division between a European context and a South African context', pointing out that the local 'experience' remained 'largely colonial': 'Our literary products are flown to the metropolitan centre and re-exported to us from there at a vastly increased price ... That very fact should give people pause before they start talking about a South African literature.'[10] He reiterated his suspicions in 1983, wondering whether it was merely 'that vast and wholly ideological superstructure constituted by publishing, reviewing and criticism' which had, rather unjustly, forced on him 'the fate of being a "South African novelist"'.[11] Coetzee's apparent insistence on publishing a local, very specifically South African version of his second novel, the first of his novels to be published abroad, and to do so despite (and after) British and American publication, nonetheless raises questions about his apparent disavowal of the national category. It also supports the ongoing re-evaluation of the extent to which his commitment to radical politics in the country in the wake of the Soweto riots of 1976 is legible in the early novels – specifically in the circumstances of their publication.

Jarad Zimbler's consideration of the institutional publishing contexts of Coetzee's fifth novel, *Foe* (1986), demonstrates how the South African edition of that novel, also published by Ravan, and its 'interaction' with a South African 'cultural milieu' have largely been elided in extant criticism focused primarily on the novel's metropolitan publishing contexts.[12] This is also the case with *In the Heart of the Country*, although its textual biography further complicates issues. The extent to which critics' engagements with the novel have unjustly ignored its twin texts is illustrated usefully by the case of Derek Attridge's otherwise richly suggestive and astute work on Coetzee. Attridge argues that works of literature 'resist the immediacy and transparency of language', and so 'engage the reader ethically', and that Coetzee's work does this preeminently, forcing encounters which, in the act of reading, do justice to the strangeness both of the writing and of the world created in it.[13] Central to Attridge's analysis is his contention that 'the otherness which makes demands on us as we read Coetzee's novels' does not exist '*outside* language or discourse', but is 'brought into being by language'.[14] It thus seems regrettable that Attridge's discussion of *In the Heart of the Country* – in an essay in *Poetics Today* and in his 2004 monograph – does not acknowledge the extensive use of Afrikaans dialogue – an*other* language bringing otherness into being – in the Ravan edition.[15] Attridge's examination of Coetzee's representation of the servants in the novel is especially compromised by this omission. His claim that, while 'Magda's language for describing or speaking to the servants is relatively free of the conventional formulas' (of, for example, the 'pioneer' Jacobus Coetzee's discourse in *Dusklands*), the servants 'remain problematic presences, never wholly grasped by the machinery of the text, never securely "in their place"', also needs to be nuanced rather more carefully in light of their tonally complex speech in the Afrikaans.[16] How and why, then, was this novel published in two versions, and what are the implications of this fact and of the different contexts in which the novel's texts have circulated?

A 'good South African of the period': Coetzee and local publication

After apparently having had the manuscript of *Dusklands* rejected by a number of foreign publishers, Coetzee took it to Peter Randall at Ravan, a small independent press in Johannesburg.[17] Because it was not published abroad until 1983 (in the wake of the success of *Waiting for the Barbarians* and in the year *Life & Times of Michael K* won the Booker Prize), most accounts of Coetzee's oeuvre suggest that this first novel made few waves. However, it received excited reviews in South African journals,[18] and was also adopted as a set text for first-year students in the English Department at the University of Natal in Durban. The resulting order, for 600 copies, confirmed the viability of Coetzee's works for a small press in a market seldom able to account for more than 1,000 copies of literary fiction.[19] Mike Kirkwood, a radical young academic, was instrumental (with his colleague Tony Morphet) in securing that institutional validation, all the more remarkable because the department, like many others in South Africa at the time, was staffed largely by Leavisites teaching a canon-driven course of mostly British writing. Kirkwood had electrified the audience at a poetry conference in the same year as the publication of *Dusklands*, with an attack on Guy Butler, the old man of South African letters, and on the 'bourgeois–colonial' heritage of much English-language writing (particularly poetry).[20] Three years later, having arrived at Ravan on a sabbatical to study black writing and undertake a series of writing initiatives with black writers, Kirkwood took over the running of the press after Randall was proscribed by the apartheid Government, and took the press – originally sponsored by the Christian Institute and the 'Study Project on Christianity in Apartheid Society' (Spro-Cas) – in an altogether more overtly radical direction.

Kirkwood founded the influential journal *Staffrider* in March 1978, along with associated history and literature series.[21] 'Staffrider' was a colloquial term for a black youth who defied the railway authorities by riding the township trains without paying (like 'staff', boarding as the train departed); it also suggested, Kirkwood recalls, a 'mobile, disreputable bearer of tidings', which suited the magazine's intentions.[22] Coetzee himself noted, in an entry on the journal in *The African Book Publishing Record* in 1979, that *Staffrider* carried 'associations of the precarious and exhilarating as well as of the lifestyle of young urban blacks'.[23] *Staffrider* appears to have been supportive of Coetzee's writing, too; a short review of *Dusklands* in 1978 urged the journal's intended audience, urban blacks, to read the novel 'to understand the psychology of colonialism and oppression'.[24] Ravan continued to publish Coetzee's novels for a decade, providing a significant institutional context for Coetzee's writing, given its association, through *Staffrider*, with 'black consciousness' ideology, a self-consciously Marxist dedication to engaged writing, and scepticism about aesthetic validations and categories of literariness.

That Coetzee chose to continue publishing with Ravan, in South Africa, is surely important. His British publishers, Secker & Warburg, insisted on publishing *In the Heart of the Country* (Coetzee's international debut), as well as his subsequent novels, in Britain first, before leasing the rights back to Ravan for a local edition. Kirkwood recalls that the growing success of writers like Coetzee enabled Ravan to sell about 3,000 hardback copies of a title in South Africa, helping to keep the company afloat. When Secker's Tom Rosenthal tried, in 1982, to withdraw Ravan's rights to publish local editions, claiming that the economics of publishing made it imperative that Secker distribute its own edition of *Life & Times of Michael K* in South Africa, Kirkwood informed Coetzee, who offered (Kirkwood recalls) to 'phone Tom and throw some of his moral rhetoric back at him'.[25] Rosenthal called Kirkwood half-an-hour later with 'second thoughts', and, on that basis, Ravan was able to continue publishing Coetzee in South Africa. Coetzee wanted local publication for his novels, and used his growing international reputation to secure it. In doing so he was, Kirkwood maintains, 'acting as a committed opponent of the apartheid structure', supporting local publishing, and specifically a press with a progressive, even radical agenda.[26]

Kirkwood recalls, too, that Randall, although banned and strictly prohibited from engaging in publishing activities, remained involved in Ravan business; Randall and Coetzee together agreed that, despite an English version having been published abroad, the South African edition of *In the Heart of the Country* should be distinctive, and distinctively South African, including Afrikaans passages from the original manuscript (which had been amended for the novel's foreign editions). This did not necessarily mean that Coetzee considered 'the Afrikaner' the 'principal target reader' for the Ravan edition, as suggested by Dominic Head (and some English-speaking reviewers in South Africa at the time).[27] Most South African English speakers would, at this point, have had some facility with Afrikaans. Coetzee, of course, has always been appropriately questioning about the idea of intended audiences, declaring in 1983: 'I am hesitant to accept that my books are addressed to readers. Or at least I would argue that the concept of the reader in literature is a vastly more problematic one than one might at first think.'[28] In this instance, it is clear that very different reading communities *would* encounter different texts; Coetzee may have wished to claim that this particular work was not addressed to specific readers, but a restricted set of readers – those in South Africa – would undoubtedly have had a different reading experience from those encountering the version available abroad.[29] Quite how different is a matter that remains to be examined.

Carrying 'the full freight of ... history': reading Ravan's edition of *In the Heart of the Country*

Magda's claim to have grown up with the farm servants' children, to have 'spoke[n] like one of them' before learning 'to speak like this', has greater potency in the Ravan edition, in which the reader encounters the vernacular.[30] The adult Magda is exhausted by the performance expected of her – as mistress and overseer – by the servants, her lips (she declares) 'tired of all the articulating they have had to do since they were babies, since it was revealed to them that there was a law'.[31] This invocation of the Lacanian symbolic order is not accidental: as Teresa Dovey has suggested, much of Coetzee's interest in language, authority, performance and variously interpreted psychoses, political and personal, is clearly influenced by – or has affinities with – Lacan.[32] The law, racial hierarchy and the consequent control of access to certain forms of enunciation define Magda's sense of self, and she struggles to articulate a separate identity. Hers is an 'antique feudal language', one 'of hierarchy, of distance and perspective'.[33] It is, she declares, 'my father-tongue' (which makes her father's betrayal of the hierarchy it encodes doubly disabling), the enabled inequalities of which she regrets: 'I feel too much the pathos of its distances, but it is all we have.'[34] The reader encountering the novel in its English-language version has to take Magda at her word: interactions with the servants illustrate her higher status, but not even Coetzee's own translations of the Afrikaans dialogue quite convey the accuracy of another of Magda's descriptions of the language as one of 'nuances, of supple word-order and delicate participles, opaque to the outsider, dense to its children[,] with moments of solidarity, moments of distance'.[35]

Those characteristics are clear in Magda's engagements with her father. She uses *pappie*, the child's version of 'father', both in addressing him and instead of using a personal pronoun, so in the Ravan text she asks: '*Pappie* ... Kan *pappie* my hoor?' The English-language version reads: '*Daddy* ... Can *you* hear me?'[36] Magda is, Susan Fitzmaurice observes, performing 'the role of the little girl appealing to her father', enacting 'a semblance of intimacy which also masks an uncertain deference'.[37] Similarly, interactions with the servants display that solidarity and distance, little of which is conveyed in the English. For example, the single word *hoor* (listen), used in colloquial speech with familiars and with children, or adults with the same relative status, and so both ambiguously affectionate and condescending (even racist), is used by Magda in dismissing Klein-Anna in the Ravan, but not the English-language, version. Her direction 'kom weer môre, hoor. Gaan asseblief nou huis toe' is rendered 'come back tomorrow. Now go away, please', where a literal translation might be: 'come again tomorrow, [you] *hear*. Now go *home*, please.'[38] Somewhat differently, words used by the servants in Afrikaans and not translated into English convey a practised affection which is also transparently a performance of subservience: '"Die mies is 'n ware engel aan haar volkies!" they say, their flatterers' eyes keen.'[39] The translation, 'An angel from heaven!', omits the final three words, 'to her [*volkies*]', which uses a diminutive of *volk* (race, people), used in colloquial speech both affectionately *by* and dismissively *of* 'Coloured' South Africans. Other instances of sly performance on the part of the servants are likewise incapable of completely suggestive translation, Magda's representation of Hendrik's first encounter with her father providing perhaps the best example. The English version does not translate the possessive used repeatedly by Hendrik – as in 'my baas' (*my* master; Coetzee leaves *baas* untranslated). It also translates some of Hendrik's use of *nee* (no) as 'yes', English struggling to convey the specific resonances of the negative used in the affirmative in specific contexts, particularly in deferring to those of higher status or in situations of social bonding.[40]

Some other suggestive ambiguities which cannot be translated include, for example, the translation of 'Wat maak jy hier in die huis?', addressed by Magda to Klein-Anna, found hiding in the sewing-room after the first attempted parricide, as: 'What have you been up to here in the house?' The original might also be translated as 'What are you doing in the house?', suggesting outrage at the mere presence of the racial other in the main house, not only an enquiry about her actions there.[41] Elsewhere, Hendrik, demanding his salary from Magda, is initially subservient, but his Afrikaans dialogue is more suggestive of the *solidarity* and *distance* of the relationship than the English-language version. Magda's rebuke does not, in the latter, include *Jong*, a dismissive, racist epithet (calling a grown man a boy). *Oubaas* (old master) becomes *baas*, removing the former's sense of affection (it is widely used thus) which both parties maintain for their own purposes.[42] The bargain they conclude is also translated in a manner which does not capture the mocking subtext of Hendrik's response. The statement 'Mies sê mos ons sal ons geld kry' (more or less idiomatically: 'Miss says we will get our money, doesn't she') is translated as a conditional clause appended to the previous statement: '[we must wait,] if Miss promises us our money'.[43]

Coetzee offered some thoughts on his dealings with his novels' translators in an essay in the Australian journal *Meanjin*, in 2005, providing oblique commentary on his own acts of translation: 'I sometimes use words with the full freight of their history behind them, and that freight is not easily carried across to another language', he observes, noting that dialogue is especially problematic, 'particularly when it … incorporates regional usages' (among other things). His dialogue is infrequently of this kind, he notes, except where it 'comes from the mouths of children or of characters for whom English is not a first language', in which cases it is 'aberrant' and 'best … translated not word for word but by speech typical of children in the language translated into … or by the speech of a foreigner making typical foreign slips'.[44] He has clearly followed that advice himself, although not without the inevitable loss it involves in a context in which language usage is also racially inflected.[45]

The racial and linguistic orders to which Magda is accustomed break down with her father's act of border-crossing: he sleeps with Hendrik's wife, Klein-Anna. Magda imagines them 'exchanging forbidden words':

> *Ons*, he is saying to her, *ons twee*; and the word reverberates in the air between them. *Kom jy saam met my*, he is saying to her. There are few enough words true, rock-hard enough to build a life on, and these he is destroying. He believes that he and she can choose their words and make a private language, with an *ek* and *jy* and *hier* and *nou* of their own. But there is no private language. Their *jy* is my *jy* too.[46]

The English-language version has 'we'; 'we two'; 'Now: come with me now'; 'I', 'you', 'here', 'now'; 'you', 'you' for the italicised Afrikaans in this passage, but this elides the specific potency of Magda's father's use of *jy* (you), a pronoun reserved for children or intimates.[47] The English-language version does not make clear why this use of the second-person pronoun challenges her authority. As Fitzmaurice explains, English's pronominal usage patterns are governed by gender and number, those in Afrikaans by 'sociolinguistic parameters of distance and familiarity'.[48] Magda muses that her trauma is potentially 'simply rage at the violations of the old language, the correct language, that takes place when he exchanges kisses and the pronouns of intimacy' with a servant, and a non-white servant at that:[49] 'subverted', it 'cannot be recovered'; she has 'no words left to exchange whose value' can be trusted.[50]

Nonetheless, Magda's father's act does not free her from the constraints of the hierarchical society her language encodes; she knows that the servants know that her continued use of the 'harsh language' is a performance, 'to keep [them] at a distance'.[51] Her – and the servants' – linguistic performances resolve into 'parody': Hendrik 'duck[s] and grin[s] secretly' while offering 'the old locutions', addressing Magda formally while using *jy* impertinently behind her back; Klein-Anna hides behind Hendrik, singing 'Jy, jy, jy'.[52] Coetzee is acutely concerned in this novel (indeed, in his entire oeuvre) with what David Attwell calls 'the poetics of reciprocity', and nowhere is this clearer than here, in the loaded uses of personal pronouns in the Afrikaans dialogue.[53]

Eager to find a way out of this linguistic and existential impasse, Magda attempts sisterly intimacy with Klein-Anna. In section 203, she bombards her with questions, musing (in English): 'This is not going to be a dialogue, thank God, I can stretch my wings and fly where I will.'[54] In the monologue which follows, she mixes, in the Ravan edition, Afrikaans and English, often appearing to offer her own English translation of the Afrikaans. The English-language version predictably omits the passages which constitute such repetition, usually by retaining Magda's English translations and translating any Afrikaans not translated by her.[55] Crucially, however, the English-language version omits a significant statement which occurs in the Ravan edition *in English*: 'I have never learned the speech of men'. It only translates what follows (in Afrikaans), offering 'I only wanted to talk, I have never learned to talk with another person' for 'ek wou slegs praat, ek het nooit geleer hoe 'n mens met 'n ander mens praat nie', the final section of which, literally translated, might read: 'I never learned how a person talks to another person'.[56] The English-language version thus not only offers an indirect translation of an Afrikaans sentence (Coetzee must be said in this instance to be offering other than merely an English translation of his original), but, in omitting Magda's English and being unable to convey the effect of her movement between languages, it in effect excises a section whose complex linguistic manoeuvring arguably calls into question the relative fictional, metafictional and fantastic status of Magda's English narration and Afrikaans dialogue.

Jane Kramer's review of *Waiting for the Barbarians* in the *New York Review of Books*, in 1982, looking back to *In the Heart of the Country*, suggested that 'consciousness (if that is what it is) is in English and dialogue in Afrikaans'.[57] Susan Fitzmaurice's explanation is, however, perhaps more compelling. She suggests that Coetzee's use of two languages in the Ravan text signifies two worlds: 'Magda's truth – her subjective, phenomenal world' and 'the fictional life she creates for herself – a structural epic world which lies outside her experience'.[58] For Fitzmaurice, the languages correspond broadly to two levels of reality: English is the language of private commentary about *the real* – although

Magda's commentary repeatedly demonstrates the impossibility of assessing reality independently from its representation in language – and Afrikaans the language of (Magda's) fiction. Consequently, Fitzmaurice suggests, in section 203, 'the narrator's (English) reveries take over the persona's (Afrikaans) speech, removing it from the realm of human interaction'. A movement 'in and out of what appears to be the fictional frame' is marked by Magda's switching between languages.[59] Fitzmaurice's interpretation makes judgements about the sections' occasion(s) of narration which are nonetheless plausible, and accommodate most of the narrative's contradictions and alternative accounts.[60]

The single instance which (potentially) resists this neat explanatory scheme comes at the very end of the novel, when we see Magda sitting beside her father on the verandah, laying him 'out on his bed', feeding him broth – episodes which suggest that both of the earlier parricides exist at the level of fantasy. The crucial difference, however, specifically in section 262, is that, in the Ravan edition, Magda addresses her father in English for the first and only time.[61] Is this because what Magda records here is *real*, and everything previously, including both parricides, *fiction*? Or because it is not strictly dialogue or, at least, is a monologue in which another present party appears to be unable (unlike Klein-Anna in section 203) to reply (her father appears to be dying)? Or are we to read the Afrikaans dialogue elsewhere as more *real* (in a loose sense) than this, which is merely imagined (in the pages of a diary, for example), indicating that one or other of the parricides may have existed in that level of *reality*, rendering this *final* sequence fantasy?

Ultimately, these are pointless questions: Coetzee's novel foregrounds the artifice of any narrative pretending to a coherence or claim on reality existing outside of language. The multilingual nature of the Ravan edition adds considerably to the complexity of this endeavour, the only *other* language dramatising the novel's concern with language, power and textuality in the English-language version being in the sections in which Magda attempts to communicate, in cod-Spanish, with imagined extraterrestrials, but the pathos of failed communication seems less marked there than in a text in which the reader literally witnesses the failure of a language in which interaction with real people is attempted (and one different from that in which Magda appears to narrate her failures to herself).

Whose heart, which country? Local and global reception

In March 1978, in one of the earliest reviews of the Ravan edition, Philip Cohen remarked that important questions were raised by Coetzee's novel's twin texts. Would the 'South African reader (or critic)' appreciate the Ravan text more than 'an outsider'?; 'what, if anything', made *In the Heart of the Country* 'a South African novel?'; had 'the liberal inclusion of Afrikaans in the South African edition' in any way affected 'the quality of the work' (or, conversely, had the 'exclusion of Afrikaans from the London edition emasculated the original work')?[62] Even the cursory glance above at the nuances present in the Afrikaans passages and not completely conveyed by their English translations suggests that South African readers and critics *were* likely to have had access to a richer, more suggestive text than were *outsiders*. Whether or not the inclusion of Afrikaans dialogue makes a work 'South African' is, of course, a more difficult question; it certainly rendered the South African edition a different version of the work. Critics in South Africa and abroad naturally encountered the versions in different material forms, too. Each of the British, American and South African first editions bore different dust-jacket or cover designs, with different blurbs.

Secker & Warburg's dust-jacket featured, against a black background, Coetzee's initials and surname in white capitals above the novel's title, in large capitals, each letter white at the top and fading, through yellow, to deep red. Just as those colours might suggest a conflict (red, blood, yellow fire) between white(s) and black(s), so the blurb draws attention to the racial nature of the plot: a white farmer, 'trapped with his serfs in a web of reciprocal oppression', commits an act of miscegenation, a 'lurch across the colour bar' into 'the arms of a black concubine'. The blurb ends by suggesting that the novel's real focus is Magda's inner turmoil – it is 'a fable of a consciousness adrift', Magda a 'passionate, obsessed and absurd woman'. Racial politics is both foregrounded and simultaneously down-played by the blurb's explicit naming of 'colonial South Africa' (colonial in terms of its 'feudal' power structures, but also potentially '*colonial*-era', so in the past), and by its final focus on Magda's trauma.[63]

Harper & Row's dust jacket, alone among the first editions, seems consciously calculated to suggest the novel's geographical setting: its colourful, stylised, 'Bushman' rock-art figures, human and animal, invoke an iconically 'African' aesthetic.[64] The blurb, however, mostly paraphras-es or repeats the British jacket's copy – although Magda's father 'seeks comfort', rather than 'makes a bid for private salvation' with a black woman; Magda is an 'embittered spinster daughter' in both, but in the American blurb tries 'to create an eventful life for herself out of empti-ness', rather than being 'a consciousness trying to construct itself out of nothing'.[65] Both blurbs draw attention to the uncertain status of Magda's narrative, the British suggesting that she 'play[s] out, with the two witnesses of her shame, the doom of the family', the American more sensationally that she plays out 'her sexual fantasies and final degrada-tion'. Both, however, are quick to question the status of her narrative, chorusing: 'Or does she?'.[66]

All three editions cast Magda as mad. The British edition's blurb claims that 'madness' is her 'response to an Africa that will not respond to her', arguably casting *her* exercise of racially determined power as less objec-tionable than her father's – 'in the end', the blurb asserts, 'we cannot help feeling sympathy' for her.[67] Many of the review extracts quoted on the American jacket refer to Magda's (in)sanity, the front inside flap quoting Martyn Goff, in the *Daily Telegraph*, on Magda's 'growing madness', and Susan Hill's comment, in *The Times*, that the novel offers Coetzee's 'disconcertingly acute' 'insight into the hysterical female'.[68] The Ravan cover features a review extract telling the reader that 'a white woman ... is going mad' in the novel, while the cover illustration is a line drawing, by Richard Smith, of a woman's shoulders and contorted face gazing upwards.[69]

The South African edition also offers the most direction to readers, chiefly through a lengthy excerpt from Maev Kennedy's *Irish Times* review, on the back cover, serving as both endorsement and lesson. It stresses that, while 'the setting is South Africa', the period is 'unspecified' but 'with the feel of' the late nineteenth-century, that 'neither political nor historical events impinge' on the farm, that the 'book' has a 'deliberately artificial' form and that Magda's account of events is not trustworthy.[70] It may have been thought that the South African reading public required more guidance about the novel's form, although the careful elision of racial politics is more likely to have been with the censors in mind. All three editions, in fact, seem cautious about promoting the novel as a work of political protest or of casting Coetzee as critical of the apartheid (a word not once used) Government.

The novel's versions' different material appearances and paratextual representations encode usefully some of the broad categories of response it is possible to track in the local and global reception of the novel. Most foreign reviews of *In the Heart of the Country* shared the concerns of those cited on the American dust-jacket: to invoke South African politics without suggesting that the novel was a protest novel (or even about *contemporary* South Africa); and to suggest its potential universal appeal (and allegorical nature) by focusing attention on its exploration of an individual's tortured consciousness. *Publishers Weekly*, for example, described it as 'a book about race' and 'about fantasy' (although it was not complimentary, crediting the novel with 'little plot, less purpose and much confusion'); Anatole Broyard, in the *New York Times*, read the novel apolitically as being about Magda's breakdown, and called Coetzee 'a master of deft hysteria'.[71]

A restrained balance is what most British and American reviewers were keen to convey. As Clive Barnett suggests, foreign non-academic reviewers tended to read Coetzee's novels positively, as allegories with 'universal, moral' resonances, casting what might otherwise seem too politically engaged or country-specific as broadly fitting a liberal humanist tradition.[72] This has repeatedly been the case with Coetzee's works, no less than it was for Paton's *Cry, the Beloved Country*: South Africa is identified as the 'context and referent', but is simultaneously 'idealised as a stage for more general moral dramas of human suffering and violence',

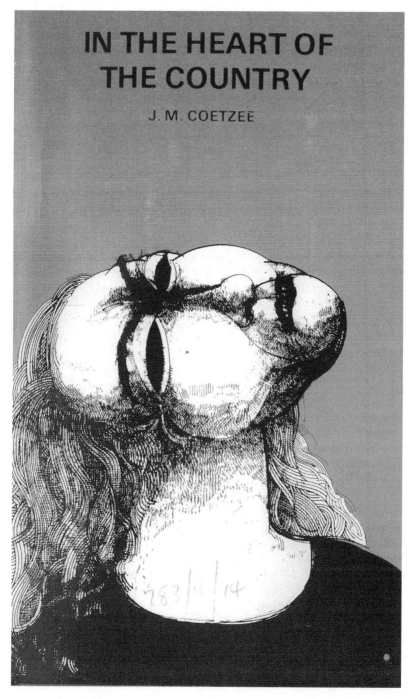

6.1 Ravan Press cover, *In the Heart of the Country*, 1978

with the reality of suffering in the country kept at a safe distance.[73] Kramer's 1982 *New York Review of Books* review of *Waiting for the Barbarians* (which she praised) and Brink's *A Chain of Voices* (which she thought 'bad') ventriloquised for the prevailing critical mood: 'We judge South African writers ... by the risks they take in putting the wall of their own dissidence between ourselves and the black Africa we praise and fear. We love them for being South African *for* us. They are our surrogates in resistance.'[74] Only a minority of readers construing Coetzee's novels as allegories were critical, thinking allegory 'a politically duplicitous escape from historical reality'; this did, however, became a comparatively more frequent response in the wake of Gordimer's well-known critique of *Life & Times of Michael K*.[75] Most early British reviews of *In the Heart of the Country* sought to gesture to the South African context, but elicit its broader appeal. Some, like Blake Morrison's review in the *Times Literary Supplement*, commented more specifically on Magda's unreliability, her putative 'jealousy and madness' (although he also noted the novel's treatment of miscegenation, citing a 'cross-cultural seduction' as the 'pivotal event' of the novel).[76] Others read it as unavoidably 'South African', including expatriate South African playwright Ronald Harwood, who suggested in the London *Sunday Times* that the novel exemplified the entrapment of South African writers in the particular theme of life in an oppressive country and society.[77]

South African reception of *In the Heart of the Country* was varied. Liberal English-language newspapers looked actively for an engagement with contemporary politics, the *Weekend World* remarking, for example, that it was 'a powerful novel of sex across-the-colour-line' which had been published in the midst of protests against the Immorality and Mixed Marriages Acts (which prohibited interracial relationships).[78] Left-leaning English-language intellectuals offered a nuanced sense of Coetzee's uses of 'allegory', including a view of his political engagement through form as much as through content. Isabel Hofmeyr, for example, reviewing the Secker & Warburg edition in *Africa Perspective*, in July 1977, suggested that Magda was 'socially paradigmatic', but argued crucially that the novel historicised her 'predicament', and was thus both allegory and historically engaged critique of ideological formations in South Africa.[79] Poet Robert Berold, writing in the first issue of the small journal *Inspan* in 1978, went further, suggesting that the novel's unreliable narrative enacted Coetzee's insightful critique of the forms of the 'English literary tradition' in South Africa, whose 'moral filter' – its desire for relevance – had become 'like a skin between the "inner" and "outer" world[s]' of the writer, Berold charged, one which separated the writer's imagination and environment, rendering imaginative introspection as 'fantasy' and accounts of the 'outer' world as merely journalism, while their 'amalgam' was too often indiscriminately 'offered as literature'. *In the Heart of the Country*, however, took this dilemma as its 'central concern', he suggested: 'By making his central character struggle with the dialectics of fantasy and reality, Coetzee does not have to fall into the trap himself.'[80]

Two reviews by leading Afrikaans writers suggest how the novel was read by a white, Afrikaans-speaking, cultural and intellectual elite in the country, and associated with a high modernist, nationalist, literary and cultural moment. Novelist Anna M. Louw published reviews in two local newspapers, *Die Burger* and *Beeld*, later reworking and expanding these for a 1987 essay in the British journal *PN Review*.[81] She argued that Coetzee's novel was a Calvinist allegory, and Coetzee an interesting hybrid writer, part English, part Afrikaans, with insights into the psyche of 'the Afrikaner people and their half-blood [*sic*] labourers' (which she ascribed to his childhood experiences on his paternal grandfather's Karoo farm). Louw concluded that the novel was 'an allegory', and that Coetzee was disinterested in 'writing or reading politically committed literature'.[82] Barend Toerien's review of *From the Heart of the Country*, in the American journal *World Literature Today* in 1978, called it a 'spiritual search for God', a 'reaching out beyond the restrictions imposed by Calvinism'. Specifically, however, Toerien was at pains to stress Coetzee's apparent non-partisanship, that he was 'not one for easy answers or for cashing in on the market for the slick novel on the South African "racial problem"'.[83]

Those reviews are interesting beyond their evident investment in disavowing political intent: Louw's were revised from the reader's report she prepared on the novel as a member of the State's censorship bureaucracy; while Toerien's assessment invites us to consider an often overlooked site in which he and Coetzee were published together, yet another material context framing the novel and exercising on it particular interpretative energies. Toerien contributed a column, including comments on the reputation of Afrikaans writers abroad (specifically in the USA) and among black writers, to the August 1976 issue of the South African quarterly *Standpunte* (Standpoints). The same issue included sections 85–94 of Coetzee's *In the Heart of the Country*.[84] Founded in 1945 (and running until 1986) largely to promote the development of a mature Afrikaans culture and literature, *Standpunte*'s tone betrayed many Afrikaner intellectuals' ambiguous self-definition as European-in-Africa.[85] Among its founders were 'Dertigers' (Thirty-ers – Afrikaans writers who came to prominence in the 1930s), principally N. P. Van Wyk Louw and W. E. G. Louw, who largely set its agenda. Michael Chapman suggests critically that they mastered a 'European inheritance in guard against their own sectarian commitments', urging too that the 'aesthetic formalism' which *Standpunte* sanctioned and encouraged might be viewed likewise.[86] The excerpt from *In the Heart of the Country* chafed against many of the journal's defining artistic imperatives, although it is likely that, like much of Coetzee's writing (but perhaps specifically in this context), its level of subversiveness was not immediately apparent, and what might have been construed as its high modernism appealed. *Standpunte*'s high literary ethos appeared to provide a sympathetic venue for Coetzee's text, which would have appeared self-consciously formally experimental. Its apparently creative re-imagining of the *plaasroman* could also appear to answer Van Wyk Louw's own critique, in 1958, of the genre's 'genial local realism', 'dreary … chronological sequences' and 'flights of fantasy'.[87] Magda's narrative pushes just those characteristics to their limits, but in order to deconstruct not merely the genre, but also an entire racially constructed psyche and a Calvinist sense of election – an impulse heavily foregrounded in the excerpted sections.[88]

The co-texts or circumtexts in the context of which Coetzee's excerpt appeared yield other productive ironies. The journal's sense of the aesthetic may have had as a corollary a desire on the part of its supporters to read apolitically, but *Standpunte* itself was never apolitical, nor did it offer unqualified support for the conservative political establishment, providing a forum for early (if circumscribed) critique and provocation.[89] The issue in which Coetzee's extract appeared was published in the month after the start of the Soweto student uprising, and it contained muted political commentary (I. L. de Villiers's poem 'Notre Dame de Paris', for example, included a prayer for Africa), and a direct engagement with inequality (an essay on the responsibilities of universities to promote equality) and with the censorship regime (an essay by André Brink suggesting that all great art is objectionable because it tests the limits of readers' expectations, expanding the borders of form).[90] Brink attacked the censors as an 'anonymous committee-of-three' presuming, absurdly, to protect 'the people [*volk*]'.[91]

Brink could not have known that just such a Committee was about to be constituted to consider whether *In the Heart of the Country* was objectionable according to section 47(2) of the Publications Act.[92] One member of the Committee appointed by the deputy director of publications, its chair, was H. van der Merwe Scholtz, professor of Afrikaans and Nederlands at the University of Cape Town (hence technically a colleague of Coetzee, then senior lecturer in the English department), whose new collection of poetry had been advertised in the issue of *Standpunte* preceding that carrying extracts from the novel he was to be asked to judge.[93] Anna M. Louw was the second reader; another languages professor, F. C. Fensham, the third.[94] Neither Scholtz nor Louw, though bearing the most impeccable Afrikaner intellectual and social credentials, was an apologist for the State. Both would resign from their posts as censors after the banning (on appeal, by the Directorate), in November 1977, of Etienne Leroux's *Magersfontein, O Magersfontein!*, which, during January 1977, they both judged should *not* be banned.[95] All three readers found *In the Heart of the Country* 'not undesirable', considering its objectionable elements (sexual and other violence, blasphemy, scatological detail, miscegenation), and even the 'traces of protest literature' (*versetliteratuur*)

detected by Fensham, to be tempered by the novel's striking – even difficult – narrative style.[96] It was unlikely to be a best-seller, its artistic merit
outweighed other objections and, as Peter McDonald suggests (about *all*
of Coetzee's works considered by the censor, none of which was banned),
'real or imagined spatiotemporal displacements' both 'deemphasized' and
(or) 'overwhelmed' the work's likely 'relevance to contemporary South
Africa'.[97]

Conclusion

While for Toerien and Louw, *In the Heart of the Country* was *not* a politically engaged work, for Berold and others it was, chiefly because of its
formal engagement with an English (as much as with an Afrikaans) literary tradition in South Africa. Coetzee's own response to the criticism that
formal experimentation was no act of political engagement is consonant
with that reading: 'an unquestioning attitude toward forms or conventions is as little radical as any other kind of obedience'.[98] *In the Heart of
the Country* is important not least because of its fiercely astute indictment
of the disabling discourses of power and privilege, the violent acquisitive-
ness of European epistemologies. Its place among Coetzee's texts displays
his recurrent concern with the topos of the farm in the white South
African psyche and its exploration of the ethics of responsibility. Chiefly,
however, it is important in this book-historical study for its multi-textual-
ity: its different versions evidence the necessity of concerning ourselves
with the multivalency of meaning in diverse material contexts.

On the basis that *In the Heart of the Country* (apparently) achieved
widespread international notice only after the success of *Waiting for the
Barbarians*, with a Penguin reissue in the USA in 1982, Josephine Dodd
claims that the novel achieved 'full citizenship' of Coetzee's oeuvre only
after the commercial viability of his fiction had been proven. That, she
says, renders Magda doubly colonised – both as character (subject to
'patriarchal domination', and to 'the cultural hegemony of the First
World') and on a textual level, with 'meanings thrust upon her by the
representatives of the same orders' (chiefly critics and reviewers).[99]
Despite an investment in character unfaithful to Coetzee's conception of
Magda and others as merely 'I-figures in books', this is a productively
polemical suggestion.[100] Reading is always akin to colonising. This
chapter's insight is that the *Country* being colonised has not had a single
identity. *In the Heart of the Country*, in its different printed versions (this
chapter has not ventured to consider its 1985 adaptation for film), has
been constructed differently, by readers with different investments,
responding to different texts.[101] Most significantly, that it exists as a
multi-textual work suggests that Coetzee, at least in the late 1970s, in
publishing a distinctly 'South African' version, tacitly recognised that he
was contributing to a 'South African' literature – even as his novel

contributed to his ongoing project of rendering such a category problematic.

Notes

1 Head, *J. M. Coetzee*, 66; see Coetzee, *White Writing*, 12–114.
2 Coetzee, *Doubling the Point*, 62; see 60–2.
3 Coetzee, *In the Heart of the Country* (Ravan, 1978; hereafter *Heart* [R]); (Secker & Warburg, 1977; hereafter *Heart* [S]); *From the Heart of the Country* (Harper & Row, 1977; hereafter *Heart* [H]), all 70–1 (section 136).
4 Head, *J. M. Coetzee*, 67.
5 Coetzee, *Doubling the Point*, 97, 98; see also 61.
6 Coetzee, *Heart* (R, S, H), 62 (section 122).
7 Watson, 'Colonialism and the Novels of J. M. Coetzee', 17. Much of Coetzee's writing from the 1970s, critical as well as creative, attests to his reading of Roland Barthes.
8 Coetzee, *Heart* (S, H), iv.
9 Glenn, Dodd and Fitzmaurice are exceptions who prove the rule, but of these only Fitzmaurice ('Aspects of Afrikaans') deals in any sophisticated way with some of the effect of the variations. Glenn ('Game Hunting', 120) and Dodd ('Naming and Framing', 153) erroneously suggest that the novel appeared in South Africa first. The Ravan edition states explicitly: 'English-language edition published in U.K. by Secker & Warburg (cloth) 1977'; 'First South African edition by Ravan Press ... 1978'. Coetzee, *Heart* (R), ii; see also *Heart* (H), iv.
10 Quoted in Watson, 'Colonialism and the Novels of J. M. Coetzee', 13; see Watson, 'Speaking: J. M. Coetzee', 23–4.
11 Morphet, 'Two Interviews', '1983', 460.
12 Zimbler, 'Under Local Eyes', 47.
13 Attridge, 'Ethical Modernism', 653, 654.
14 *Ibid.*, 669.
15 *Ibid.*; Attridge, *J. M. Coetzee and the Ethics of Reading*, 21–31.
16 Attridge, 'Ethical Modernism', 668.
17 Kirkwood, Interview. Dodd claims that 'Nadine Gordimer tried to interest her British publishers [Gollancz] in accepting' Coetzee's manuscript in 1976, 'but they declined'. She does not specify on what evidence this claim is based: Dodd, 'Naming and Framing', 153.
18 For example: Abrahams, 'Reflections in a Mirror' (in *Snarl*); Wilhelm, 'Vietnam, SA Powerfully Linked' (in the Johannesburg *Star*); Temple, 'City Man's Novel of Violence' (in Cape Town's *Argus*); Bowers, 'First SA Modern Novel?' (in the *Cape Times*); Fletcher, 'Dusklands' (*Reality*); Tony Morphet, Review of *Dusklands* (*Bolt*).
19 Kirkwood, Interview. Kirkwood recalls Randall having to scramble around remaindered bookshops to collect the required number of copies.
20 On Kirkwood's attack, see Chapman, *Southern African Literatures*, 340.
21 See *ibid.*, 370–2; Lewis, Review (online); Zimbler, 'Under Local Eyes', 49. The Staffrider Book Series, edited by Mothobi Mutloatse, published work by, among others, Miriam Tlali, Modikwe Dikobe, Achmat Dangor, Mongane Serote and Njabulo Ndebele; see also Mpe and Seeber, 'The Politics of Book

Publishing'; and Cloete, 'Alternative Publishing in South Africa'.

22 Kirkwood, '*Staffrider*', 23; see Chapman, *Southern African Literatures*, 340; McClintock, 'Azikwelwa', 598–9.

23 Coetzee, 'Staffrider', 235.

24 Anon., '*Dusklands*', 60.

25 Kirkwood, Interview.

26 *Ibid*.

27 Head, *J. M. Coetzee*, 49; see Marquard, 'Strength Lies in Using Novel', 1. Peter Temple, after reviewing *In the Heart of the Country* in the Cape Town *Argus* in May, published a feature on Coetzee in the same paper in June which was keen to dispel an apparently growing assumption that Coetzee was an Afrikaner: Temple, 'J. M. Coetzee: Major Talent in S African Literary Scene', B3. The assumption that Coetzee was an Afrikaner persisted, however, especially abroad: Roger Owen's review of the 1983 edition of *Dusklands* in the *Times Literary Supplement*, for example, called him a 'young Afrikaner' (and wondered why the novel had taken so long to arrive in Britain): Owen, 'Sunset in the West', 30.

28 Morphet, 'Two Interviews', '1983', 456.

29 The British edition was clearly read inside South Africa, though; Isabel Hofmeyr's review 'The Frenzy of Desire' was most likely of the Secker & Warburg edition (and does not, incidentally, make mention of the Afrikaans).

30 Coetzee, *Heart* (R, S, H), 6 (section 16).

31 *Ibid.*, 84 (section 163).

32 See Dovey, 'Coetzee and His Critics', 24; Dovey, *Novels of J. M. Coetzee*.

33 Coetzee, *Heart* (R, S, H), 43 (section 89) and 97 (section 195).

34 *Ibid.*, 97 (section 195).

35 *Ibid.*, 30 (section 58); *Heart* (R) alone has the [,].

36 Coetzee, *Heart* (R, S, H), 54 (section 101), my emphases; see also sections 130–1, 145–6.

37 Fitzmaurice, 'Aspects of Afrikaans', 182.

38 Coetzee, *Heart* (R, S, H), 14 (section 32).

39 *Ibid.*, 5 (section 13).

40 Coetzee, *Heart* (R), 20–1 and (S, H), 20 (section 41); see also exchanges in sections 248, 251. Hendrik's agreement (not to slaughter sheep for the house until so directed) becomes 'Yes, miss', rather than the more expressive 'Nee mies' ('No miss') of the Afrikaans in section 196.

41 Coetzee, *Heart* (R, S, H), 73 (section 140).

42 *Ibid.*, 94 (section 186). Similarly, the British and American editions omit translation of 'Jong' in section 196 (98). In section 205, during their confrontation, Magda's exclamation 'Jong' (103) becomes merely 'You' in the English text (104).

43 Coetzee, *Heart* (R, S, H), 95 (section 186).

44 Coetzee, 'Roads to Translation', 143.

45 There are numerous anomalies, not entirely a product purely of a prepared translation, including spelling variations: in section 14, 'debâcle' in the Ravan (5) and 'débâcle' in the Secker and the Harper (5); while the American edition mostly follows the British edition's English spellings, Ravan unaccountably has 'color' where the Harper text has 'colour' (62). The Ravan edition's 'werf' is translated throughout the English-language version as 'yard' (in sections

23, 48, 86, 90, 95, 149, 178), while 'veld-flower' (74; and 'veld-flowers', 41) and 'baas' are nowhere translated into English in the English-language texts, which likewise retain the Afrikaans 'muishond, meerkat' ('muishond' might have been usefully translated as 'mongoose'), but italicised – which they are not in the Ravan edition (9, section 23). The English-language version has inverted commas for the Ravan text's italics in section 84, and generally has more punctuation.

46 Coetzee, *Heart* (R), 35 (section 74).
47 Coetzee, *Heart* (S, H), 35.
48 Fitzmaurice, 'Aspects of Afrikaans', 182.
49 Coetzee, *Heart* (R, S, H), 43 (section 89).
50 *Ibid.*, 97 (section 195).
51 *Ibid.*, 86 (section 167).
52 *Ibid.*, 97 (section 195); see Fitzmaurice, 'Aspects of Afrikaans', 181.
53 Attwell, in Coetzee, *Doubling the Point*, 58. Coetzee's own translation of a sonnet sequence by Dutch poet Achterberg is, again in Attwell's words (with which Coetzee appears to concur), preoccupied 'with person as a grammatical category, particularly the relationship between *I* and *You*'; similarly, Attwell contends, 'Magda in *In the Heart of the Country* ... dramatizes the vicissitudes of the *I–You* relation, showing its implications for the subject in a deeply divided society where a language of equal exchange seems to be unavailable': *ibid.*, 7.
54 Coetzee, *Heart* (R, S, H), 101 (section 203).
55 *Ibid.* There are other instances in this passage of the English-language version omitting lines appearing in the Ravan text in English but *not* in Afrikaans.
56 Coetzee, *Heart* (R, S, H), 101 (section 203).
57 Kramer, 'In the Garrison', 8.
58 Fitzmaurice, 'Aspects of Afrikaans', 179.
59 *Ibid.*, 183.
60 For example, we are unsure whether Magda's father brings home a new wife or whether this is Magda's fantasy based on Hendrik's bringing home a wife (which may itself be imagined, in Fitzmaurice's explanation). Alternative accounts of one (or more) rape(s) are also given.
61 Coetzee, *Heart* (R) 135–6 (section 262); see 136–7.
62 Cohen, 'Mies Is die Mies', 25.
63 Coetzee, *Heart* (S), dust-jacket front inside flap.
64 See plate 2.
65 *Ibid.* and Coetzee, *Heart* (H), dust-jacket front and rear inside flaps.
66 *Ibid.*, both editions.
67 Coetzee, *Heart* (S), dust-jacket front inside flap.
68 Coetzee, *Heart* (H), dust-jacket rear; dust-jacket front inside flap.
69 Coetzee, *Heart* (R), back cover. See fig. 6.1. Readers familiar with *Dusklands* would have known not to trust the cover of a Coetzee novel, however. As Pauline Fletcher commented in *Reality* in 1974 about that novel: 'Don't be misled by the black exterior of this slim volume, with its dusk jacket reproduction of a painting by Thomas Baines. Title and painting might seem to suggest that here we have yet another inoffensive piece destined for the Africana shelves: something interesting to send to Aunt Mary overseas. Aunt Mary would be horrified by its contents, and many South Africans, whatever

their political affiliations, are going to be equally horrified': Fletcher, '*Dusklands*', 11.

70 Coetzee, *Heart* (R), back cover.

71 Anon., Review of *From the Heart of the Country* (*Publishers Weekly*); Broyard, 'One Critic's Fiction'.

72 Barnett, 'Constructions of Apartheid', 292.

73 *Ibid.*, 294, 290; see 292, 288; see Levin, 'On the Edge of the Empire'. Laura Chrisman discusses this imperative in 'Transnational Productions', 4–6.

74 Kramer, 'In the Garrison', 8.

75 Barnett, 'Constructions of Apartheid', 292; Gordimer, 'The Idea of Gardening'; see also Enright, 'The Thing Itself'.

76 Morrison, 'Veldschmerz'.

77 Harwood, 'An Astonishing First Novel' – he thought this Coetzee's first novel.

78 Anon., 'New SA Novel Explores Black–White Sex'.

79 Hofmeyr, 'The Frenzy of Desire', 84.

80 Berold, 'White South African Psyche', 173–4.

81 McDonald, 'The Writer, the Critic and the Censor', 287, 299; see Louw, ''n Onvergeetlike Indruk' (An Unforgettable Impression, *Die Burger*), ''n Fyn Geslypte Metafoor' (A Finely Polished Metaphor, *Beeld*).

82 Louw, 'A Calvinist Allegory?', 51, 50.

83 Toerien, Review of *From the Heart of the Country*, 510.

84 The extracts appeared with a note that the novel would be published by Secker & Warburg in London the following year: Coetzee, 'From *In the Heart of the Country*', *Standpunte*, 16; see Toerien, 'Enkele Aantekeninge' (Sundry Notes).

85 Dekker, *Afrikaanse Literatuurgeskiedenis*, 182–3. In 1976, the editorial board included established literary luminaries from several generations, including the venerable W. E. G. Louw and D. J. Opperman, as well as A. P. Grové, T. T. Cloete, Ernst van Heerden and Chris Barnard.

86 Chapman, *Southern African Literatures*, 196.

87 *Ibid.*, 193, 201 note 31; Chapman quotes from Louw's 'Stilstand in Ons Prosa?' (reprinted in *Vernuwing in die Prosa*, 1963).

88 In section 88, for example, she muses on losing her 'sense of election', and in section 89 considers the nature of 'that election', determining 'not to … figure in a bucolic comedy' or 'be explained away by poverty, degeneracy, torpor, or sloth': Coetzee, 'From *In the Heart of the Country*', *Standpunte*, 11, 12.

89 It courted controversy, for example, with the 1952 publication of Opperman's 'Kersliedjie' (Christmas Carol), whose depiction of a black – strictly, 'Coloured' – Christ, outraged conservatives: see Chapman, *Southern African Literatures*, 197–8, 202 note 40. On Louw's compromised critiques of the apartheid Government (*lojale verset*, or loyal opposition), see Sanders, *Complicities*, 57–91.

90 Brink, 'Die Kuns Is Aanstootlik!', 18, 20, my translation; see also De Villiers, 'Notre Dame', and Sinclair and Roodt, 'Dosent en Student'.

91 Brink, 'Die Kuns Is Aanstootlik!', 26, my translation.

92 See chapter 6, above, and Merrett, *A Culture of Censorship*, 79–90.

93 Tafelberg advertised new anthologies ('nuwe digbundels') in issues 29.3,

including *Grimas*, a new collection by Merwe Scholtz, 'one of our foremost literary scholars': see McDonald, 'The Writer, the Critic and the Censor', 287.

94 McDonald, 'Not Undesirable', 14.

95 *Ibid.*

96 *Ibid.*, 15; McDonald quotes from the archive files PCB, P77/7/103.

97 McDonald, 'The Writer, the Critic and the Censor', 293. A 1980 review of *Waiting for the Barbarians* astutely speculated on Coetzee's escape from the censors: 'The South African authorities have banned many books that seem to me to be far more harmless than this one. Probably they thought it was too modern, too difficult and would not reach the masses': Stuckert, 'The Heart of the Matter', 48.

98 Coetzee, *Doubling the Point*, 64.

99 Dodd, 'Naming and Framing', 153, 160.

100 Although Dodd develops it incoherently by suggesting that effectively decolonising the text requires mounting a defence of Magda's sanity, and so mistakes the significance (despite drawing attention to it) of the explanation Coetzee himself gives of Magda: Dodd, 'Naming and Framing', 157; see Watson, 'Speaking: J. M. Coetzee', 23; Glenn, 'Game Hunting', 122.

101 *Dust*, directed by Marion Hänsel, 1985. The film won the Silver Lion award at the 1985 Venice Film Festival; Coetzee expressed his disappointment with it in *Doubling the Point*, 60.

7

Zakes Mda's novel educations

Not 'a state-of-the-nation report': Mda and the post-apartheid novel

In a polemical review of Zakes Mda's *Ways of Dying* and *The Heart of Redness* in the *New York Review of Books* in January 2003, American novelist Norman Rush suggested that, because 'serious' – implicitly, North American and European – readers so keenly wanted the 'voices' of white novelists like Gordimer, Brink and Coetzee 'to be matched' or even 'surpassed' by 'new black voices', far too much had been expected from 'post-apartheid black literature', too soon. Inevitably, he wrote, 'the first fruits by writers creating in the new era' had attracted 'overpraise driven by the emotion of welcome', and this had happened in particular in the case of Mda.[1] While Mda was increasingly heralded as the most promising black South African novelist, and his work had attracted major literary awards, it did not deal adequately with the realities of the new nation, Rush contended: Mda seemed relatively uninterested in the violent spectacle of the transition, and did not mention AIDS – rendering his work more 'fable' than 'parable', and ultimately 'an escapist dream'.[2] Rush's own work (set in Botswana, where he lived between 1978 and 1983) by contrast, takes delineating socio-political reality very seriously indeed – although, in the National Book Award-winning *Mating*, arguably merely as backdrop for an erotic novel-of-ideas meets CIA thriller.[3]

Rush's judgement suggests a fascinating expectation that, even in the post-apartheid era, black writers *should* continue to document social conditions or produce allegories in which those conditions are the subject of didactic or moralising treatment. It echoes, although partly to invert, Lewis Nkosi's famous critique of some black South African writing in the 1960s as 'journalistic fact parading outrageously as imaginative literature', writing which exploited apartheid's 'ready-made plots', while making no attempt 'to transcend or transmute these given "social facts" into artistically persuasive works of fiction'.[4] Rush seems determined to demand representation of exactly those 'social facts' – along with 'artistic persuasiveness' – as a necessary condition for a new, sufficiently South African, literary culture. Nonetheless, he simultaneously finds fault with a lingering instrumentalism in Mda's writing, misreading the exploration in *The Heart of Redness* of the relative merits of past and present, local and global as 'a literary gesture against modernity'.[5] It is true that few of Mda's characters are directly engaged in 'the struggle' against apartheid: *The Heart of Redness*, for example, simply glosses the twentieth century as an era of tribulations for the 'Middle Generations'. Nonetheless, very many characters feel daily the after-effects of apartheid's social engineering, and Mda's focus on 'ordinary' characters' extraordinary lives, Richard Samin argues, 'generates a social knowledge that is richer, more varied and more contradictory than the spectacular writing which "protest writing" delivered'.[6]

Rush is, however, not alone in critiquing Mda's apparent turn from engagement: Grant Farred, an expatriate South African academic in the USA, for example, characterises as problematic Mda's attempt, in *Ways of Dying*, to develop 'a mode liberated from the incessant political demands placed upon disenfranchised authors in the anti-apartheid struggle'. This wishes into existence, he argues, a 'conception of the black artist' based on a 'fallacious commensurability between the achievement of the postapartheid state and the upliftment of the historically disenfranchised black underclass'.[7] As long as there are poor, badly housed, HIV-positive, black citizens in the post-apartheid nation, these critics appear to argue, no black artist can responsibly *not* write about such 'social facts'.

Mda, unsurprisingly, dismisses such criticisms; he chides Rush (whom he describes as 'hermeneutically challenged') for wanting 'a novel that speaks to him like an article in *The Daily News*'.[8] It is precisely an escape from this political overdetermination – whether historical and state-authored or a contemporary globalised construction of modernity – which Mda's fiction appears to celebrate, although never naively. During the apartheid era, he notes (in an echo of Nkosi, and of Ndebele's prescription of the 'rediscovery of the ordinary'), 'supreme authorship rested with apartheid', and many South African writers consequently 'became reporters'.[9] The first democratic elections, of April 1994, afforded Mda 'the luxury to write novels', he claims: 5 appeared in the decade following his return to South African from 30 years in exile – *Ways of Dying* (1995), *She Plays with the Darkness* (1995), *The Heart of Redness* (2000), *The Madonna of Excelsior* (2002) and *The Whale Caller* (2005).[10] Mda's novels are not 'state-of-the-nation report[s]', he argues, although this does not mean that South African writers can or should no longer engage with contemporary conditions: 'We still create immediate art'; '[w]e still have immediate problems ... I am still a practitioner of that kind of art'.[11]

Mda had been known since the late 1970s as an award-winning dramatist with more than thirty plays to his name. In the late 1980s, he ran a successful 'theatre-for-conscientisation', or 'participatory theatre', company, the Marotholi Travelling Theatre, in Lesotho.[12] He has strong family connections with the leaders of the liberation movement – those whom his character Camagu, in *The Heart of Redness*, testily styles the 'Aristocrats of the Revolution'.[13] His father, A. P. Mda, was an influential early president of the ANC Youth League and a significant power-broker in the liberation movement throughout the 1950s and 1960s. Born Zanemvula Kizito Gatyeni Mda, in Herschel in the Eastern Cape, in 1948, and raised there and in Orlando, Johannesburg, Mda followed his father into exile in Lesotho in 1964, later studying in the USA. He worked as a broadcaster and an academic in Lesotho between 1985 and 1991, thereafter holding a series of visiting positions in American universities, including Yale and Princeton, but returned to South Africa in 1995. He has since been a visiting academic at the University of the Witwatersrand and dramaturge at the Market Theatre in Johannesburg, and now divides his time between theatrical and community projects in South Africa, and creative-writing teaching in the USA (at the time of writing, at his alma mater, Ohio University).[14]

Mda's novels, thematically and in their implication in variously inflected publication and reception contexts, focus on a range of issues pertinent to this study. They explore, and attempt to approximate, particular constructions of (South) African modes of storytelling, some of which entertain scant separation between individual and communal or between visible reality and the spirit world. 'I tell my story the way my grandmother told me stories', with 'magic and the supernatural' operating 'in the context of the real', Mda explains.[15] Each of his novels also features at least one artist figure, often endowed with apparently supernatural powers. In *She Plays with the Darkness*, Dikosha is a gifted dancer and seer whose apprehension of an alternative reality in the mountains of Lesotho offers a diaglossic parallel narrative to the representation of domestic and national politics in the mountain kingdom. Toloki, in *Ways of Dying*, is a professional mourner whose affecting performances act as an unexpected source of aesthetic *and* political agency in the midst of chaos; David Attwell suggests that he 'embodies' an 'experimental practice', dramatising 'the power of non-instrumental art to awaken listeners to their precariousness', and 'remind[ing] them that despite the brutalisation which is their daily lot, they are still agents of culture'.[16] In *The Madonna of Excelsior*, Father Frans Claerhout, the painter, translates the mundane into vibrant, engaging canvases. In the same novel, Niki communes with bees, while in *The Whale Caller*, the eponymous protagonist communicates with whales and rock rabbits. Mda's narration also often invokes or embodies received and constructed (regional) philosophical or spiritual explorations of identity, using, for example, a chorus-like voice of the community to offer comment or act as a narrator – most noticeably in *Ways of Dying* and *The Madonna of Excelsior*.[17] About its use in the latter novel, André Brink noted in a review in November 2002 that the resulting 'detachment' prevented the novel from 'lapsing into melodrama and sentimentality', but Philip John, writing in the Afrikaans-language *Die Burger* in January 2003, judged the technique a complete failure, arguing that it precluded the development of individual characters' psychological depth, was 'a hindrance and a disappointment for the reader accustomed to the modern European prose tradition' and resulted in 'caricature-like, one-dimensional characters', which gave 'the novel the appearance of a moralising tract'.[18] If the demands of local and regional identifications, and the construction of a stylistic *South African-ness*, are recurring concerns in the fiction, so, it is clear, are ambivalent critical responses in the novels' reception; as one might expect, given the history of critical responses to colonial and postcolonial writing generally (illustrated, to varying extents, in the preceding chapters), there is considerable anxiety in some circles about the *literariness* of Mda's fiction.

Two exemplary constructions will serve to introduce Mda's works' institutional entanglements: Farrar, Straus & Giroux's marketing copywriters confidently touted *The Heart of Redness* to an American readership, in 2002, as 'arguably ... the first great novel of the new South Africa'; a review of *The Madonna of Excelsior* in the South African women's magazine, *Fair Lady*, in November of the same year, declared Mda 'a true post-struggle author – and *absolute* storyteller, focused on the art and not bogged down by message'.[19] Both representations speak to anxieties about the demands of social documentary, and evidence the predilection, on the one hand, of mainstream (white) audiences in South Africa to privilege a non-political understanding of aesthetics and, on the other, of international critics, publishers and reviewers to cast proto-postcolonial writing as national allegory or respond to it as literature of affect and displaced identification. Meanwhile, Mda appears highly marketable both to the growing number of black middle-class readers *in* South Africa (where he is almost certainly more widely read than is Coetzee or Gordimer) and to international Anglophone publishers – particularly in the USA.

As with each of the writers considered in this book, Mda's work satisfies differently inflected desires in different markets, confirming and challenging constructions of 'South Africa' in the global media. This chapter sets out to offer the first account of how some of those constructions have come to be made, before assessing, through a reading of *The Heart of Redness*, how Mda's work embodies – and engages with – national, transnational and *contra*-national transactions in an exemplary manner.

Pedagogy, politics or prose fiction? Early publication and reception

Mda initially submitted the manuscript of *Ways of Dying* to the AWS, but Heinemann suggested it be rewritten – which he refused to do (he claims they called it a 'feminist diatribe').[20] He took offence at the publisher's refusal because, in his opinion, the AWS had not published a great deal of exciting writing ('a lot of rubbish') since its few early 'gems'; his response suggests a decline in the prestige of a series conceived primarily as an educational imprint.[21] Ironically, the press which eventually published the novel, Oxford University Press South Africa, clearly seems to have done so with an eye on the book's likely educational market in Southern Africa (despite Mda's eagerness to characterise his publication by the Press as its unheralded departure from academic publishing). *Ways of Dying* also appeared in specifically *educational* Oxford University Press editions.[22] This was not, however, before Mda, while working at Yale, had sent the manuscript to a New York agent suggested by a fellow South African writer Mike Nicol. Mda recalls that the agent declined it 'on the basis that "African literature does not sell in the USA"'. Nicol suggested in explanation that, 'in her eyes and in the eyes of the US publishing houses at the time, African literature was produced by black writers', while those authors who sold copies – white writers – were, like Nicol, 'probably stateless in their terms' or, at least, not obviously alien.[23] That observation, astute if perhaps an over-reading, suggests both how 'white writing' from South Africa – in Coetzee's sense of the description, but particularly *by* white writers – was long received in the USA, and also highlights the mainstream tendency to expect national allegories from (non-white) postcolonial writers.

Oxford University Press South Africa's commissioning editor approached Mda for unpublished play scripts for a school anthology, and the Press agreed to consider his novel's manuscript when he offered to send it instead – 'they liked it, and published it immediately', Mda recalls.[24] Oxford South Africa also published his third novel, *The Heart of Redness*, in late 2000 (Mda claims that he needed the money Oxford offered as an advance). Subsequently engaging an agent, Isobel Dixon (incidentally an expatriate South African and a published poet) at the London firm Blake Friedmann, his work has always since, in his words, been 'in demand enough to be auctioned'.[25] *The Heart of Redness* did not find a British publisher, but was sold to Farrar, Straus & Giroux (FSG), for publication in hardcover in the USA in August 2002. Picador published a paperback edition in the USA in August 2003 – although not before publishing a paperback of *Ways of Dying*, to coincide with the FSG *Heart of Redness* (many American reviews combined comment on the two novels). A paperback edition of *She Plays with the Darkness* followed, in 2004, and *The Madonna of Excelsior* appeared from the same presses in South Africa (2002) and the USA (2004, 2005). *The Whale Caller* became the first of Mda's novels to be published by a British press, Penguin South Africa having outbid Oxford South Africa and sold the title on to the British Viking–Penguin list.[26] FSG and Picador remained the American publishers.[27]

Both FSG and Picador are high-quality *literary* trade publishers. The former's star-studded list includes, for example, Gordimer, Derek Walcott, Seamus Heaney, Paul Muldoon, Susan Sontag, Jonathan Franzen, Michael Cunningham and Jeffrey Eugenides, to name only a few (all of whom have won either the Nobel Prize, the American National Book Award or a Pulitzer Prize, since 1990).[28] Picador launched as a literary imprint in America in 1995, and began publishing trade paperbacks with FSG in 1999; both firms are part of the same larger publishing conglomerate, the Stuttgart-based German Verlagsgruppe Georg von Holtzbrinck, who bought FSG in November 1994, and gained partial control of the Macmillan Group (and so, the Picador imprint, which it owns) in 1995 and complete control in 1999.[29] Mda's publication with Picador thus followed automatically from his FSG deal. His publication by apparently distinct highly *literary* presses with considerable cachet in the literary marketplace, might be said, then, to complement but also mask his works' status as commodities invested in, and traded by, a significant multinational multimedia giant with extremely efficient international promotional and distribution capacities.

Ways of Dying was not the first of Mda's novels to be noticed in the press: *She Plays with the Darkness*, written while he was a visiting academic in Burlington, Vermont, appeared from the small Johannesburg-based Vivlia in late 1995, shortly after having won the prestigious South African SANLAM prize for fiction, in July 1995, while still in manuscript.[30] This marked the first appearance of Mda the novelist, and the novel's critical reception suggests some of the concerns which would predominate in the construction of his novelistic public persona. The South African press was keen to emphasise an apparent break with the past, *The Sunday Times*, for example, printing Mda's claim that he was 'disillusioned with South African theatre' and determined to write *fiction* to continue his fascination with the theatre of the absurd.[31] The *Sunday Times* review also usefully suggests the concerns which would dominate the critical reception of Mda's work: its levels of documentary and its contested status as *literature*. It refers to the novel as a 'book' with a 'story', rather than a 'novel' with a narrative or plot. It suggests that it is both 'shockingly real and subtly surreal', and calls it implicitly valuable because it '*chronicles* life in village communities that may soon disappear'. 'Like an African Hemingway', the review concludes puzzlingly, Mda 'deals with stark facts, leaving us to absorb the phrases and then interpret them according to our own emotions'.[32]

Some reviews cast Mda's representation of social conditions in *She Plays with the Darkness* more thoughtfully, as an exploration of rural society's challenging negotiations with modernity. Tumo Mokone, for example, writing in the *City Press* (a newspaper aimed chiefly at black readers), constructed it as a record of the struggles of rural communities in modern-day Lesotho to 'grapple with changes brought on by westernisation'. Mokone noted significantly, too, that Mda's novel had 'taken great care to explain several Basotho [Mosotho] craft forms, thereby revealing a people within the threads of their culture'.[33] Negotiating a balanced assessment of traditional and modern has become an abiding concern in Mda's fiction, and in the more nuanced reviews of his work.[34] Local reviews of *Ways of Dying* also drew attention to the novel's combination of social engagement with what some reviewers were beginning to call Mda's magical realism. The *Sunday Independent* suggested that 'magic and fantasy' provided a 'rich backdrop' to representations of 'natural disasters and ongoing hardship'; the *Cape Times* noticed both documentary impulses and aesthetic transformation, suggesting that even 'shockingly violent' events were 'poetically describe[d]', and that Mda's readers became 'participant[s]' in a 'tale of reconciliation'.[35] With the Truth and Reconciliation Commission in everyone's mind, this last observation is highly significant.

Despite mostly positive early notices, some reviewers were clearly anxious about the *literariness* of Mda's writing from the first. John Michell's *Sunday Times* review of *She Plays with the Darkness* reminded the reader that English was Mda's second language. It called Mda 'a quirky writer', and described his writing as 'stilted, as if, like his characters, he is still feeling his way'.[36] Writing in the *Sunday Independent* in February 1996, novelist Achmat Dangor criticised *Ways of Dying* for not seeming committed enough (by, paradoxically, appearing too documentary), but also alleged a stylistic awkwardness. The critiques are related: Dangor found Mda's apparently 'unblushing authorial political judgments' unpalatable because they interrupted 'the flow of fictional narrative'; as a government employee and veteran of the struggle, Dangor perhaps thought Mda's equivocal representation of power politics in South Africa unjustly non-committal, but it is the stylistic consequences of an overdetermining narrative consciousness, exacerbated by 'clichéd images and laboured language', and a 'proliferation of badly constructed sentences and malapropisms', which he appears to find most troubling. Dangor went as far as to suggest that to have published the novel without the editorial interventions *he* would have made evidenced the 'venal lack of respect that many publishers have for the work of (black?) South African writers'.[37] Such attacks have not ceased, but their vehemence has waned with Mda's rising status in the literary marketplace. It is true, however, that his is sometimes not the kind of English expected by *northern* Anglophone readers. He admits willingly that his 'is not the Queen's English', but a South African English which draws on his first language, isiXhosa, and on Sesotho, in which he became fluent while in Lesotho.[38] Generically and stylistically, Mda also self-consciously invokes the models of literary isiXhosa, and the work of Sesotho writers like Thomas Mofolo and J. J. Machobane, and suggests that his work offers, in part, 'a transliteration' of their modes of expression.[39]

For some readers, Mda's tone and language suggested that his writing, particularly his early work, was juvenile fiction: Brenda Cooper, for example, writing in *World Literature Today* in 1996, suggested that *Ways of Dying* was not an adult novel.[40] It *is* the case that *Ways of Dying* was marketed by Oxford South Africa, an educational press, as an 'education-al edition', and later in a 'School Notes Edition', and Mda's assertion that the press's publication of his work was an unheralded departure from school-level academic publishing thus displays a degree of revisionism.[41] There is, nonetheless, a degree of condescension in the assumption that non-standard English usage signifies that the intended audience is a juvenile one. Mda *has* published juvenile fiction,[42] and what he and his publishers construe as his adult novels are frequently prescribed for study in South African schools and universities, but his use of names from several of South Africa's indigenous languages, and their influence on his English, foreground the question of intended and likely audience – and the response of the latter, if not the same as the former, to unfamiliarity. Mda insists that he writes 'primarily for the South African audience', and claims to insist that his work is published there first. [43] So adamant is he that he will not pander to international sensibilities or horizons of expectation and competence that he has, in his words, refused to adapt 'linguistic and cultural codes that are particularly South African to suit the needs and even the tastes of American or European readers'.[44] This has led to conflict. Mda recalls his editor, Helen Moffatt, at Oxford University Press South Africa, complaining that some expressions were 'too South African' and would not be understood by his foreign readers. He states that he insisted his '"overseas readers" were not morons', that if they failed to understand 'South African expressions in a South African novel they would go out and find out', and he 'certainly was not going to refashion [his] novels to suit American or European tastes'.[45]

'The problems of redness!'[46] *The Heart of Redness* and the claims of local and global

All of these concerns are most usefully considered by focusing on the case of *The Heart of Redness*, Mda's third novel, which offers an engagement, both in its plot and its material manifestations, with the hybrid transactions between local and transcultural imperatives. In other words, it is a novel *about*, as well as a work implicated *in*, national and transnational processes of interpretation and validation.[47] I wish to suggest that the novel interrogates and actually embodies the imbrication of indigenous (African or South African) and imported (European, North American) representational systems and aesthetic values. This section departs slightly from the method of the preceding chapters in order to do justice to this double engagement, offering both a reading of the novel – as text – and of the processes in which the novel has been implicated – as work.

After four years in the 'new' South Africa (having returned from exile in the USA in 1994), the novel's chief protagonist, Camagu, has lost 'his enthusiasm for this new democratic society', and decides that he would rather go back to America.[48] On the eve of his departure, he stumbles on a wake on the roof of his apartment building, in Johannesburg, and encounters an intriguing young woman from the Eastern Cape. She disappears into the crowd, prompting Camagu to postpone emigrating and set out to find her. Her name, NomaRussia, introduces the novel's concern to demonstrate a pervasive hybridity in supposedly pure, indigenous cultures. Following her to Qolorha-by-Sea, a village on the 'Wild Coast' of the former Transkei homeland, Camagu discovers that NomaRussia is not an uncommon name: it celebrates and records the amaXhosa nation's identification with Russia during the mid-nineteenth century on hearing that a recent British Governor of the Cape Colony, Sir George Cathcart (who had defeated the amaXhosa in the War of Mlanjeni, or the Seventh Frontier War, in the early 1850s), had been killed at the hands of the Russians during the Crimean War, in 1854.[49] The connection with Russia takes on a different form during the apartheid era, when the Soviet Union 'armed and trained [the] sons and daughters of the nation' – the liberation guerrillas who brought 'an end to the sufferings of the Middle Generations'.[50]

In Qolorha, Camagu encounters another act of identification with a foreign power: Xoliswa Ximiya, a chief representative of the village faction advocating a wholesale and unquestioning embrace of Western, free-market capitalism, idolises the USA, which she calls 'a fairytale country, with beautiful people. People like Dolly Parton and Eddy Murphy.'[51] Xoliswa regards amaXhosa cultural dress and beliefs as 'an embarrassment', declaring the iconic red ochre of traditional amaXhosa blankets and decoration the 'curse of redness'.[52] The novel's title, referencing Conrad's *Heart of Darkness*, draws similarly on this traditional icon. Camagu is drawn into a struggle between these groups who ascribe different values to the past, and to the relative merits of a modernity associated, largely, with America. Those factions, the 'Believers' and 'Unbelievers', take their names from their ancestors' responses to perhaps the most significant emblematic episode in the history of the amaXhosa nation: the Great Cattle Massacre of 1857. This was prompted by a teenager, Nongqawuse, who, inspired by a vision beside a pool near present-day Qolorha, prophesied that the spirits of the ancestors would rise and help drive into the sea the British colonial administration and the white settlers it protected, should the people kill all their cattle and burn their crops. Many did so, and thousands starved to death or were forced into service in the Cape Colony.[53] The descendants of those who gave credence to the prophecy form the Believers, under the patriarch Zim. Their relatives, descendants of those who did not act on the prophecy, are led by Bhonco Ximiya, and blame the Believers for the woes of colonisation and, ultimately, for apartheid: Nongqawuse, the Unbelievers declare, was 'a fake', 'used by white people to colonise us'.[54]

Mda's novel moves between the time of the cattle massacre and the present, in which the divisions between the earlier generations are refocused through an immediately pressing question: whether to embrace or reject a casino and hotel development plan which could bring employment to the area, but would destroy its delicate local ecosystem and cultural traditions. Bhonco and Xoliswa Ximiya, the chief Unbelievers, support the plans. Zim and his daughter, Qukezwa, both ardent conservationists, oppose them.[55] After flirting with the Unbelievers, Camagu comes to see the strengths of the Believers' arguments (and becomes romantically involved with Qukezwa), revaluing the insights of traditional culture, and reviling the cynicism of the casino developers – white engineers and black-empowerment front-man alike.[56] It is 'wrong to dismiss those who believed in Nongqawuse as foolish', says Camagu: 'Her prophecies arose out of the spiritual and material anguish of the amaXhosa nation.'[57] It remains for the Believers, once more, to save the land, and the way of life, from the Unbelievers, who, in this construction, were in the historical period, the 'selfish and greedy men who wanted to hoard their cattle and thereby rob the entire amaXhosa nation of the sweet fruits of the resurrection', and in the present are those whose well-intentioned compliance with an intrusive modernity risks losing the amaXhosa of Qolorha the little which they have left.[58]

The other models open to the community appear to be *cultural* tourism and *eco*-tourism. Camagu sets up a collective of local women to cater, non-exploitatively, to the former, and starts a backpackers' lodge to facilitate the development of the latter.[59] As the novel ends, both the collective's holiday camp (grown out of the backpackers' lodge) and a cultural village run by the local white trader, Dalton, featuring performances of local cultural practices, co-exist uneasily.[60] Dalton has previously, in what reads like an echo of James Jarvis's dam-building undertaking in *Cry, the Beloved Country*, attempted a water project for the village: as in Paton's novel, the beneficent white man chooses a committee, invites a government expert, and imposes his plan on the local people.[61] In a passage which approximates the kind of 'set-piece debates' which, as David Attwell notes, are 'typical of theatre-for-development', Camagu criticises Dalton's cultural village as 'an attempt to preserve folk ways ... to reinvent culture. When you excavate a buried precolonial identity of these people ... a precolonial authenticity that is lost ... are you suggesting that they currently have no culture ... that they live in a cultural vacuum?'[62] Camagu – and through him, Mda – declares: 'I am interested in the culture of the amaXhosa as they live it today, not yesterday. The amaXhosa people are not a museum piece. Like all cultures their culture is dynamic.'[63]

That is the novel's key insight, that culture is dynamic and identities are never pure. *The Heart of Redness* repeatedly foregrounds this sense of hybridity. As Anthony Vital observes, its 'references to precolonial cultural exchanges and intermarriage among the Khoikhoi and amaXhosa' – in the mid-nineteenth-century narrative, the Believers' ancestor, Twin, marries a Khoihkoi woman, Qukezwa (after whom Zim's daughter is named) – 'frames the amaXhosa encounter with the British in terms of a cultural hybridisation already in process'.[64] Furthermore, the clicks in isiXhosa have been traced to contact with Khoisan languages, and Mda's self-conscious ascription of names with the range of isiXhosa clicks to characters in the novel seems to gesture to this legacy of contact, marking a determination to force (specifically white South African and foreign Anglophone) readers to engage with the cultural specifics of a particular place. (Some readers protested: Robyn Cohen, writing in the *Cape Times* in November 2000, noted that colleagues had labelled the novel a difficult book, and remarked that the '"difficult" part, for the non-Xhosa-speaking reader, is Mda's use of Xhosa names'.[65] A February 2004 review of *The Madonna of Excelsior* in the *Economist* claimed that *The Heart of Redness* was too difficult for non South Africans, 'daunted by [Mda's] fondness for Xhosa expressions and … difficult names'.[66]) The central historical event in the novel, the Great Cattle Massacre, is also linked directly to a process of contact and conceptual syncretism: Nongqawuse's uncle, Mhlakaza, with whom she lives, was formerly a servant of the Anglican Bishop of Grahamstown, under whose auspices he became familiar with the Christian belief in the resurrection of a messianic figure.[67] Dalton makes the connection explicit: Nongqawuse 'had vaguely heard of the teachings … about the resurrection', and about its 'Christian version', and 'decided to concoct her own theology'.[68] The novel's open-ended but generally optimistic conclusion suggests that local people need to find their own solutions to their uniquely inflected situations; in Attwell's words, Mda 'foregrounds the encounter with modernity, not as completed event, but as unfinished business, over which the amaXhosa … must take charge' – a process of 'incomplete, fugitive, yet necessary reinvention'.[69]

A review of the American edition in *World Literature Today*, in 2003, noticed this 'pertinent social criticism' and 'postcolonial vindication of a third way between tradition and Western ideas'.[70] Immediately on publication in South Africa, the *Sowetan*, one of the largest daily newspapers aimed at black readers, was keen to downplay any impression of sectarianism, claiming that the novel 'isn't about Xhosas only', but spoke to 'all black people in the country'.[71] The Port Elizabeth-based *Eastern Province Herald* suggested that its blend of 'magic with reality and today with yesteryear' gave 'white readers a better understanding of the Xhosa culture', making 'a delightful easy read'.[72] Both claims demonstrate fascinating assumptions about the novel's literariness – or lack thereof – and likely audience, addressing its own largely white audience and assuming, perhaps, that the novel would not attract a large black readership (or assuming that one did not exist). The country's premiere English-language weekly, the *Mail & Guardian*, praised the novel's ambition in a positive review which called it 'a history book, a rural comedy, an environmental treatise, a cultural manual, and a love story'.[73] Some South African reviews focused on Camagu's criticism of corruption and on several other characters' unhappiness at having politicians imposed on their communities by far-away administrators.[74] Nonetheless, it is worth noting that Mda has always remained a committed ANC supporter, and despite the novel's critiques of the excesses of some elites, *The Heart of Redness* secured something like the official stamp of approval when Tourism Minister Valli Moosa discussed its representation of sustainable development in Parliament.[75]

The material presentation of the novel's first South African edition, an Oxford University Press South Africa paperback, explains the preoccupation of many of the South African reviews with the specifically regional focus of the novel, and its (partial) concern with indigenous cultures and belief systems. The cover features a photograph of an isiXhosa woman in full and stereotypical traditional costume – draped in a red-ochre blanket, with a child on her back, and smoking a traditional long-stemmed pipe – as well as an iconically South African aloe.[76] The back cover repeats the aloe, with a reversed (and pipe-less) image of the woman's head and shoulders, along with a pull-quote from the novel which draws attention to the historical period setting, and a description which emphasises its concern with 'fascinating history, powerful myth, and faithful depiction of people and place'. As if to reinforce the historical veracity of the novel's source material, the rear inside cover reproduces a black-and-white photograph of the historical Nongqawuse. The American FSG hardcover, by contrast, is less specifically South African, and does not foreground the novel's historical sections. The front of the dust-jacket features a black-and-white photograph of a young woman in dress of indeterminate cultural or historical provenance. The Picador paperback opts for an abstract illustration of a woman's head, over which is superimposed an abstract outline of another head – suggesting the novel's concern with the simultaneity of two temporal periods, the presence of the past in the present.

The FSG dust-jacket's copy also emphasises that the novel is about *contemporary* South Africa. It quotes praise for *Ways of Dying* on the rear, one source calling it a 'strange and terrifying account of the realities of the new South Africa'. The front inside flap quotes Nadine Gordimer's assessment of 'Mda's fascinating narrative skill' as revelatory of 'the past as a powerful presence in the present', not only 'of his characters' but 'of all of us, as we live'. Gordimer's statement is particularly suited to the novel's placement in a sphere of universal resonance, and material details support this de-emphasising of the novel's *South African* status: the rear of the dust-jacket features a photograph of the 'Mandara Mountains, Africa' (credited on the inside rear flap), which are in Nigeria and Cameroon, while geometric details on the dust-jacket's spine and in the box housing each chapter number *in* the text suggest central African (particularly

7.1 Mda's *The Heart of Redness*, Oxford University Press South Africa, 2000

7.2 *The Heart of Redness*, Picador America, 2003

Congolese Kuba or Kongo) design.[77] Universalising, pan-Africanising gestures arguably aid the novel's marketing to a larger audience in the USA, specifically to African-American readers. A small error in the dust-jacket's copy supports this, indicating the revisioning of the novel's South African landscape in terms of a mainland North American geographic imagination: Camagu is said to travel 'to Qolorha *on* the remote Eastern Cape', refiguring as a peninsula a province, in terms of an American sense of a 'cape' (as in Cape Cod).[78]

7.3 *The Heart of Redness*, Farrar, Straus & Giroux, 2002

If the novel's thematic engagements with the simultaneous and complex demands of local and global, past and present, indigenous and foreign illustrate convincingly that 'South African' cultural 'texts' (like Nongqawuse's prophecy, a central absent 'text' in the novel, as it were) are always already local and global, then the material implications of the novel (its publication and reception circumstances) suggest something similar about the country's textual cultures: that the local is inevitably and always already globalised. James English notes that symbolic capital is 'less and less tightly bound to national markets' in this era of globalisation, observing astutely that while an 'erosion of the value of specifically national cultural prestige has opened up some new opportunities both for the agents of "local" cultural production and for "interstitial" artists from the former colonies' (Mda has a larger market now, arguably, than he would have done had he been a 'protest' novelist in the 1960s), it is also the case that 'the institutions and marketplaces of global prestige have been at best a mixed blessing for those engaged in the ongoing project of cultural postcolonization'.[79] Local postcolonial concerns are inevitably reinterpreted – and repositioned – by the global marketplace. Postcoloniality, Graham Huggan argues, a condition in which postcolonial cultural products – 'culturally "othered" artefacts and goods' – have become objects of consumption in the West, has turned the cultural expressions of postcolonialism ('oppositional practices' seeking to undermine or replace 'imperial epistemologies and institutional structures') into commodities able to generate commercial value in the West.[80] Mda's work, not unlike Coetzee's – but less self-consciously contestative in its relation to the demands or felicities of its historical moment, or the category of a national literature – seems an extremely suggestive example of such a commodity among early twenty-first-century South African writing.

Notes

1 Rush, 'Apocalypse When?', 29.
2 *Ibid.*, 31. *The Heart of Redness* won the 2001 Commonwealth Writers' Prize (Africa Region) and the South African *Sunday Times* Fiction Award, and was shortlisted for the Hurston–Wright Legacy Award in the USA in 2003. *The Madonna of Excelsior* was shortlisted for the same award in 2005. It was also longlisted for the IMPAC Dublin Literary Award in 2004, named one of the 'Top Ten Titles for the Decade of Democracy' by the Library and Information Association of South Africa in 2004 and was one of twenty-six titles on the Notable Books List in the USA in 2005. *The Whale Caller* was shortlisted for the Commonwealth Prize (Africa Region) in 2006: Dixon, Interview.
3 Rush is author of *Whites* (stories, 1986), and two novels, *Mating* (1991) – winner of the US National Book Award and the *Irish Times* International Fiction Prize – and *Mortals* (2003): see Hope, 'Our Man in Botswana' and Updike, 'Botswana Blues' (online).

4 Nkosi, 'Fiction by Black South Africans', 212.

5 Rush, 'Apocalypse When?', 31.

6 Samin, 'Marginality and History', 192.

7 Farred, 'Mourning the Postapartheid State', 187.

8 Wark, 'Interview' (online).

9 Mda, 'Babel's Happiness' (online); Wark, 'Interview' (online).

10 Wark, 'Interview' (online).

11 *Ibid.*

12 See Mda, *When People Play People*, 98. Michael Chapman comments that Mda's 'theatre art, whether on the professional stage or in the rural clearing', always 'has societal dedication': *Southern African Literatures*, 361.

13 Mda, *Heart of Redness*, 36; all quoted matter is from the first Oxford University Press South Africa edition (2000).

14 Wark, 'Interview' (online); Mda, *When People Play People*, 'About the Author' (unpaginated).

15 Mda, Interview with Eaton (online).

16 Attwell, 'The Experimental Turn', 170. Toloki returns in Mda's sixth novel, *Cion* (2007).

17 See for example Mda, *Ways of Dying* (1997), 8; *Madonna of Excelsior* (2004), 241. Mervis calls this voice 'a homodiegetic, witness–narrator which defines itself early in the text as the (first-person plural) voice of the community', and suggests that this usage is part of Mda's development of a 'fiction for development' akin to his theatre-for-development ideas: Mervis, 'Fiction for Development', 48.

18 Brink, 'Novel's tightrope', 18. John, 'Oprakelings Nie Altyd Letterkunde', 9, my translation. John argues further that this kind of prose raises the question of whether attempts to retain links with the 'collective, premodern (African) world' can ever produce anything more than didactic or cultural-historical documentary.

19 Mda, *Heart of Redness* (2002), inside dust-jacket cover; Cordell, 'Where the Heart Is', 185.

20 Mda, Interview with Eaton (online).

21 Mda, Interview with Van der Vlies.

22 Mda casts it as such: *ibid.*

23 Mda, 'Zakes Mda in Conversation' (online).

24 Mda, Interview with Van der Vlies.

25 Mda, Interview with Eaton (online). Isobel Dixon represents a number of other South African writers, including Achmat Dangor, Ivan Vladislavić and Marlene van Niekerk.

26 Mda, Interview with Van der Vlies; Dixon, Interview.

27 Mda's work has been widely translated, with European and Asian publishers often buying the rights to translate a new novel in addition to one or more titles from the backlist. *She Plays with the Darkness* has not been translated, but the others all have French (initially Musée Dapper, now the prestigious Le Seuil) and Italian (Edizioni E/O) editions, and one, two or three titles have appeared (respectively) in: Spain and Norway; Korea, Sweden, Germany and Serbia; and the Netherlands. Four of the novels are optioned for film: *Ways of Dying* (by Ross Devenish); *The Heart of Redness* (Ben Horowitz); *The Madonna of Excelsior* (Jonathan Parkinson); *The Whale Caller* (Zola

Maseko): Dixon, Interview.

28 The firm also manages the North Point Press and the Hill and Wang imprints, and Faber & Faber in the USA.

29 Holtzbrinck Group, Verlagsgruppe Georg von Holtzbrinck and Pan Macmillan: online information.

30 Mda, 'Damon Galgut in Conversation' (online).

31 Collins, 'Playwright a Dab Hand'.

32 Michell, 'Local Hemingway'.

33 Mokone, 'Mda Mixes Styles'.

34 See Kgositsile, 'History, Myth and Magic'.

35 Fourie, 'SHE PLAYS WITH DARKNESS'; Rutter, 'Metamorphosis'. Fionuala Dowling used the term 'magic realism' in her review of the novel in the *Sunday Independent* ('Zakes Mda's Magic'); Brink used it in his review of *The Madonna of Excelsior* in the same newspaper in 2002 ('Novel's Tightrope').

36 Michell, 'Local Hemingway'.

37 Dangor, 'Mda's No Match'; the question mark is Dangor's.

38 Wark, 'Interview' (online).

39 Mda, 'Babel's Happiness' (online).

40 See Cooper, Review of *Ways of Dying*.

41 It appeared as an 'educational edition (Southern African Writing)' in July 1995 (ISBN 0195711068) and later in an Oxford University Press 'School Notes Edition', with Robin Malan and Mncedisi Mashigoane credited on the cover alongside Mda (ISBN 0195717511), before finally being released with an Oxford 'Southern African Writing' cover in August 1997 (ISBN 0195714989).

42 Vivlia published *Melville 67: A Novella for Youth* in 2002.

43 Wark, 'Interview' (online).

44 *Ibid.*

45 *Ibid.*; Mda, Interview with Van der Vlies.

46 Mda, *Heart*, 183; all references are to the 2000 South African edition.

47 A great deal might be said, too, about book club, serial, film, and audio 'versions' of Mda's works.

48 Mda, *Heart*, 32. He accuses 'the black empowerment boom' of, among other things, 'merely enriching the chosen few' Mda, *Heart*, 197. Camagu is, by Mda's admission, a 'consciously and overtly' semi-autobiographical character: Wark, 'Interview' (online); his upbringing and training in America mirror Mda's: *Heart*, 31, 65.

49 Mda, *Heart* 70.

50 *Ibid.*, 204.

51 *Ibid.*, 71,

52 *Ibid.*, 48, 184.

53 See Lloyd, 'The Modernization of Redness', 35.

54 Mda, *Heart*, 165; see also 4.

55 Both are apparently able supernaturally to commune with birds and animals: *Heart*, 41, 122, 135.

56 *Ibid.*, 229.

57 *Ibid.*, 283.

58 *Ibid.*, 98.

59 *Ibid.*, 109, 185, 275.

60 *Ibid.*, 314–15.
61 *Ibid.*, 207.
62 *Ibid.*, 286; ellipses Mda's. See Attwell, 'The Experimental Turn', 171.
63 Mda, *Heart*, 286.
64 Vital, 'Situating Ecology', 308; see, for examples, Mda, *Heart*, 23, 26.
65 Cohen, 'Delving into the *Heart of Redness*'.
66 Anon., 'Beyond the Pale', 81.
67 Mda, *Heart*, 54.
68 *Ibid.*, 283; see Vital, 'Situating Ecology', 308.
69 Attwell, 'The Experimental Turn', 172; Attwell, *Rewriting Modernity*, 204.
70 Stynen, Review of *The Heart of Redness*.
71 Molakeng, 'Wide-Ranging Debate'.
72 Anon., 'Appealing African tale'.
73 Rossouw, 'Mda's Twin Peak'.
74 Molakeng, 'Wide-Ranging Debate'; see Mda, *Heart*, 189: 'the ruling party ... imposed its own people nominated by party bosses from some regional head-quarters far away ... '.
75 Moosa, 'Lend a Hand'; see Isaacson, 'The Free State Madonnas' (online); Wark, 'Interview' (online).
76 See fig. 7.1.
77 See, for example, Phillips, *Africa*, 275; Gillow, *African Textiles*, 190–1, 196–7.
78 My emphasis. This error, interestingly, has been repeated on the dust-jacket of the 2005 British Penguin hardcover edition of *The Whale Caller*, which uses the same construction ('on South Africa's Eastern Cape') in addition to placing Hermanus in the Eastern, rather than the Western Cape.
79 English, *Economy of Prestige*, 263.
80 Huggan, *Postcolonial Exotic*, 28; see viii–ix, 6.

Afterword: white(s) and black(s), read all over

Lewis Nkosi recalls that when, during an address to a conference on the subject in Oxford, in 1991, he suggested that 'South African literature' did not exist, his remarks 'provoked an outraged reaction from delegates determined to defend at all costs the existence of at least *something*'.[1] 'In the absence of a single national identity', he continues, reflecting on that position (in 2002), 'South Africa's "house of fiction"' had long 'served merely as a "War Room"'; the 'absence of any signified' which might 'correspond to the idea of the nation' had become the country's 'almost generic condition, our particular affliction, bequeathed to us by ... [a] history of racial division and racial oppression'.[2] As Nkosi, Ndebele, Mda and others observed, writing by black South Africans was long determined by the spectacular subjects of apartheid: the state, in effect, directed the themes (and even, in various protest genres, the form) of much literary production. Writing by white South Africans was overdetermined, too, by the spectacle of race, with works often being judged – at home and abroad – by their willingness to interrogate adequate responses to oppression. As Jane Kramer noted, in reviewing Coetzee and Brink in the *New York Review of Books* in 1982, the country's literary cultures had been 'mortgaged to apartheid'.[3] 'South African' writing dealt with black and white issues, quite literally: produced by white(s) and black(s), in largely isolated traditions, race was its omnipresent concern – it was literally about white and black.

Any study using the designation 'South African literature' as shorthand necessarily engages, as this study has made clear, not only with a field riven with definitional problems, but one which inevitably also invites (in Leon de Kock's useful formulation) 'questions about the colonisation of culture; about canonisation and tradition formation; and about literary critical-historiography ... the materiality of discursive regimes ... and the relations of power to cultural production'.[4] To ask, then, what South African literature might *be*, requires asking not only what *makes* a work 'South African' (what makes it tentatively the work of a national category), but also what criteria, institutions and protocols of reading have effected its reception and construction, both as South African – or problematically 'South African' – and as *literature*.

Fredric Jameson suggested famously that third-world texts were always 'to be read as ... *national allegories*'.[5] In fact, his polemic suggested how those works had at least always seemed to Western critics to present themselves in such a way as to invite being read as allegory, highlighting, in Julie McGonegal's words, how 'First World literary criticism ... remains blithely unaware, for the most part, of the ways its own historical and social conditions impart various givens to [its] interpretive situation'.[6] This study has frequently had to address the problematic nature of aesthetic judgements in colonial and postcolonial contexts. It has become clear that, for many nineteenth- and twentieth-century writers from Southern Africa, the literary was construed as a category authorised and validated by complex, multi-polar, fragmented, often inconsistent and at best self-interested Anglophone metropolitan (both British and North American) fields of publishers, reviewers and readers, and debated and modified variously by nationalist, anti-colonialist and determinedly postcolonial impulses in Southern Africa itself. Cultural and political processes (national, transnational, even contra-national in their impulses and operations) have long structured the field.

The nation has, Simon Gikandi reminds us, been 'both the form that structures modern identities and the sign of their displacement and alienation'.[7] So, while this study has explored how, in practice, the textual and material histories of particular works evidence the nature of national cultural identity as ambivalent, as effectively in performance, it has also taken the measure of different moments, from the late nineteenth to the early twenty-first century, in which the idea of the nation has been regarded as worthy of creative investment. John Comaroff suggests insightfully that South Africa's prominence in the global mediascape in the mid-1990s had much to do with its model of an 'heroic, hopeful effort to build a modernist nation-state under postmodern postmortem conditions; at just the time, that is, when the contradictions of modernity were becoming inescapable'.[8] Those contradictions continue to challenge the South African polity, and to provoke an ever-growing body of creative writing in the country – which continues to be published both there and abroad, and to invite and resist description in national terms.

Notes

1 Nkosi, 'The Republic of Letters', 318.
2 *Ibid.*, 315, 323.
3 Kramer, 'In the Garrison', 8.
4 De Kock, 'South Africa in the Global Imaginary', 7.
5 Jameson, 'Third-World Literature', 69; see Szeman, *Zones of Instability*, 48–64.
6 McGonegal, 'Postcolonial Metacritique', 253.
7 Gikandi, 'Globalization and the Claims', 635.
8 Bhabha and Comaroff, 'Speaking of Postcoloniality', 32. Comaroff contin-

ues: 'As Eric Hobsbawn said ... the African National Congress was perhaps the last great Euronationalist movement. He was not altogether wrong': all quoted in Attwell, *Rewriting Modernity*, 7; see Brown, 'National Belonging', 758.

Bibliography

Archival material

Alan Paton Centre, University of KwaZulu-Natal, Pietermaritzburg (APC)

PC1/1/1/5
Typescript (TS), Charles Dunn. Letter to Alan Paton. 30 January 1948.
TS, Henry S. Canby. Letter to Alan Paton. 18 April 1949.
TS, William Plomer. Reader's Report. 'CRY, THE BELOVED COUNTRY by? Paton'. 12 March 1947.
TSS, D.G. (Daniel George Bunting) and L.L. (Lois Lamplugh). 'Two Reader's Reports on CRY, THE BELOVED COUNTRY by – Paton'. March 1947.
TS, copy. Alan Paton. Letter to Charles Scribner. 13 February 1948.
TS, copy. Alan Paton. Letter to Wallace Meyer. 14 March 1948.
TS, Charles Scribner. Letter to Alan Paton. 5 February 1948.

PC1/1/1/6–3
TS, copy. Alan Paton. Letter to Jan Juta. 12 May 1948.

PC1/4/1/1
TS, G. Wren Howard. Letter to Alan Paton. 30 May 1956.
TS, copy. Alan Paton. Letter to G. Wren Howard. 6 June 1956.
TS, G. Wren Howard. Letter to Alan Paton. 21 March 1957.

PC1/4/1/2
TS, copy. Alan Paton. Letter to Michael S. Howard. 30 December 1968.
TS, Gaye Poulton. Letter to Alan Paton. 30 January 1974.

PC1/4/1/4
TS, Gaye Poulton. Letter to Alan Paton. 12 January 1982.
TS, Ruth Logan. Letter to Anne Paton. 26 June 1986.
TS, Jean Mossop. Letter to Alan Paton. 18 December 1984.
TS, copy. Alan Paton. Letter to Jean Mossop. 1 January 1985,

TS, copy. Alan Paton. Letter to Jean Mossop. 13 July 1985.

PC1/4/2/1
TS, Charles Scribner, Jnr. Letter to Alan Paton. 13 August 1959.
TS, Charles Scribner, Jnr. Letter to Alan Paton. 14 February 1961.

Blanche La Guma private collection, Claremont, Cape Town
Royalty statements 1978–1990.
TS, copy. Blanche La Guma. Letter to Rachel Calder. 2 May 1996.

British Library (BL)
MS Add. 58079J. Roy Campbell. Letter to Michael Roberts. Undated (July 1934).

Harry Ransom Humanities Research Center, University of Texas at Austin (HRHRC)
MSS letters. Olive Schreiner. Letters to Philip Kent. 30 March 1883, 19 April 1883, 1, May 1883, 26 May 1883, 30 May 1883. Copies in British Library, R.P. 1189.

Macmillan Archive, British Library (MABL)

MS Add. 55935. Reader Reports, Vol. 4. Anon (John Morley)
'Saints and Sinners (Ralph Iron) Miss Olive Schreiner'. November 1881, 104.
'Windabyne'. December 1880, 30–1.
'Wild Birds of Kileevy'. 1881 (early), 35–6.
'Damaris'. April 1881, 56.
'A Woman's Love'. May 1881, 60.
'Chronicles of Glenbuckie'. May 1881, 59–60.
'Princess Eithne'. June 1881, 71–2.
'Ostrich Farming. Mrs Carey Hobson'. October 1881, 84–5.
'Story of an African Farm. Ralph Iron. Olive Schreiner'. January 1882, 109.

MS Add. 55413. Letterbooks. Macmillan & Co.
(George Macmillan) Letter to Olive Schreiner. 1 November 1881, Part 1, 141–2.
Letter to 'Ralph Iron'. 19 January 1882, Part 2, 756.

National English Literary Museum, Grahamstown (NELM)
MS Havelock Ellis Letters. Ms. Olive Schreiner. Letter to Havelock Ellis. (5) April 1889.
Doc. 98.30.2.33. TS copy. Roy Campbell. Letter to Percy Wyndham Lewis. Undated (late 1931).

William Plomer files
MS William Plomer. Letter to Harold Monro. 14 January 1922.
MS William Plomer. Letter to Harold Monro. 2 October 1921.
091 PLO 530/35–36. Transcript. William Plomer. 'South African Poetry: II – After 1900'. BBC General Overseas Service, 8 June 1953, 14h45–15h15.

National Library of South Africa, Cape Town (NLSA)
MSB 76. Box 1/192. MS Tristan. Autograph MS Roy Campbell. 'Tristan da Cunha'. 1926.

Poetry Collection, University Libraries, State University of New York, Buffalo (SUNY Buffalo)
MS Roy Campbell. Letter to Maurice Wollman. Undated (February 1934).
MS Roy Campbell. Letter to Maurice Wollman. Undated (late 1936).

Publications Control Board Archive, National Archives of South Africa, Cape Town (PCB)
TS and MS copy. W. A. Joubert. 'Report of Reader'. Report on *A Walk in the Night*. 22 and 28 November 1962.
TS copy. Chair, Board of Censors. Letter to the Secretary of Home Affairs. 3 December 1962.
TS Department of Home Affairs. Letter to Chair, Board of Censors. 21 January 1963.
1/70. Vol. 2. MS copy. A. H. Murray. Report on *The Stone Country*. 9 March 1970.

P76/9/166
TS and MS C. J. W. Du Plooy. Application for a Review. 17 May & 2 June 1976.
TS and MS J. P. Jansen. 'Reader's/Expert's Report'. Report on *And a Threefold Cord*. 17 October 1976.

P76/11/146
TS Directorate of Publications. Letter to E. Steytler. 10 December 1976.
TS copy. Directorate of Publications. Letter to E. Steytler. 14 March 1977.
TS and MS E. Steytler. Letter and forms. To Directorate of Publications. Review of *A Walk in the Night*. 21 September 1976.
TS and MS M. M. Wiggett. 'Reader's Report'. Review of *A Walk in the Night*. 7 December 1976.

P80/1/148
TS and MS J. P. Jansen. 'Reader's Report' on *Time of the Butcherbird*. 6 February 1980.

TS and MS J. P. Jansen. Chairman's Report. 27 February 1980.

MS T. Hicks. 'Reader's Report' on *Time of the Butcherbird*. Undated (early 1980).

MS R. E. Lighton. 'Reader's Report' on *Time of the Butcherbird*. Undated (early 1980).

Anon. Schedule. 24 March 1980. Publications Control Board Archive, National Archives of South Africa, Cape Town.

P82/3/59

TS and MS J. W. Price. Letter to the Director of Publications. 1 March 1982.

TS copy. J. W. Price. Letter to the Director, Department of Justice. 26 July 1982.

TS and MS S. C. Biermann. 'Chairman's Report'. Review of *A Walk in the Night*. 16 June 1982.

TS and MS S. C. Biermann. 'Reader's Report'. Review of *A Walk in the Night*. 16 June 1982.

TS and MS J. A. Scholtz. Review of *A Walk in the Night*. 10 April 1982.

TS copy. Directorate of Publications. Notification of Appeal to Clerk of Publications Appeal Board. 6 June 1982.

TS copy. Director of Publications. Letter to J. W. Price. 28 June 1982.

P86/7/121

Archive file. *And a Threefold Cord* review.

P86/7/120

Archive file. *In the Fog of the Seasons' End* review.

P86/10/51

Archive file. *Time of the Butcherbird* review.

P88/02/59

Archive file. *A Walk in the Night* review.

Robben Island Mayibuye Archive, University of the Western Cape, Belville (Mayibuye)

MCH118/1/B.1

TS Begum Hendrickse. Letter to Alex La Guma. 3 July 1962.

TS Tom Maschler. Letter to Alex La Guma. 29 October 1962.

TS Kay Pankey. Letter to Alex La Guma. 19 November 1962.

TS and MS. N. J. A. Jordaan. Letter to Alex La Guma. 15 November 1962.

University Library, University of Reading, Reading
Heinemann Educational Books Archive (HEB)
3/8
TSS Begum Hendrickse. Letters to Keith Sambrook. 11 May & 18 July 1963.
TS Chinua Achebe. Letter to Keith Sambrook. 27 March 1963.
TS copy. Keith Sambrook. Letter to Chinua Achebe. 3 April 1963.
TS copy. Keith Sambrook. Letter to Ulli Beier. 3 April 1963.
TS copy. Keith Sambrook. Letter to Begum Hendrickse. 17 December 1963.
TS copy. Keith Sambrook. Letter to Ulli Beier. 8 May 1964.
TSS Begum Hendrickse. Letters to Keith Sambrook. 13 & 20 May 1964.
TS Gertrude Gelbin. Letter to Judith Verity. 27 July 1966.
TS copy. Judith Verity. Letter to Ulli Beier. 23 February 1966.
TS copy. Judith Verity. Letter to David Machin. 14 April 1964.
TS David Machin. Letter to Keith Sambrook. 28 May 1964.
TS copy. Judith Verity. Letter to David Farrer. 8 December 1966.
TSS John B. Putnam. Letters to Hilary Birley. 14 February & 8 March 1967.
TS and MS Alex La Guma. Publicity questionnaire for *A Walk in the Night*. 1966.
TS copy. James Currey. Letter to Alex La Guma. 8 November 1972.
TS copy. James Currey. Letter to Alex La Guma. 28 January 1970.

12/8
TS T. G. Rosenthal. Letter to James Currey. 3 January 1973.
TSS Hope Leresche. Letters to James Currey. 6 & 15 October 1971, 13 April 1973.
TS copy. James Currey. Letter to Alex La Guma. 15 July 1972.
TS James Currey. Letter to Hope Leresche. 5 January 1973.

18/3
TS copy. James Currey. Letter to Alex La Guma. 27 January 1970.
TS T. G. Rosenthal. Letter to Keith Sambrook. 30 July 1971.

Hogarth Press Archive (RUL Hogarth)

MS 2750, file 342
MS William Plomer. Letter to John Lehmann. 30 June 1931.
TS John Lehmann. Letter to R. R. Clarke. 20 April 1932.

Jonathan Cape Archive (RUL Cape)

A Files
MS Roy Campbell. Letter to P. Gilchrist Thompson. Undated (March or April 1930).
TS P. Gilchrist Thompson. Letter to Roy Campbell. 27 March 1930.

Special Collections (RUL)

MS 1979
MS Roy Campbell. Letter to R. L. Mégroz. 14 July 1935.
TS R. L. Mégroz. Letter to Roy Campbell. 17 July 1935.

Online material

Barnard, Rita. Online answer, Oprah's Book Club. www.oprah.com /obc_classic/featbook/ctbc/qa/ctbc_qa_display.jhtml?contentId =20031202_04.xml. Accessed 15 December 2003.

Bothma, Gabriël. '"Cry" op die Verhoog Kasty, Streel – Genees'. *Die Burger* (10 July 2003). http://152.111.1.251/argief/berigte/dieburger/2003/07 /10/DB/12LDN/10.html. Accessed October 2003.

Holtzbrinck Group. 'Who We Are'. www.holtzbrinckus.com/about /about_who.asp. Accessed 23 May 2006.

Hope, Christopher. 'Our Man in Botswana'. *Guardian* (26 July 2003). http://books.guardian.co.uk/reviews/generalfiction /0,6121,1005846,00.html. Accessed 16 May 2006.

Isaacson, Maureen. 'The Free State Madonnas Prevail in Mda's New Novel'. *Sunday Independent.* www.theconnection.org/features/zakesar-ticle.asp. Accessed 21 June 2005.

Lewis, Simon. Review of G. E. de Villiers (ed.) *Ravan Twenty-Five Years (1972–1997): A Commemorative Volume of New Writing.* Randburg: Ravan, 1997. H-AfrLitCine, H-Net Reviews, February 2000. www.h-net.org/reviews/showrev.cgi?path=29198949945111. Accessed 22 June 2006.

Mandela, Nelson. Remarks at the Miramax Films World Premiere of *Cry, The Beloved Country*, 23 October 1995, Ziegfeld Theater, New York City. Open Book Systems. http://archives.obs-us.com/obs/english /films/mx/cry/speech4m.htm. Accessed 20 April 2006.

Mda, Zakes. 'Babel's Happiness'. Zakes Mda website. www.zakesmda .com/pages/oraltradition.html. Accessed 13 February 2006.

—— 'Damon Galgut in conversation with Zakes Mda'. 19 July 2005. The ABSA/LitNet Chain Interview. LitNet. www.oulitnet.co.za/chain /damon_galgut_vs_zakes_mda.asp. Accessed 20 March 2006.

—— Interview with Tom Eaton. 5 July 2005. LitNet. http://oulitnet .co.za/nosecret/zakes_mda.asp. Accessed 14 February 2006.

—— 'Zakes Mda in Conversation with Mike Nicol'. 2 August 2005. The ABSA/LitNet Chain Interview. LitNet. www.oulitnet.co.za/chain/zakes _mda_vs_mike_nicol.asp. Accessed 20 March 2006.

Oxford English Dictionary. 2nd edn. Ed. J. A. Simpson and E. S. C. Weiner. Oxford: Clarendon, 1989. *OED Online.* Oxford University Press. Entry for 'South African, *n.* and *a.*' http://dictionary.oed .com/cgi/entry/50231693. Entry for 'voorloper, *n.*' http://dictionary

.oed.com/cgi/entry/50279145. Entry for 'voorslag, *n.*' http://diction-ary.oed.com/cgi/entry/50279147. All accessed 27 August 2006.

Pan Macmillan. 'About Us Homepage'. www.panmacmillan.com /about%20us/. Accessed 23 May 2006.

University of Reading. 'Papers of R. L. Mégroz'. The Library, Special Collections. www.rdg.ac.uk/library/colls/special/megroz.html. Accessed 1 April 2006.

Updike, John. 'Botswana Blues: Orgies of Talk in Africa'. *New Yorker* (26 June 2003). www.newyorker.com/critics/books/?030602crbo_books1. Accessed 16 May 2006.

Van der Merwe, Annari. 'Did the First Democratic Elections of 1994 also Democratise South African Publishing and Literature?' www .univ-reunion.fr/~ageof/text/74c21e88–333.html. Accessed May 2004.

Verlagsgruppe Georg von Holtzbrinck. 'The Group'. www.holtzbrinck .de/artikel/778433&s=en. Accessed 23 May 2006.

Wark, Julie. 'Interview with Zakes Mda'. 15–16 October 2004. www.zakesmda.com/pages/Interview_Wark.html. Accessed 13 February 2006.

Other material

Reviews consulted as cuttings – with page numbers obscured – in archives are listed with archival references. Original issue numbers of journals are given in square brackets.

Abrahams, Cecil. *Alex La Guma*. Boston: Twayne, 1985.

Abrahams, Lionel. 'Reflections in a Mirror'. Review of *Dusklands*. *Snarl* 1.1 (1974), 2–3.

Adhikari, Mohamed. Introduction. In Alex La Guma, *Jimmy La Guma*. Cape Town: Friends of the South African Library, 1997, 7–12.

—— *Not White Enough, Not Black Enough: Racial Identity in the South African Coloured Community*. Athens: Ohio University Press; Cape Town: Double Storey, 2005.

Alexander, Lucy, and Evelyn Cohen. *150 South African Paintings Past and Present*. Cape Town: Struik, 1990.

Alexander, Peter F. *Roy Campbell: A Critical Biography*. Cape Town: David Philip; Oxford: Oxford University Press, 1982.

—— *William Plomer: A Biography*. Oxford: Oxford University Press, 1990.

—— *Alan Paton: A Biography*. Oxford: Oxford University Press, 1994.

Alexander, Peter F. (ed.) Introduction. In Roy Campbell, *The Selected Poems of Roy Campbell*. Oxford: Oxford University Press, 1982, xi–xvi.

Allen, Walter. 'New Novels'. *New Statesman and Nation* 36.924 (20 November 1948), 445–6.

Anderson, Benedict. *Imagined Communities: Reflections on the Origin and Spread of Nationalism*. 1983. Rev. edn. London: Verso, 1991.

Anderson, Maxwell. *Lost in the Stars: The Dramatization of Alan Paton's Novel* Cry, the Beloved Country. 1950. London: Jonathan Cape and Bodley Head, 1951.

Anon. 'Alan Paton's Significant Scrutiny of South Africa'. *Jewish Affairs* 3.11 (November 1948), 53, 55.

Anon. (Canon McColl) 'An Agnostic Novel'. *Spectator* (13 August 1887), 1091–3.

Anon. 'Appealing African Tale'. *Eastern Province Herald* (31 January 2001), 'La Femme', 4.

Anon. 'At Bloemfontein Africans Choose Between – Congress and Convention'. *The African Drum* 2.2 (February 1952), 14–16.

Anon. 'Beyond the Pale: *The Madonna of Excelsior*, By Zakes Mda'. *Economist* (28 February 2004), 81–2.

Anon. 'Censorship in South Africa'. *Sechaba* 10 (Fourth Quarter 1976), 59–62.

Anon. 'The Censorship Threat'. *Spark* (7 February 1963). Mayibuye, MCH/118/1/B.1.

Anon. '"Cry, the Beloved Country": An Analysis'. *Fighting Talk* (December 1951), 5.

Anon. 'Death of Mrs Carey Hobson'. *South Africa* 89.1152 (21 January 1911), 167.

Anon. '*Dusklands*: J. M. Coetzee'. *Staffrider* 1.4 (1978), 60.

Anon. Editorial Note. *The South African Book Buyer: A Monthly Guide to Literature* 1 (September 1906), 3.

Anon. 'Ein Buch mit einer Moral'. *Jewish Family Magazine* (October 1948), 4–5.

Anon. 'Illumination'. *Time and Tide* (24 September 1926), 850.

Anon. 'Journalist's Book Banned'. *Cape Argus* (9 March 1965). Mayibuye, MCH/118/1/B.1.

Anon. 'More Fiction'. *New Adelphi* (December 1927), 191.

Anon. 'New Books'. *Daily Despatch* (2 October 1948). APC, PC1/1/1/3.

Anon. 'New SA Novel Explores Black–White Sex'. *Weekend World* (31 July 1977), 7.

Anon. 'News and Ideas'. *College English* 16.3 (December 1954), 190–3.

Anon. Opinion. *The African Drum* 1.2 (April 1951), 1.

Anon. Review of Cry, the Beloved Country. *Femina* (November 1948), 19.

Anon. Review of From the Heart of the Country. *Publishers Weekly* (11 April 1977), 73.

Anon. Review of In the Heart of the Country. *Observer* Review (7 August 1977), 29.

Anon. Review of The Flaming Terrapin. *Liverpool Daily Post and Mercury* (25 June 1924), 4.

Anon. 'S.A. Novel Meets with High Praise: Impact of Black and White in an Impressive Setting'. *Natal Mercury* (30 October 1948). APC, PC1/1/1/3.

Anon. '"She Was Our South Africa, Africa All Over": The Vast Land Whose Mysterious Charm Calls to All Gallant Adventurers'. *Vogue* 65.8 (April 1925), 76–7, 112.

Anon. '"Solving" the South African Native Problem'. *New Statesman* 30.789 (9 June 1928), 282–4.

Anon. 'Some New Novels'. *Daily Telegraph* (15 October 1948), 3.

Anon. 'South Africa, the Land of Gold and Sunshine: Some Varied Aspects of the Life in a Land Prodigal of All Good Things'. *Vogue* 63.4 (February 1924), 60–1, 80.

Anon. 'South Africa's "White" Problem'. *New Statesman* 34.869 (21 December 1929), 358–9.

Anon. (Philip Kent) 'The Story of an African Farm'. *Life* (8 February 1883), 107–8.

Anon. 'The Story of an African Farm, by Ralph Iron'. *The Englishwoman's Review of Social and Industrial Questions*, n.s. 14.124 (15 August 1883), 362–4.

Anon. 'The Story of Bethal'. *The African Drum* 2.3 (March 1952), 4, 7.

Anon. Translation of the Minority Report (pp. 13–14). In Gordimer et al. *What Happened to* Burger's Daughter. Emmarentia: Taurus, 1980, 15.

Anon. 'Voorslag'. *Cape Times* (15 June 1926), 8.

Arac, Jonathan. Introduction. *Boundary 2* 11.1–2 (fall–winter 1982–83), 1–4.

—— *Huckleberry Finn as Idol and Target*. Madison: University of Wisconsin Press, 1997.

Ardis, Ann. 'Organizing Women'. In Nicola Diane Thompson (ed.) *Victorian Women Writers and the Woman Question*. Cambridge: Cambridge University Press, 1999, 189–203.

Aschman, George. 'Distinguished New South African Novel Acclaimed in America'. *Cape Times* (24 March 1948), 8.

Ashcroft, Bill, Gareth Griffiths and Helen Tiffin. *The Empire Writes Back: Theory and Practice in Post-Colonial Literatures*. London: Routledge, 1989.

Ashcroft, Bill, Gareth Griffiths and Helen Tiffin (eds) *The Post-Colonial Studies Reader*. London: Routledge, 1995.

Astrachan, Anthony M. 'The Names Are Fictitious'. *Black Orpheus: A Journal of African and Afro-American Literature* 14 (February 1964), 59.

Attridge, Derek. 'Ethical Modernism: Servants as Others in J. M. Coetzee's Early Fiction'. *Poetics Today* 25.4 (winter 2004), 653–71.

—— *J. M. Coetzee and the Ethics of Reading: Literature in the Event*. Chicago: University of Chicago Press, 2004.

Attwell, David. *J. M. Coetzee: South Africa and the Politics of Writing*.

Berkeley: University of California Press; Cape Town: David Philip, 1993.

—— 'The Experimental Turn in Black South African Fiction'. In Leon de Kock, Louise Bethlehem, and Sonja Laden (eds) *South Africa in the Global Imaginary*. Pretoria: University of South Africa Press; Leiden: Koninklijke Brill NV, 2004, 154–79.

—— *Rewriting Modernity: Studies in Black South African Literary History*. Scottsville: University of KwaZulu-Natal Press, 2005.

Aveling, Edward B. 'A Notable Book'. *Progress, a Monthly Magazine of Advanced Thought* 2 (September 1883), 156–5.

B. P. B. 'Alex La Guma's First Novel: Banned by the Sabotage Act'. *New Age* (August 1962). Mayibuye, MCH118/1/B.1.

Bain, Bruce, 'Four New Novels'. *Tribune* 613 (8 October 1948), 18–19.

Baker, Sheridan. 'Paton's Beloved Country and the Morality of Geography'. *College English* 19.2 (November 1957), 56–61.

—— 'Introduction'. In Baker, Sheridan (ed.) *Paton's* Cry, the Beloved Country. New York: Scribner's, 1968, 1–3.

Baldick, Chris. *The Modern Movement. The Oxford English Literary History, vol. 10: 1910–1940*. Oxford: Oxford University Press, 2004.

Banham, Martin. 'South Africa'. *Books Abroad* 36.4 (autumn 1962), 458.

Barash, Carol (ed.) *An Olive Schreiner Reader: Writings of Women and South Africa*. London: Pandora, 1987.

Barkham, Margot. 'South African's FIRST NOVEL is a Best-Seller'. *Outspan* (16 April 1948), 31, 77.

Barnard, Rita. 'Oprah's Paton, or South Africa and the Globalization of Suffering'. *English Studies in Africa* 47.1 (2004), 85–107.

Barnett, Clive. 'Constructions of Apartheid in the International Reception of the Novels of J. M. Coetzee'. *Journal of Southern African Studies* 25.2 (June 1999), 287–301.

Barnicoat, Constance A. 'The Reading of the Colonial Girl'. *The Nineteenth Century and After* 60.358 (December 1906), 939–50.

Barrett, Franklin T. (comp.) *Catalogue of the Central Libraries (Lending and Reference)* (Fulham Public Libraries). London: Eyre & Spottiswoode, 1899.

Barthes, Roland. *Writing Degree Zero* (*Le degré zéro de l'écriture*). 1953. Trans. Annette Lavers and Colin Smith. New York: Hill & Wang, 1968.

Beier, Ulli. Letter to Andrew van der Vlies. 25 August 2002. TS, private correspondence.

Beittel, Mark. '"What Sort of Memorial?" *Cry, the Beloved Country* on Film'. In Isabel Balseiro and Ntongela Masilela (eds) *To Change Reels: Film and Culture in South Africa*. Detroit: Wayne State University Press, 2003, 70–87.

Benson, Peter. '"Border Operators": *Black Orpheus* and the Genesis of Modern African Art and Literature'. *Research in African Literatures* 14.4 (winter 1983), 431–73.

—— Black Orpheus, Transition, *and Modern Cultural Awakening in Africa*. Berkeley: University of California Press, 1986.

Berold, Rob. 'White South African Psyche'. *Inspan* 1.1 (1978), 171–4.

Bhabha, Homi K. 'DissemiNation: Time, Narrative and the Margins of the Modern Nation'. In Homi K. Bhabha (ed.) *Nation and Narration*. London: Routledge, 1990, 291–322.

—— *The Location of Culture*. London: Routledge, 1994.

Bhagat, Dipti. 'The Poetics of Belonging: Exhibitions and the Performance of White South African Belonging, 1886–1936'. Unpublished Ph.D thesis, University of London, 2002.

Bickford-Smith, Vivian. 'Words, Wars and World Views: The Coming of Literacy and Books to Southern Africa'. *Bulletin du Bibliophile* 1 (2003), 9–22.

Blacksell, J. E. Introduction. In Alan Paton, *Cry, the Beloved Country*. Abr. J. E. Blacksell. London: Longmans, 1962, 5–6.

Boehmer, Elleke. *Colonial and Postcolonial Literature: Migrant Metaphors*. Oxford: Oxford University Press, 1995.

—— *Empire, the National and the Postcolonial, 1890–1920: Resistance in Interaction*. Oxford: Oxford University Press, 2002.

Boehmer, Elleke and Bart Moore-Gilbert. Introduction. *Interventions* 4.1 (2002), 7–21.

Bolitho, Hector. 'Culture and South Africa'. *The South African Nation* 3.131 (9 October 1926), 12.

—— (ed.) *The New Countries: A Collection of Stories and Poems by South African, Australian, Canadian and New Zealand Writers*. London: Jonathan Cape, 1929.

—— *My Restless Years*. London: Max Parrish, 1962.

Booker, M. Keith. *The African Novel in English: An Introduction*. Portsmouth, NH: Heinemann; Oxford: James Currey, 1998.

Bornstein, George. *Material Modernism: The Politics of the Page*. Cambridge: Cambridge University Press, 2001.

Boumelha, Penny. 'The Woman of Genius and the Woman of Grub Street: Figures of the Female Writer in British *Fin-de-Siècle* Fiction'. *English Literature in Transition 1880–1920* 40.2 (1997), 164–80.

Bourdieu, Pierre. *The Field of Cultural Production: Essays on Art and Literature*. Ed. and intro. Randal Johnson. Cambridge: Polity, 1993.

Bowers, Frances. 'First SA Modern Novel?' *Cape Times* (5 June 1974), 5.

Brennan, Timothy. 'The National Longing for Form'. In Homi K. Bhabha (ed.) *Nation and Narration*. London: Routledge, 1990, 44–70.

Bright, J. A. 'The Bridge Series: Its Aim and Purpose'. In Alan Paton, *Cry, the Beloved Country*. Ed. and abr. G. F. Wear and R. H. Durham. London: Longmans, Green, 1953, v–vii.

Brink, André P. 'Die Kuns is Aanstootlik!' *Standpunte* [124] 3rd series, 29.4 (August 1976), 17–28.

—— 'Novel's Tightrope of Entertainment and Depiction of Trauma a

Testimony to Mda's Art'. *Sunday Independent* (10 November 2002), 18.

Bristow, Joseph. *Empire Boys: Adventures in a Man's World*. London: Harper Collins Academic, 1991.

—— Introduction. In Olive Schreiner, *The Story of an African Farm*. Oxford: Oxford University Press, 1992, vii–xxix.

Brown, Duncan. 'National Belonging and Cultural Difference: South Africa and the Global Imaginary'. *Journal of Southern African Studies* 27.4 (December 2001), 757–69.

Broyard, Anatole. 'One Critic's Fiction'. *New York Times Book Review* (18 September 1977), BR4, 2.

Bunting, Brian. Foreword. In Alex La Guma, *And a Threefold Cord*. Berlin: Seven Seas, 1962, 9–16.

—— *The Rise of the South African Reich*. Harmondsworth: Penguin, 1964.

Burdett, Carolyn. *Olive Schreiner and the Progress of Feminism: Evolution, Gender, Empire*. Basingstoke: Palgrave, 2001.

Burns, Aubrey. 'Mirror to the South'. *Southwest Review* (autumn 1948), 408–10.

Butler, Guy. (ed.) *A Book of South African Verse*. Cape Town: Oxford University Press, 1959.

—— *Essays and Lectures 1949–1991*. Ed. Stephen Watson. Cape Town: David Philip, 1994.

Cairncross, A. S. (ed.) *Longer Poems Old and New*. London: Macmillan, 1934.

Calder-Marshall, Arthur. 'In the Soil Are Life and Death'. *Reynolds News* (10 October 1948), 6.

Callan, Edward. *Cry, the Beloved Country: A Novel of South Africa*. Boston: Twayne, 1991.

Campbell, Ethel. *Sam Campbell: A Story of Natal*. Durban: privately published, 1949.

Campbell, Roy. *The Flaming Terrapin*. London: Jonathan Cape, 1924.

—— 'The Significance of *Turbott Wolfe*'. *Voorslag* 1.1 (June 1926), 39–45.

—— (as Lewis Marston) '"Eunuch Arden" and "Kynoch Arden" (Two Tendencies in Modern Literature)'. *Voorslag* 1.2 (July 1926), 32–8.

—— 'Fetish Worship in South Africa'. *Voorslag* 1.2 (July 1926), 3–19.

—— 'The Serf'. *The Nation* 40.5 (6 November 1926), 183.

—— 'The Zulu Girl'. *New Statesman* 28.709 (27 November 1926), 206.

—— 'Tristan da Cunha'. *New Statesman* 30.755 (15 October 1927), 14.

—— 'Tristan da Cunha'. *The Waste Paper Basket of the Owl Club, 1926*. Cape Town: Horton, 1927, 4–7.

—— 'Tristan da Cunha'. In Thomas Moult (ed.) *Best Poems of 1928*. London: Jonathan Cape; New York: Harcourt, Brace, 1928, 33–6.

—— 'Tristan da Cunha'. In Harold Monro (ed.) *Twentieth-Century*

Poetry. London: Chatto & Windus, 1929, 197–200.

—— *Adamastor*. London: Faber & Faber, 1930.

—— 'Tristan da Cunha'. In Dorothy Wellesley (ed.), *A Broadcast Anthology of Modern Poetry*. London: Hogarth, 1930, 49–53.

—— *Poems*. London: Benn, 1931.

—— 'Tristan da Cunha'. *Poems*. London: Benn, 1931, 16–19.

—— 'Tristan da Cunha'. In J. C. Squire (ed.) *Younger Poets of To-Day*. London: Martin Secker, 1932, 95–9.

—— *Broken Record: Reminiscences by Roy Campbell*. London: Boriswood, 1934.

—— 'Tristan da Cunha'. In A. S. Cairncross (ed.) *Longer Poems Old and New*. London: Macmillan, 1934, 236–9.

—— 'Tristan da Cunha'. In *The Modern Muse*. London: English Association, 1934, 56–9.

—— *Mithraic Emblems*. London: Boriswood, 1936.

—— 'Tristan da Cunha'. In R. L. Mégroz (ed.) *A Treasury of Modern Poetry: An Anthology of the Last Forty Years*. London: Pitman, 1936, 37–40.

—— 'Tristan da Cunha'. In Maurice Wollmann (ed.) *Poems of Twenty Years: An Anthology, 1918–1938*. London: Macmillan, 1938, 62–5.

—— 'Tristan da Cunha'. In Francis Carey Slater (ed.) *The New Centenary Book of South African Verse*. London: Longmans, Green, 1945, 175–8.

—— 'Tristan da Cunha'. In Margaret and Ronald Bottrall (eds). *Collected English Verse: An Anthology*. London: Sidgwick and Jackson, 1945, 554–8.

—— *Light on a Dark Horse*. London: Hollis & Carter, 1951. Rev. edn. Harmondsworth: Penguin, 1971.

—— *Collected Works*. Ed. Peter F. Alexander, Michael Chapman and Marcia Leveson. 4 vols. Johannesburg: Donker, 1985–88. Volume 4: *Prose*.

Cape Times Reporter. 'La Guma Novel Too Hot to Hold'. *Cape Times* (4 August 1962), 3.

Carey, John. *The Intellectuals and the Masses: Pride and Prejudice Among the Literary Intelligentsia, 1880–1939*. London: Faber & Faber, 1992.

Carey-Hobson, Mrs Mary Ann. *The Farm in the Karoo; Or, What Charley Vyvyan and His Friends Saw in South Africa*. London: Juta, Heelis, 1883.

Carlin, Murray. 'Cry, the Beloved Country'. *Student Review: A Journal for Liberals* (29 October 1948), 10–11.

'Castor'. 'In Darkest Johannesburg'. *Church Times* 131.4471 (15 October 1948), 581.

Central News Agency. 'A Best-Seller Is Born!' Advertisement. *Rand Daily Mail* (18 September 1948), 10.

Chapman, Michael (ed.) *A Century of South African Poetry*. Johannesburg: Donker, 1981.

—— *South African English Poetry: A Modern Perspective*. Johannesburg: Donker, 1984.

—— 'Roy Campbell, Poet: A Defence in Sociological Terms'. *Theoria* 68 (1986), 79–93.

—— (ed.) 'More than Telling a Story: *Drum* and its Significance in Black South African Writing'. In *The 'Drum' Decade: Stories from the 1950s*. Pietermaritzburg: University of KwaZulu-Natal Press, 1989, 183–232.

—— *Southern African Literatures*. London: Longman, 1996; Scottsville: University of Natal Press, 2003.

Chapman & Hall. Advertisement. *The Publishers' Circular* (15 February 1883), 154.

—— Advertisement. *The Publishers' Circular* (16 July 1883), 617.

—— Advertisement. *The Torch and Colonial Book Circular* 2.6 (31 December 1888), rear cover.

—— Advertisement. *The Torch and Colonial Book Circular* 2.7 (30 March 1889), 11.

Chisholm, Anne. *Nancy Cunard*. London: Sidgwick & Jackson, 1979.

Chrisman, Laura. *Rereading the Imperial Romance: British Imperialism and South African Resistance in Haggard, Schreiner, and Plaatje*. Oxford: Clarendon, 2000.

—— 'Transnational Productions of Englishness: South Africa in the Post-Imperial Metropole'. *Scrutiny 2: Issues in English Studies in South Africa* 5.2 (2000), 3–12.

—— *Postcolonial Contraventions: Cultural Readings of Race, Imperialism and Transnationalism*. Manchester: Manchester University Press, 2003.

Clarke, Becky. 'The African Writers Series: Celebrating Forty Years of Publishing Distinction'. *Research in African Literatures* 34.2 (summer 2003), 163–74.

Clark, Reynold. Introduction. In Alan Paton, *Cry, the Beloved Country*. London: Longman, 1966, 251–66.

Clarkson, T. E. 'A Lash for Us'. *The South African Nation* 3.116 (26 June 1926), 21.

Clayton, Cherry. *Olive Schreiner*. New York: Twayne, 1997.

Clery, E. J. Caroline Franklin and Peter Garside (eds) Introduction. In *Authorship, Commerce and the Public: Scenes of Writing, 1750–1850*. Houndmills: Palgrave Macmillan, 2002, 1–26.

Cloete, Dick. 'Alternative Publishing in South Africa in the 1970s and 1980s'. In Nicholas Evans and Monica Seeber (eds) *The Politics of Publishing in South Africa*. Scottsville: University of Natal Press, 2000, 43–72.

Coetzee, J. M. 'Alex La Guma and the Responsibilities of the South African Writer'. *Journal of the New African Literature and the Arts* 9–10 (September 1971), 5–11.

—— 'From *In the Heart of the Country*'. *Standpunte* [124]. 3rd series,

29.4 (August 1976), 9–16.

—— *From the Heart of the Country: A Novel*. New York: Harper & Row, 1977.

—— *In the Heart of the Country: A Novel*. London: Secker & Warburg, 1977.

—— *In the Heart of the Country*. Johannesburg: Ravan Press, 1978.

—— 'Staffrider'. *The African Book Publishing Record* 5.4 (1979), 235–6.

—— *Waiting for the Barbarians*. London: Secker & Warburg, 1980.

—— 'SA Authors Must Learn Modesty'. *Die Vaderland* (1 May 1981), 16.

—— *Foe*. Johannesburg: Ravan Press; London: Secker & Warburg, 1986.

—— 'The Novel Today'. *Upstream* 6.1 (summer 1988), 2–5.

—— *White Writing: On the Culture of Letters in South Africa*. New Haven, CT: Yale University Press, 1988.

—— *Doubling the Point: Essays and Interviews*. Ed. David Attwell. Cambridge, MA: Harvard University Press, 1992.

—— 'Roads to Translation'. *Meanjin* 64.4 (2005), 141–51.

Cohen, Philip. 'Mies Is die Mies'. Review of *In the Heart of the Country*. *Speak: Critical Arts Journal* 1.3 (1978), 25–6.

Cohen, Robyn. 'Delving into the *Heart of Redness* with Zakes Mda'. *Cape Times* (30 November 2000), 11.

Cohen, Tim and Rehana Rossouw. 'Search for SA's Best Book Is a Story in Itself'. *Weekender* (17–18 June 2006), Weekend Review, 1–2.

Colebrook, Claire. *New Literary Histories: New Historicism and Contemporary Criticism*. Manchester: Manchester University Press, 1997.

Colleran, Jeanne. 'South African Theatre in the United States: The Allure of the Familiar and of the Exotic'. In Derek Attridge and Rosemary Jolly (eds) *Writing South Africa: Literature, Apartheid and Democracy, 1970–1995*. Cambridge: Cambridge University Press, 1998, 221–36.

Collins, Harold R. '"Cry, the Beloved Country" and the Broken Tribe'. *College English* 14.7 (April 1953), 379–85.

Collins, Mandy. 'Playwright a Dab Hand at Novels. *SHE PLAYS WITH THE DARKNESS* by Zakes Mda (Unpublished Manuscript)'. *Sunday Times* (9 July 1995), 23.

Cooper, Brenda. Review of *Ways of Dying*. *World Literature Today* 70.1 (winter 1996), 228–34.

Comaroff, Jean and John Comaroff. *Of Revelation and Revolution: Christianity, Colonialism, and Consciousness in South Africa*. Chicago: Chicago University Press, 1991.

—— *Of Revelation and Revolution: The Dialectics of Modernity on a South African Frontier*. Chicago: Chicago University Press, 1997.

Comaroff, John and Homi K. Bhabha. 'Speaking of Postcoloniality, in the Continuous Present: A Conversation'. In D. T. Goldberg and A. Quayson (eds) *Relocating Postcolonialism*. Oxford: Blackwell, 2002, 15–46.

Coppard, A. E. 'The Ark Afloat'. *Saturday Review* 138 (16 August 1924), 171–2.

Cordell, Kirsten. 'Where the Heart Is'. *Fair Lady* (6 November 2002), 185.

Cowling, Lesley. 'The Beloved South African: Alan Paton in America', *Scrutiny 2* 10.2 (2005), 81–92.

Crehan, Stewart. 'Broken History'. *Southern African Review of Books* 8.4 (1996), 16–17.

Crewe, Jonathan. 'The Specter of Adamastor: Heroic Desire and Displacement in "White" South Africa'. *Modern Fiction Studies* 43.1 (spring 1997), 27–52.

Cronin, Jeremy. 'Turning Around: Roy Campbell's "Rounding the Cape"'. *English in Africa* 11.1 (May 1984), 65–78.

Cronwright-Schreiner, S. C. *The Life of Olive Schreiner*. London: Unwin, 1924.

—— Introduction. In Olive Schreiner, *The Story of an African Farm*. London: Unwin, 1924, 1–7.

Cunard, Nancy (ed.) *Negro: An Anthology*. 1934. abr. edn. ed. Hugh Ford. New York: Fred Ungar, 1970.

Cunningham, Valentine. *British Writers of the Thirties*. Oxford: Oxford University Press, 1988.

Currey, James. Interview with Andrew van der Vlies. Oxford, 18 September 2001.

—— 'Chinua Achebe, the African Writers Series and the Establishment of African Literature'. *African Affairs* 102 (2003), 575–85.

—— 'Publishing Bessie Head: Memories and Reflections'. *Wasafiri* 46 (winter 2005), 19–26.

Danby, Frank. 'The Case of Olive Schreiner'. *The Saturday Review of Politics, Literature, Science and Art* 83.2163 (10 April 1897), 388–9.

Dangor, Achmat. 'Mda's No Match for the Rich Fabric from Which He Draws His Material'. *Sunday Independent* (4 February 1996), 22.

Darnton, Robert. *The Kiss of Lamourette: Reflections in Cultural History*. London: Faber & Faber, 1990.

Davenport, T. R. H. and Christopher Saunders. *South Africa: A Modern History*. 5th edn. Houndmills: Macmillan, 2000.

Davies, David. E-mail to Andrew van der Vlies. 30 May 2002.

Davis, Peter. *In Darkest Hollywood: Exploring the Jungles of Cinema's South Africa*. Randburg: Ravan Press; Athens: Ohio University Press, 1996.

Dawson, W. J. 'Books That Have Moved Me: *The Story of an African Farm*'. *The Young Man* 5.50 (February 1891), 42–5.

De Kock, Leon. 'A Central South African Story, or Many Stories?'. *English Academy Review* 10 (1993), 45–55.

—— *Civilising Barbarians: Missionary Narrative and African Textual Response in Nineteenth-Century South Africa*. Johannesburg:

Witwatersrand University Press; Lovedale: Lovedale Press, 1996.

—— 'The Pursuit of Smaller Stories: Reconsidering the Limits of Literary History in South Africa'. In Johannes A. Smit, Johan van Wyk and Jean-Philippe Wade (eds) *Rethinking South African Literary History*. Durban: Y Press, 1996, 85–92.

—— 'An Impossible History'. *English in Africa* 24.1 (May 1997), 103–17.

—— 'South Africa in the Global Imaginary: An Introduction'. In Leon de Kock, Louise Bethlehem, and Sonja Laden (eds) *South Africa in the Global Imaginary*. Pretoria: University of South Africa Press; Leiden: Koninklijke Brill NV, 2004, 1–31.

De Lange, Margreet. *The Muzzled Muse: Literature and Censorship in South Africa*. Amsterdam and Philadelphia, PA: John Benjamins, 1997.

De Villiers, I. L. 'Notre Dame de Paris'. *Standpunte* [124] 3rd series, 29.4 (August 1976), 1–4.

Dekker, G. *Afrikaanse Literatuurgeskiedenis*. 12th edn. Cape Town: Nasou, 1974.

Deutsch, Karl W. 'The Growth of Nations: Some Recurrent Patterns of Political and Social Integration'. *World Politics* 5.2 (January 1953), 168–95.

Dick, Archie. 'Building a Nation of Readers? Women's Organizations and the Politics of Reading in South Africa, 1900–1914'. *Historia* 49.2 (2004), 23–44.

Dixon, Isobel. Interview with Andrew van der Vlies. London, 8 June 2006.

Dodd, Josephine. 'Naming and Framing: Naturalization and Colonization in J. M. Coetzee's *In the Heart of the Country*'. *World Literature Written in English* 27.2 (1987), 153–61.

Dovey, Teresa. 'Coetzee and His Critics: The Case of *Dusklands*'. *English in Africa* 14.2 (1987), 15–30.

—— *The Novels of J. M. Coetzee: Lacanian Allegories*. Johannesburg: Donker, 1988.

Dowling, Fionuala. 'Zakes Mda's Magical Sleight of Mind Reveals Our Way of Dying as Our Way of Living: *Ways of Dying* by Zakes Mda'. *Sunday Independent* (15 June 1997), 22.

Dugard, John. 'Censorship in South Africa: The Legal Framework'. In Gordimer et al. *What Happened to Burger's Daughter: Or, How South African Censorship Works*. Emmarentia: Taurus, 1980, 67–73.

Easley, Alexis. *First-Person Anonymous: Women Writers and Victorian Print Media, 1830–1870*. Aldershot: Ashgate, 2004.

'Ebony Awards for 1948'. *Ebony* 4.5 (March 1949), 34–5.

Eggert, Paul. '*Robbery Under Arms*: The Colonial Market, Imperial Publishers, and the Demise of the Three-Decker Novel'. *Book History* 6 (2003), 27–46.

Ehmeir, Walter. 'Publishing South African Literature in English in the

1960s'. *Research in African Literatures* 26.1 (spring 1995), 111–31.

Eliot, T. S. 'Tristan da Cunha' (Letter). *New Statesman* 30.756 (22 October 1927), 44.

Ellis, Havelock. *My Life*. London: Heinemann, 1940.

Ellis, Mark Spencer. Introduction. In Alan Paton, *Cry, the Beloved Country*. Ed. Mark Spencer Ellis. London: Longman, 1986, vii–xxi.

—— E-mail to Andrew van der Vlies. 8 March 2002.

—— Interview with Andrew van der Vlies. London, 29 May 2002.

Ellison, Ralph. 'The Art of Fiction: An Interview'. 1955. In *The Collected Essays of Ralph Ellison*. Ed. John F. Callahan. New York: Modern Library 1995, 210–24.

Emerson, Jacqueline. E-mail to Andrew van der Vlies. 28 May 2002.

English, James F. *The Economy of Prestige: Prizes, Awards, and the Circulation of Cultural Value*. Cambridge, MA, and London: Harvard University Press, 2005.

Enright, D. J. 'The Thing Itself'. *Times Literary Supplement* (20 September 1983), 1037.

Evans, David. *The Novel as Political Tract: A Reassessment of Alan Paton's* Cry, the Beloved Country, Working Paper. Liverpool: University of Liverpool School of Extension Studies, 1986.

Farred, Grant. 'Mourning the Postapartheid State Already? The Poetics of Loss in Zakes Mda's *Ways of Dying*'. *Modern Fiction Studies* 46.1 (spring 2000), 183–206.

Fausset, Hugh I. A. 'Books of the Day'. *Manchester Guardian* (8 October 1948), 3.

Ferguson, Margaret, Mary Jo Salter and Jon Stallworthy (eds) *The Norton Anthology of Poetry*. 4th edn. New York: W. W. Norton, 1996.

Finkelstein, David and Alistair McCleery (eds) Introduction. *The Book History Reader*. London: Routledge, 2002, 1–4.

First, Ruth and Ann Scott. *Olive Schreiner*. London: André Deutsch, 1980. Repr. London: Women's Press, 1989.

Fitzmaurice, Susan. 'Aspects of Afrikaans in South African Literature in English'. In J. J. Cribb (ed.) *Imagined Commonwealths: Cambridge Essays on Commonwealth and International Literature in English*. Houndmills: Macmillan, 1999, 166–90.

Fletcher, Pauline. '*Dusklands*'. *Reality* (July 1974), 11–13.

Flint, Kate. *The Woman Reader: 1837–1914*. Oxford: Clarendon, 1993.

—— 'The Victorian Novel and its Readers'. In Deidre David (ed.) *The Cambridge Companion to the Victorian Novel*. Cambridge: Cambridge University Press, 2001, 17–36.

Fourie, Bobby. 'SHE PLAYS WITH DARKNESS and WAYS OF DYING BY ZAKES MDA'. *Sunday Independent* (14 July 1996), Sunday Life, 29.

Frankel, Max. 'Seven Seas East of the Wall'. *New York Times* (10 January 1965), Section 7.2, 3, 32–33.

Galloway, Francis. 'Statistical Trends in South African Book Publishing During the 1990s'. *Alternation* 9.1 (2002), 202–25.

—— and Rudi M. R. Venter. 'Book History, Publishing Research and Production Figures: The Case of Afrikaans Fiction Production During the Transitional Period 1990–2003'. *South African Historical Journal* 55 (2006), 46–65.

Gardener, J. B. 'The English-Speaking Pupil and South African Set-Books'. *English Studies in Africa* 13.1 (1970), 21–36.

Gardiner, Harold C. 'On Saying "Boo!" to Geese'. *America* (13 March 1948), 661–2.

Geertz, Clifford. *The Interpretation of Cultures: Selected Essays*. 1973. New York: Basic Books, 2000.

Genette, Gérard. *Paratexts: Thresholds of Interpretation*. Trans. Jane E. Lewin. 1987. Cambridge: Cambridge University Press, 1997.

George, Daniel. '"Evil City" Makes First Time Winner'. *Daily Express* (28 September 1948). APC, PC1/1/1/2–3.

Gikandi, Simon. 'Globalization and the Claims of Postcoloniality'. *South Atlantic Quarterly* 100.3 (2001), 627–58.

Gillow, John. *African Textiles*. London: Thames & Hudson; San Francisco: Chronicle Books, 2003.

Glenn, Ian. 'The Production and Prevention of the Colonial Author: The Case of Daphne Rooke'. *New Contrast* 22.1 (March 1994), 78–85.

—— 'Game Hunting in *In the Heart of the Country*'. In Graham Huggan and Stephen Watson (eds) *Critical Perspectives on J. M. Coetzee*. Houndmills: Macmillan, 1996, 120–37.

Gordimer, Nadine. 'The Last Colonial Poet?'. *Snarl* 1.1 (1974), 1–2.

—— 'The Prison-House of Colonialism'. *Times Literary Supplement* (15 August 1980), 918.

—— 'What Happened to *Burger's Daughter*'. In Gordimer et al. *What Happened to* Burger's Daughter. Emmarentia: Taurus, 1980. 1–3.

—— 'The Idea of Gardening'. *New York Review of Books* (2 February 1984), 3–6.

—— John Dugard, Richard Smith, Director of Publications, Committee of Publications, Publications Appeals Board and the Press. *What Happened to* Burger's Daughter: *Or, How South African Censorship Works*. Emmarentia: Taurus, 1980.

Gray, Stephen. 'The Myth of Adamastor in South African Literature'. *Theoria* 48 (1977), 1–23.

—— *Southern African Literature: An Introduction*. Cape Town: David Philip; London: Rex Collins, 1979.

—— 'Opening Southern African Studies Post-Apartheid'. *Research in African Literatures* 30.1 (spring 1999), 207–15. Reprinted in *English in Africa* 26.1 (May 1999), 107–17.

Green, Michael. 'Resisting a National Literary History'. In Johannes A. Smit, Johan van Wyk and Jean-Philippe Wade (eds) *Rethinking South*

African Literary History. Durban: Y Press, 1996, 224–35.

Green, M. S. 'Book Review: Grave and Sombre Words'. *British Africa Monthly* (October 1948), 7.

Green, Robert. 'Stability and Flux: The Allotropic Narrative of *An African Farm*'. 1982. In Cherry Clayton (ed.) *Olive Schreiner*. Johannesburg: McGraw-Hill, 1983, 158–69.

Greetham, D. C. *Textual Scholarship: An Introduction*. New York: Garland, 1992.

Griest, Guinevere L. *Mudie's Circulating Library and the Victorian Novel*. Bloomington: Indiana University Press, 1970.

Griffiths, Gareth. *African Literatures in English: East and West*. Harlow: Longman, 2000.

Grigely, Joseph. *Textualterity: Art, Theory, and Textual Criticism*. Ann Arbor: University of Michigan Press, 1995.

Gross, John. 'South Africa Presented in its Own Eloquence: Sensation Omitted as Hurt People Speak'. (Hartford, CT) *Times* (14 February 1948). APC, PC1/1/1/2.

Gross, John. *The Rise and Fall of the Man of Letters: Aspects of English Literary Life Since 1800*. 1969. Harmondsworth: Penguin, 1973.

Gross, Robert A. 'Books, Nationalism, and History'. *Papers of the Bibliographical Society of Canada* 36.2 (fall 1998), 107–23.

Gupta, Abhijit, and Swapan Chakravorty (eds) *Print Areas: Book History in India*. Delhi: Permanent Black, 2004.

Haffenden, John. *William Empson*, vol. 1: *Among the Mandarins*. Oxford: Oxford University Press, 2005.

Haggard, H. Rider. 'About Fiction'. *Contemporary Review* 51 (February 1887), 172–80.

Haggerston, W. J. (ed.) *Newcastle-upon-Tyne: Alphabetical List of Books Added to the Lending and Juvenile Departments (1887–89)*. 2nd edn. Newcastle-upon-Tyne: Andrew Reid, 1889.

Hall, David D. 'The History of the Book: New Questions? New Answers?'. *Journal of Library History Philosophy and Comparative Librarianship* 21.1 (winter 1986), 27–38.

—— *Cultures of Print: Essays in the History of the Book*. Amherst: University of Massachusetts Press, 1996.

Hall, Michael. *Francis Brett Young*. Bridgend: Seren, 1997.

Hallett, Caroline M. *Parish Lending Libraries: How to Manage and Keep Them Up. With a List of Books*. London: Walter Smith & Innes, 1888.

Hannigan, D. F. 'The Artificiality of English Novels'. *Westminster Review* 133.3 (March 1890), 254–64.

Hansen, Harry. 'A Gentle Protest'. *The Graphic Survey* (March 1948). APC, PC1/1/1/2.

Harries, Patrick. 'Missionaries, Marxists and Magic: Power and the Politics of Literacy in South-East Africa'. *Journal of Southern African Studies* 27.3 (September 2001), 405–27.

Harris, Frank. *Contemporary Portraits*. 4th series. London: Grant Richards, 1925.

Hartzenberg, Meg. E-mail correspondence with Andrew van der Vlies. 22 February 2001.

Harwood, Ronald. 'An Astonishing First Novel'. *Sunday Times* (12 June 1977), 41.

Hassam, Andrew. *Through Australian Eyes: Colonial Perceptions of Imperial Britain*. Melbourne: Melbourne University Press, 2000.

Hänsel, Marion. Dir. *Dust*. Adapted from J. M.Coetzee's *In the Heart of the Country*. Man's Films, Daska Films International, Flach Films, FR3 Production France, La Communaute Française de Belgique, De Ministerie van de Vlaamse Gemeenschap, 1985.

Head, Dominic. *J. M. Coetzee*. Cambridge: Cambridge University Press, 1997.

Herron, Shaun. 'A Great Novel Comes Out of Africa'. *British Weekly* (11 November 1948), 4.

Herwitz, Daniel. 'Modernism at the Margins'. In Hilton Judin and Ivan Vladislavić (eds) *Blank __ Architecture, Apartheid and After*. Rotterdam: NAi, 1998, 405–21.

Herzberg, Lily. 'Dr. Joseph Sachs: Aesthete'. *Southern African Jewish Times* (18 August 1961), 17.

Heywood, Christopher. *A History of South African Literature*, Cambridge and Cape Town: Cambridge University Press, 2004.

Hibberd, Dominic. *Harold Monro: Poet of the New Age*. Houndmills: Palgrave, 2001.

Hill, Alan. *In Pursuit of Publishing*. London: John Murray, 1988.

Hofmeyr, Isabel. 'The Frenzy of Desire'. *Africa Perspective* 8 (July 1978), 83–4.

—— '"Setting Free the Books": The David Philip Africasouth Paperback Series'. *English in Africa* 12.1 (May 1985), 83–95.

—— *We Spend Our Years as a Tale That Is Told: Oral Historical Narrative in a South African Chiefdom*. Johannesburg: Witwatersrand University Press; Oxford: James Currey; Portsmouth, NH: Heinemann, 1993.

—— 'Metaphorical Books'. *Current Writing* 13.2 (2001), 100–8

—— 'From Book Development to Book History: Some Observations on the History of the Book in Africa'. *SHARP News* 13.1 (summer 2004), 3–4.

—— '"Spread Far and Wide over the Surface of the Earth': Evangelical Reading Formations and the Rise of a Transnational Public Sphere – the case of the Cape Town Ladies' Bible Association'. *English Studies in Africa* 47.1 (2004), 17–29.

—— and Lize Kriel (eds) 'Book History in Southern Africa: What Is it and Why Should it Interest Historians?'. *South African Historical Journal* 55 (2006), 1–19.

—— and Sarah Nuttall, with Cheryl Ann Michael (eds) *Current Writing: Text and Reception in Southern Africa* 13.2 (2001).

Holtby, Winifred. 'The Voorloper Group'. *New Statesman* (13 August 1927), 568–9.

—— 'They Speak of Africa', *Time and Tide* (30 September 1927), 864.

—— 'Writers of South Africa'. *The Bookman* (September 1929), 279–83.

Howard, Michael S. *Jonathan Cape, Publisher: Herbert Jonathan Cape, G. Wren Howard*. London: Jonathan Cape, 1971.

Huggan, Graham. *The Postcolonial Exotic: Marketing the Margins*. London and New York: Routledge, 2001.

Huxley, Leonard. *The House of Smith Elder*. London: privately printed, 1927.

Huddleston, Trevor. *Naught for Your Comfort*. London: Collins, 1956.

Iannone, Carol. 'Alan Paton's Tragic Liberalism'. *American Scholar* 66.3 (1997), 442–51.

Iloegbunam, Chuks. 'The Write Stuff'. *West Africa* (10–16 April 1995), 561–3.

Inkster, Lawrence. *Battersea Public Libraries: Central Library, Lavender Hill, S. W. Catalogue of the Lending Library*. London: Truslove & Bray, 1890.

J. M. 'The Reviewer Reviewed'. *The Torch* (29 November 1948), 5.

Jacobson, Dan. 'Nostalgia for the Future'. *Times Literary Supplement* (29 July–4 August 1988), 830.

James, Louis. 'The Protest Tradition: *Black Orpheus* and *Transition*'. In Cosmo Pieterse and Donald Munro (eds) *Protest and Conflict in African Literature*. London: Heinemann, 1969, 109–23.

Jameson, Fredric. 'Third-World Literature in the Era of Multinational Capitalism'. *Social Text* 15 (fall 1986), 65–88.

JanMohamed, Abdul R. 'Alex La Guma: The Literary and Political Function of Marginality in the Colonial Situation'. *Boundary 2* 11.1–2 (fall–winter 1982–83), 271–90.

Jauss, Hans Robert. *Toward an Aesthetic of Reception*. Trans. Timothy Bahti. Brighton: Harvester, 1982.

John, Philip. 'Oprakelings nie Altyd Letterkunde'. *Die Burger* (13 January 2003), 9.

Johns, Adrian. *The Nature of the Book: Print and Knowledge in the Making*. Chicago: University of Chicago Press, 1998.

Johnston, Henry. *Chronicles of Glenbuckie*. Edinburgh: David Douglas, 1889.

Jolly, Rosemary. 'Rehearsals of Liberation: Contemporary Postcolonial Discourse and the New South Africa'. *Publications of the Modern Language Association of America* 110.1 (January 1995), 17–29.

Jonathan Cape. 'Threshing'. Advertisement. *Spectator* 5001 (3 May 1924), 719.

Jordan, John O. and Robert Patten (eds) *Literature in the Marketplace:*

Nineteenth-Century Publishing and Reading Practices. Cambridge: Cambridge University Press, 1995.

Joshi, Priya. *In Another Country: Colonialism, Culture, and the English Novel in India*. New Delhi: Oxford University Press, 2002.

Judd, Catherine A. 'Male Pseudonyms and Female Authority in Victorian England'. In John O. Jordan and Robert Patten (eds) *Literature in the Marketplace: Nineteenth-Century Publishing and Reading Practices*. Cambridge: Cambridge University Press, 1995, 250–68.

July, Robert W. 'African Personality: African Literature and the African Personality'. *Black Orpheus* 14 (February 1964), 33–45.

Kgositsile, Keorapetse. 'History, Myth and Magic Are Interwoven to Create a Palpable World: *She Plays with the Darkness* by Zakes Mda'. *Sunday Independent* (12 November 1995), 22.

Killam, Douglas and Ruth Rowe (eds) *The Companion to African Literatures*. Oxford: James Currey; Bloomington: Indiana University Press, 2000.

King, Bruce. 'New Centres of Consciousness: New, Post-Colonial and International English Literature'. In Bruce King (ed.) *New National and Post-Colonial Literatures: An Introduction*. Oxford: Clarendon, 1996, 3–26.

Kirkwood, Mike. '*Staffrider*: An Informal Discussion'. Interview with Nick Visser. *English in Africa* 7.2 (September 1980), 22–31.

—— Interview with Andrew van der Vlies. York, 6 June 2006.

Knight, Donald R. and Alan D. Sabey. *The Lion Roars at Wembley: British Empire Exhibition 60th Anniversary 1924–1925*. New Barnet: D. R. Knight, 1984.

Koch, Adrienne. 'Comfort in Desolation'. *The Saturday Review of Literature* (14 February 1948). APC, PC1/1/1/2.

Komai, Felicia with Josephine Douglas. *Cry, the Beloved Country: A Verse Drama Adapted from Alan Paton's Novel*. London: Edinburgh House, 1954.

Kramer, Jane. 'In the Garrison'. *New York Review of Books* (2 December 1982), 8–12.

Krebs, Paula M. *Gender, Race and the Writing of Empire*. Cambridge: Cambridge University Press, 1999.

Kruger, Loren. 'Apartheid on Display: South Africa Performs for New York'. *Diaspora* 1.2 (1991), 191–208.

—— and Patricia Watson Shariff. '"Shoo – This Book Makes Me to Think!" Education, Entertainment and "Life Skills" Comics in South Africa'. In Leon de Kock, Louise Bethlehem and Sonja Laden (eds) *South Africa in the Global Imaginary*. Pretoria: University of South Africa Press; Leiden: Koninklijke Brill NV, 2004, 214–47.

Krige, Uys (ed.) Introduction. *Olive Schreiner: A Selection*. Cape Town: Oxford University Press, 1968, 1–30.

Laden, Sonja. '"Making the Paper Speak Well", or, the Pace of Change in

Consumer Magazines for Black South Africans'. In Leon de Kock, Louise Bethlehem, and Sonja Laden (eds) *South Africa in the Global Imaginary*. Pretoria: University of South Africa Press; Leiden: Koninklijke Brill NV, 2004, 248–77.

La Guma, Alex. *A Walk in the Night*. Ibadan: Mbari, 1962.

—— *And a Threefold Cord*. Berlin: Seven Seas, 1964.

—— *A Walk in the Night and Other Stories*. London: Heinemann, 1967.

—— *The Stone Country*. Berlin: Seven Seas, 1967.

—— *A Walk in the Night and Other Stories*. African Writers Series 35. London: Heinemann Educational, 1968.

—— 'Address by Lotus Award Winner'. *Lotus: Afro-Asian Writings* (October 1971), 195–7.

—— Interview with Robert Serumaga, London (October 1966). In Dennis Duerden and Cosmo Pieterse (eds) *African Writers Talking: A Collection of Interviews*. London: Heinemann, 1972. 90–3.

—— *In the Fog of the Seasons' End*. African Writers Series 110. London: Heinemann Educational, 1972.

—— *The Stone Country*. African Writers Series 152. London: Heinemann Educational, 1974.

—— *Time of the Butcherbird*. African Writers Series 212. London: Heinemann Educational, 1979.

—— *A Walk in the Night and Other Stories*. Africasouth. Cape Town: David Philip, 1991.

—— 'The Real Picture: Interview with Cecil Abrahams'. In Cecil Abrahams (ed.) *Memories of Home: The Writings of Alex La Guma*. Trenton, NJ: Africa World, 1991, 15–29.

La Guma, Blanche. 'Alex La Guma: A Wife's Memory'. In Cecil Abrahams (ed.) *Memories of Home: The Writings of Alex La Guma*. Trenton, NJ: Africa World, 1991, 7–14.

—— Interview with Andrew van der Vlies. Cape Town, 7 September 2001.

Lambert, John. 'South African British? Or Dominion South Africans? The Evolution of an Identity in the 1910s and 1920s'. *South African Historical Journal* 43 (November 2000), 197–222.

Land, S. 'The State of Book Development in South Africa'. *Journal of Education* 29 (2003), 93–124.

Larson, Charles R. *The Ordeal of the African Writer*. London: Zed Books, 2001.

Lazarus, Neil. *Nationalism and Cultural Practice in the Postcolonial World*. Cambridge: Cambridge University Press, 1999.

Leistikow, Nicole. 'Marketing Bessie Head: Collections, Classifications and the Negotiation of History'. Unpublished M.Phil thesis. Oxford: Oxford University, 2001. Bodleian Library. MS M.Phil.c.2462.

Levin, Bernard. 'On the Edge of the Empire'. *Sunday Times* (23 November 1980), 44.

Lewis, Ethelreda. 'The State of Literature'. *The South African Nation* 3.131 (9 October 1926), 13–14.

Lindfors, Bernth. 'Post-War Literature in English by African Writers from South Africa: A Study of the Effects of Environment upon Literature'. *Phylon* 27.1 (1966), 50–62.

Lloyd, David. 'The Modernization of Redness'. *Scrutiny 2* 6.2 (2001), 34–9.

Locke, Alain. 'Dawn Patrol: A Review of the Literature of the Negro for 1948: Part 1'. *Phylon* 10.1 (1949), 5–14.

Louw, Anna M. ''n Onvergeetlike Indruk'. *Die Burger* (2 December 1977), 2.

—— ''n Fyn Geslypte Metafoor'. *Beeld* (23 January 1978), 10.

—— '*In the Heart of the Country*: A Calvinist Allegory?' *PN Review* 14.2 (1987), 50–2.

Low, Gail. '"Finding the Centre?" Publishing Commonwealth Writing in London: The Case of Anglophone Caribbean Writing 1950–1965'. *Journal of Commonwealth Literature* 37.2 (2002), 21–38.

—— 'In Pursuit of Publishing: Heinemann's African Writers Series'. *Wasafiri* 37 (winter 2002), 31–5.

Lynch, Deidre and William B. Warner (eds) 'Introduction: The Transport of the Novel'. *Cultural Institutions of the Novel*. Durham, NC, and London: Duke University Press, 1996, 1–10.

Macnab, Roy. *The Story of South Africa House – South Africa in Britain: The Changing Pattern*. Johannesburg: Jonathan Ball, 1983.

Maja-Pearce, Adewale. 'Publishing African Literature – in Pursuit of Excellence: Thirty Years of the Heinemann African Writers' Series'. *Research in African Literatures* 23.4 (winter 1992), 125–32.

Marquard, Jean. 'Strength Lies in Using Novel as Critical Tool'. *Oggendblad* (28 April 1978), 1. Reprinted (revised) as 'Novel as Critical Tool'. *Contrast* [45] 12.1 (1978), 83–6.

Marx, Eleanor. 'Underground Russia'. *Progress* 2 (September 1883), 172–6.

Matlaw, Myron. 'Alan Paton's *Cry, the Beloved Country* and Maxwell Anderson's/Kurt Weill's *Lost in the Stars*: A Consideration of Genres'. *Arcadia: Zeitschrift für Vergleichende Literaturwissenschaft* 10.3 (1975), 260–72.

Matz, B. W. 'George Meredith as Publishers' Reader'. *The Fortnightly Review*, n.s. 92.512 (August 1909), 282–98.

McClintock, Anne. '"Azikwelwa" (We Will Not Ride): Politics and Value in Black South African Poetry'. *Critical Inquiry* 13.3 (spring 1987), 597–623.

McDonald, Peter. D. *British Literary Culture and Publishing Practice 1880–1914*. Cambridge: Cambridge University Press, 1997.

—— 'Implicit Structures and Explicit Interactions: Pierre Bourdieu and the History of the Book'. *The Library* 6th series 19.2 (June 1997), 107–21.

—— '"Not Undesirable": How J. M. Coetzee Escaped the Censor'. *Times Literary Supplement* (19 May 2000), 14–15.

—— 'Modernist Publishing: "Nomads and Mapmakers"'. In David Bradshaw (ed.) *A Concise Companion to Modernism*. Oxford: Blackwell, 2003, 221–42.

—— 'The Writer, the Critic and the Censor: J. M.Coetzee and the Question of Literature'. *Book History* 7 (2004), 285–302.

McGann, Jerome J. *The Beauty of Inflections: Literary Investigations in Historical Method and Theory*. Oxford: Clarendon, 1985.

—— *The Textual Condition*. Princeton, NJ: Princeton University Press, 1991.

McGonegal, Julie. 'Postcolonial Metacritique: Jameson, Allegory and the Always-Already-Read Third World Text'. *Interventions* 7.2 (2005), 251–65.

McKenzie, D. F. *The Panizzi Lectures, 1985: Bibliography and the Sociology of Texts*. London: British Library, 1986.

Mda, Zakes. *When People Play People: Development Communication Through Theatre*. Johannesburg: Witwatersrand University Press; London and New Jersey: Zed Books, 1993.

—— *She Plays with the Darkness*. Johannesburg: Vivlia, 1995; New York: Picador, 2004.

—— *Ways of Dying*. Cape Town: Oxford University Press, 1995, 1997; New York: Picador, 2002.

—— *The Heart of Redness*. Cape Town: Oxford University Press South Africa, 2000.

—— *Melville 67: A Novella for Youth*. Johannesburg: Vivlia, 2002.

—— *The Heart of Redness*. New York: Farrar, Straus & Giroux, 2002.

—— *The Madonna of Excelsior*. Cape Town: Oxford University Press, 2002; New York: Farrar, Straus & Giroux, 2004; New York: Picador, 2005.

—— *The Heart of Redness*. New York: Picador, 2003.

—— *The Whale Caller*. Cape Town: Penguin South Africa; London: Viking Penguin; New York: Farrar, Straus & Giroux, 2005.

—— Telephone interview with Andrew van der Vlies, 6 April 2006.

Medalie, David. '"Keeping History Open": Studies in South African Literary History'. *Journal of Southern African Studies* 25.2 (June 1999), 303–10.

Mégroz, R. L. (ed.) *A Treasury of Modern Poetry: An Anthology of the Last Forty Years*. London: Pitman, 1936.

Meredith, George. *The Letters of George Meredith*. 3 vols. Ed. C. L. Cline. Oxford: Clarendon, 1970.

Merrett, Christopher. *A Culture of Censorship: Secrecy and Intellectual Repression in South Africa*. Cape Town: David Philip; Pietermaritzburg: University of KwaZulu-Natal Press; Macon, GA: Mercer University Press, 1994.

Mervis, Margaret. 'Fiction for Development: Zakes Mda's *Ways of Dying*'. *Current Writing* 10.1 (1998), 39–56.

Michell, John. 'Local Hemingway Has Subtle Rhythm. *She Plays with the Darkness* by Zakes Mda'. *Sunday Times* (24 September 1995), 21.

Miles, Hamish. Review of *The Flaming Terrapin*. *The Dial* 77 (November 1924), 423–5.

Millin, S. G. 'A South African Magazine: Is "Voorslag" What it Ought to Be?'. *Rand Daily Mail* (16 June 1926), 8.

Modisane, William (Bloke). 'The Dignity of Begging'. *The African Drum* 1.6 (September 1951), 4–5.

—— 'African Writers' Summit'. *Transition* 5 (August 1962), 5–6.

Mokone, Tumo. 'Mda Mixes Styles and Gets it Right: *SHE PLAYS WITH THE DARKNESS* BY ZAKES MDA'. *City Press* (3 September 1995), 24.

Molakeng, Saint P. 'Wide-Ranging Debate on SA Now and Then'. *Sowetan* (19 January 2001), 14.

Monro, Harold. Review of *The Flaming Terrapin*. *The Criterion* 3.144 (October 1924), 147–8.

—— (ed.) Introduction. *Twentieth-Century Poetry*. London: Chatto & Windus, 1929, 7–11.

—— Review of *Adamastor*. *The Criterion* 10.39 (January 1931), 352–3.

Monsman, Gerald. *Olive Schreiner's Fiction: Landscape and Power*. New Brunswick: Rutgers University Press, 1991.

Moosa, Valli. 'Lend a Hand for Sustainable Development, People, Planet and Prosperity: Budget Vote Speech of the Minister of Environmental Affairs and Tourism, Valli Moosa, 9 May 2002'. South African Ministry of Environmental Affairs and Tourism, 9 May 2002.

Morgan, Charles. *The House of Macmillan (1843–1943)*. London: Macmillan, 1943.

Morphet, Tony. Review of *Dusklands*. *Bolt* 11 (December 1974), 58–61.

—— 'Two Interviews with J. M. Coetzee, 1983 and 1987'. In David Bunn and Jane Taylor (eds) *From South Africa: New Writings, Photographs & Art*. Special issue. *TriQuarterly* 69 (spring–summer 1987), 454–64.

—— 'Stranger Fictions: Trajectories in the Liberal Novel'. *World Literature Today* 70.1 (winter 1996), 53–8.

Morrison, Blake. 'Veldschmerz' (Review of *In the Heart of the Country*). *Times Literary Supplement* (22 July 1977), 900.

Mortimer, Raymond. 'New Books for the Morning Room Table'. *Vogue* 63.12 (June 1924), 94.

Mpe, Phaswane and Monica Seeber. 'The Politics of Book Publishing in South Africa: A Critical Overview'. In Nicholas Evans and Monica Seeber (eds) *The Politics of Publishing in South Africa*. Scottsville: University of Natal Press, 2000, 15–42.

Mphahlele, Ezekiel/Es'kia. 'What the South African Negro Reads and Writes'. *Presence Africaine* 16 (1957), 171–5.

—— 'Mbari: 1st Anniversary'. *Africa Report* 7.11 (December 1962), 17.

—— *The African Image.* 1964. 2nd rev. edn. London: Faber & Faber, 1974.

—— 'Writers and Commitment'. In Ulli Beier (ed.) *Introduction to African Literature: An Anthology of Critical Writing.* New edn. London: Longman, 1979, vii–xvii.

—— *Afrika My Music: An Autobiography 1957–1983.* Johannesburg: Ravan, 1984.

Mudie's Select Library. *Catalogue of the Principal Books in Circulation at Mudie's Select Library.* London: Mudie's, 1888–1893.

Nakasa, Nat. 'Writing in South Africa'. *The Classic* 1.1 (1963). Reprinted in Michael Chapman (ed.) *Soweto Poetry.* Johannesburg: McGraw-Hill, 1982, 35–40.

Nathan, Manfred. *The South African Commonwealth.* Johannesburg and Cape Town: Speciality Press, 1919.

—— *South African Literature: A General Survey.* Cape Town and Johannesburg: Juta, 1925.

Ndebele, Njabulo S. *South African Literature and Culture: Rediscovery of the Ordinary.* Manchester: Manchester University Press, 1994.

Newbolt, Henry (ed.) Preface. *New Paths on Helicon.* London: Thomas Nelson, 1927, ix–xvi.

Ngiyeke, Bulima. ''Mlung' Ungazikhohlisi (White Man, Do Not Deceive Yourself)'. Trans. G. R. Dent. *The African Drum* 1.7 (October 1951), 11.

Nims, John Frederick. 'Grim View of Family Life in South Africa'. *Chicago Tribune* (15 February 1948). APC, PC 1/1/1/2.

Nixon, Rob. *Homelands, Harlem and Hollywood: South African Culture and the World Beyond.* New York: Routledge, 1994.

Nkosi, Lewis. 'African Fiction: Part One. South Africa: Protest'. *Africa Report* 7.9 (October 1962), 3–6.

—— 'Annals of Apartheid'. *New Statesman* (29 January 1965), 164–5.

—— *Home and Exile.* London: Longmans, Green, 1965.

—— 'Fiction by Black South Africans'. 1966. In Ulli Beier (ed.) *Introduction to African Literature: An Anthology of Critical Writing from 'Black Orpheus'.* London: Longmans, Green, 1967, 211–17.

—— 'Constructing the "Cross-Border" Reader'. In Elleke Boehmer, Laura Chrisman, Kenneth Parker (eds) *Altered State? Writing and South Africa.* Sydney: Dangeroo, 1994, 37–49.

—— 'The Republic of Letters After the Mandela Republic'. 2002. In Lindy Stiebel and Liz Gunner (eds) *Still Beating the Drum: Critical Perspectives on Lewis Nkosi.* Amsterdam and New York: Rodopi, 2005, 311–30.

Norman, Henry. 'Theories and Practices of Modern Fiction'. *The Fortnightly Review,* n.s. 34.104 (1 December 1883), 870–86.

Nowell-Smith, Simon. *International Copyright Law and the Publisher in the Reign of Queen Victoria*. Oxford: Clarendon, 1968.

Nuttall, Sarah. 'Reading in the Lives and Writing of Black Women', *Journal of Southern African Studies* 20.1 (1994), 85–98.

—— 'Literature and the Archive: The Biography of Text'. In Carolyn Hamilton, Verne Harris, Jane Taylor, Michele Pickover, Graeme Reid and Rezia Saleh (eds) *Refiguring the Archive*. Cape Town: David Philip, 2002, 283–99.

—— 'Stylizing the Self: The Y Generation in Rosebank, Johannesburg', *Public Culture* 16 (2004), 430–52.

Ofeimun, Odia. 'Challenges to the AWS'. *West Africa* 3930 (18–24 January 1993), 56.

'Om'. 'The Poetry of Roy Campbell: VI. Latest Tendencies and Future Possibilities'. *Cape Times* (1928), 148. NLSA, Campbell Collection, MSB76.

Owen, Roger. 'Sunset in the West' (Review of *Dusklands*). *Times Literary Supplement* (14 January 1983), 30.

P. H. S. 'Now the Coloured Voice'. *The Times* (31 August 1967), 401.

Pajalich, Armando. 'The Influences of Vorticism on Roy Campbell's *The Flaming Terrapin*'. *English in Africa* 15.2 (October 1988), 13–23.

Parker, Kenneth (ed.) 'The South African Novel in English'. In *The South African Novel in English: Essays in Criticism and Society*. London: Macmillan, 1978, 1–26.

Parsons, D. S. J. 'Roy Campbell and Wyndham Lewis'. *Papers on Language and Literature* 7.4 (1971), 406–21.

—— *Roy Campbell: A Descriptive and Annotated Bibliography*. New York: Garland, 1981.

Patmore, Derek. 'Florentine Interlude'. *Harper's Bazaar* 6 (July 1932), 21, 82, 84.

Paton, Alan. *Cry, the Beloved Country: A Story of Comfort in Desolation*. New York: Scribner's, 1948.

—— *Cry, the Beloved Country: A Story of Comfort in Desolation*. London: Jonathan Cape, 1948.

—— *Cry, the Beloved Country*. abr. *Reader's Digest Condensed Books Spring 1950 Selections*. Vol. 1. New York: Reader's Digest, Inc., 1950. 395–571.

—— 'Cry, the Beloved Country'. Abr. *The African Drum* 1.1–1.9 (March–December 1951) and 2.1–2.4 (January–April 1952).

—— *Cry, the Beloved Country*. Ed. and abr. G. F. Wear and R. H. Durham. London: Longmans, Green, 1953.

—— 'The Negro in America Today'. *Collier's* 134 (15 October 1954), 20, 50–6.

—— 'The Negro in the North'. *Collier's* 134 (29 October 1954), 70–80.

—— *Cry, the Beloved Country*. Abr. *Reader's Digest Condensed Books Anthology*. Vol. 2. Montreal: Reader's Digest Condensed Book Club, 1956. 195–337.

—— *Cry, the Beloved Country*. Abr. *Reader's Digest Condensed Books*. Vol. 14. London, Sydney and Cape Town: Reader's Digest Association, 1958. 345–502.

—— *Cry, the Beloved Country*. Harmondsworth: Penguin, 1958, 1959, 1987, 2001.

—— *Cry, the Beloved Country*. Abr. and intro. J. E. Blacksell. London: Longmans, 1962.

—— *Cry, the Beloved Country*. Intro. Reynold Clark. London: Longman, 1966.

—— *Kontakion for You Departed*. London: Jonathan Cape, 1969.

—— *Towards the Mountain: An Autobiography*. Oxford: Oxford University Press, 1981.

—— *Cry, the Beloved Country*. Ed. Mark Spencer Ellis. Harlow: Longman, 1986.

—— *Journey Continued: An Autobiography*. Oxford: Oxford University Press, 1988.

—— *Cry, the Beloved Country*. Ed. Jennie Sidney. Harlow: Longman, 1991.

—— *Cry, the Beloved Country*. Ed. and abr. G. F. Wear and R. H. Durham. Simplified edn. Harlow: Longman, 1996.

—— *Cry, the Beloved Country*. Ed. and abr. G. F. Wear and R. H. Durham. Simplified edn. Harlow: Longman, 1999.

Pearce, Joseph. *Bloomsbury and Beyond: The Friends and Enemies of Roy Campbell*. London: Harper Collins, 2001.

Pechey, Graham. Introduction. In Njabulo S. Ndebele. *South African Literature and Culture: Rediscovery of the Ordinary*. Manchester: Manchester University Press, 1994, 1–16.

Penny, Sarah. 'A Literary Vox Pop'. Unpublished paper delivered at the 'Letters Home Festival: Exiles and Émigrés, South Africans Writing Abroad'. St John's College, Cambridge. 5 March 2004.

Petherick, Edward Augustus (ed.) *The Colonial Book Circular and Bibliographical Record* 1.1 (September 1887).

—— *The Torch and Colonial Book Circular, including Classified Lists of New English Books and of Publications Relating to, or Issued in, the British Colonies* 1.2 (December 1887).

—— *The Torch and Colonial Book Circular, including Classified Lists of New Publications, English, American, and Colonial, in All Departments of Literature* 1.3 (March 1888).

Phillips, Tom (ed.) *Africa: The Art of a Continent*. Munich, London and New York: Prestel and Royal Academy of Arts, 1999.

Pike, Henry R. *A History of Communism in South Africa*. Germiston: Christian Mission International of South Africa, 1985.

Plomer, William. *Turbott Wolfe*. London: Hogarth, 1925.

—— 'Pop! Goes the Gun'. *The South African Nation* 3.118 (10 July 1926), 29.

—— *I Speak of Africa*. London: Hogarth, 1927.

—— 'The Scorpion'. *The Nation and Athenaeum* (10 May 1930), 170.

—— *The Case Is Altered*. London: Hogarth, 1932.

—— *The Fivefold Screen*. London: Hogarth, 1932.

—— *Cecil Rhodes*. London: Peter Davies, 1933.

—— *The Child of Queen Victoria and Other Stories*. London: Jonathan Cape, 1933.

—— 'The Scorpion'. In *The Oxford Book of Modern Verse 1892–1935*. Ed. W. B. Yeats New York: Oxford University Press, 1936, 407–8.

—— *Visiting the Caves*. London: Jonathan Cape, 1936.

—— 'The Scorpion'. In *Poems of Twenty Years: An Anthology, 1918–1938*. Ed. Maurice Wollman. London: Macmillan, 1938, 220.

—— 'Some Books from New Zealand'. In *Folios of New Writing: Autumn 1941*. Ed. John Lehmann. London: Hogarth, 1941, 55–61.

—— 'The Scorpion'. In *Modern Verse: 1900–1940*. Ed. Phyllis M. Jones. London: Oxford University Press, 1941, 162.

—— *Double Lives: An* Autobiography. London: Jonathan Cape, 1943.

—— 'Coming to London'. In John Lehmann (ed.) *Coming to London*. London: Phoenix House, 1957, 13–35.

—— 'South African Writers and English Readers'. *Proceedings of a Conference of Writers, Publishers, Editors and University Teachers of English*. Johannesburg: Witwatersrand University Press, 1957, 54–72.

—— *At Home: Memoirs*. London: Jonathan Cape, 1958.

—— 'Voorslag Days'. *The London Magazine* 6 (July 1959), 46–52.

—— 'The Scorpion'. In Nancy Cunard (ed.) *Negro: An Anthology*. Abr. edn. Ed. Hugh Ford. New York: Fred Ungar, 1970, 268.

—— 'Three Letters'. In William Plomer, *Turbott Wolfe*. Ed. Stephen Gray. 1925. Johannesburg: Donker, 1980, 128–31.

Prescott, Orville. 'Books of the Times'. *New York Times* (2 February 1948), 17.

Radway, Janice A. *A Feeling for Books: The Book-of-the-Month Club, Literary Taste, and Middle-Class Desire*. Chapel Hill and London: University of North Carolina Press, 1997.

Rainey, Lawrence. *The Institutions of Modernism: Literary Elites and Public Culture*. New Haven, CT: Yale University Press, 1998.

Raiskin, Judith L. *Snow on the Cane Fields: Women's Writing and Creole Subjectivity*. Minneapolis: University of Minnesota Press, 1996.

Ranken, George. *Windabyne: A Record of By-Gone Time in Australia*. London and Sydney: Remington, 1895.

Ravilious, C. P. '"Saints and Sinners": An Unidentified Olive Schreiner Manuscript'. *Journal of Commonwealth Literature* 12.1 (August 1977), 1–11.

Ricard, Alain. *The Languages* and *Literatures of Africa: The Sands of Babel*. Trans. Naomi Morgan. Oxford: James Currey; Trenton, NJ: Africa World; Cape Town: David Philip, 2004.

Ridge, Stanley G. M. 'The Meaning of the Map: Considerations for a History of South African Literature'. *English in Africa* 18.2 (October 1991), 87–97.

Rive, Richard (ed.) *Quartet: New Voices from South Africa*. New York: Crown, 1963; London: Heinemann Educational, 1965.

Rivers, Gertrude B. 'Cry, the Beloved Country'. *Journal of Negro Education* 18.1 (winter 1949), 50–2.

Roberts, Michael (ed.) *New Signatures: Poems by Several Hands*. London: Hogarth, 1932.

—— (ed.) Preface. *New Country: Prose and Poetry by the authors of New Signatures*. London: Hogarth, 1933, 9–21.

—— (ed.) Introduction. *The Faber Book of Modern Verse*. Ed. Michael Roberts. London: Faber & Faber, 1936, 1–35.

Roscoe, Adrian. *Uhuru's Fire: African Literature East to South*. Cambridge: Cambridge University Press, 1977.

—— 'Writers in South Africa'. *Listener* 100.2583 (26 October 1978), 533.

Rose, Jonathan. 'How to Do Things with Book History'. *Victorian Studies* 37.3 (spring 1994), 461–71.

Rossouw, Henk. 'Mda's Twin Peak. THE HEART OF REDNESS by Zakes Mda'. *Mail & Guardian* (12–18 January 2001), Friday supplement, 5.

Rush, Norman. 'Apocalypse When?'. *New York Review of Books* (16 January 2003), 29–32.

Rutter, Karen. 'Metamorphosis, and the Ways of Living. *Ways of Dying*, Zakes Mda'. *Cape Times* (25 July 1997), 12.

S. Review of *Cry, the Beloved Country*. *Rand Daily Mail* (25 September 1948). NELM, Press Files.

Sachs, Albie. 'Preparing Ourselves for Freedom'. 1989. In Derek Attridge and Rosemary Jolly (eds) *Writing South Africa: Literature, Apartheid, and Democracy, 1970–1995*. Cambridge: Cambridge University Press, 1998, 239–48.

—— Interview with Andrew van der Vlies. London, 20 November 2001.

Sachs, Joseph. 'Books of the Month'. *Trek* 12.11 (November 1948), 25.

Said, Edward. *Orientalism*. London: Routledge & Kegan Paul, 1978.

Sambrook, Keith. Interview with Andrew van der Vlies. Oxford, 6 November 2001.

Samin, Richard. 'Marginality and History in Zakes Mda's *Ways of Dying*'. *Anglophonia: French Journal of English Studies* 7 (2000), 189–99.

Sampson, Anthony. *Drum: A Venture into the New Africa*. London: Collins, 1956.

Sanders, Mark. *Complicities: The Intellectual and Apartheid*. Durham and London: Duke University Press; Scottsville: University of Natal Press, 2002.

S. C. '"Cry, the Beloved Country": Another View'. *The Torch* (1 November 1948). APC, PC1/1/1/4–1.

Schoeman, Karel. *Olive Schreiner: A Woman in South Africa, 1855–1881.* Trans. Henri Snijders. 1989. Johannesburg: Jonathan Ball, 1991.

—— *Only an Anguish to Live Here: Olive Schreiner and the Anglo-Boer War, 1899–1902.* Cape Town: Human & Rousseau, 1992.

Schreiner, Olive (as Ralph Iron). *The Story of an African Farm: A Novel.* 2 vols. London: Chapman & Hall, January 1883.

—— (as Ralph Iron). *The Story of an African Farm: A Novel.* New edn. London: Chapman & Hall, July 1883.

—— (as Ralph Iron). *The Story of an African Farm: A Novel* (cover: *A Romance*). New (3rd) edn. London: Chapman & Hall, 1887.

—— 'A Dream of Wild Bees'. *The Woman's World* (November 1888), 3–4.

—— 'Professor Pearson on the Woman's Question'. *Pall Mall Gazette* 49. 7447 (29 January 1889), 3.

—— (as Ralph Iron). *The Story of an African Farm, A Novel.* London: Chapman & Hall, 1890.

—— (as Ralph Iron). *The Story of an African Farm, A Novel.* London: Chapman & Hall, 1891, 1892.

—— (as Ralph Iron). *The Story of an African Farm, A Novel.* London: Hutchinson, 1891, 1893, 1894, 1896.

—— *Trooper Peter Halket of Mashonaland.* London: Unwin, 1897.

—— *Woman and Labour.* London: Unwin, 1911.

—— *The Story of an African Farm, A Novel.* Intro. S. C. Cronwright-Schreiner. London: Unwin, 1924.

—— *The Letters of Olive Schreiner 1876–1920.* Ed. S. C. Cronwright-Schreiner. London: Unwin, 1925.

—— *The Story of an African Farm.* Intro. Dan Jacobson. Harmondsworth: Penguin, 1971, 1993, 1995.

—— *The Story of an African Farm.* Intro. Richard Rive. Johannesburg: Donker, 1975.

—— *The Story of an African Farm.* Intro. Cherry Clayton. Johannesburg: Donker, 1986.

—— *The Story of an African Farm.* Intro. Doris Lessing. London: Century Hutchinson, 1987.

—— *Olive Schreiner Letters.* Volume 1: *1871–1899.* Ed. Richard Rive, and Russell Martin, 1987. Oxford: Oxford University Press, 1988.

—— *The Story of an African Farm.* London: Virago, 1989.

—— *The Story of an African Farm.* Ed. and intro. Joseph Bristow. Oxford: Oxford University Press, 1992.

Scribner's. 'A Best-Seller Is Born!' Advertisement. *New York Times* (9 February 1948), 17.

—— Advertisement. *The Publishers' Weekly* (14 February 1948), 943.

Seeber, Monica, and Nicholas Evans (eds) *The Politics of Publishing in*

South Africa. Scottsville: University of KwaZulu-Natal Press, 2000.

Sepamla, Sipho. 'The Black Writer in South Africa Today: Problems and Dilemmas'. *New Classic* 3 (1976). Repr. in Michael Chapman (ed.) *Soweto Poetry*. Johannesburg: McGraw-Hill, 1982, 115–21.

Sharp, Joanne P. *Condensing the Cold War*: Reader's Digest *and American Identity*. Minneapolis: University of Minnesota Press, 2000.

Shore, Herbert L. 'A Note on South African Life and Letters', *Come Back, Africa! Fourteen Short Stories from South Africa*. Ed. Herbert L. Shore and Megchelina Shore-Bos. Berlin: Seven Seas, 1968, 15–37.

Silver, Louise. *A Guide to Political Censorship in South Africa*. Johannesburg: University of the Witwatersrand, 1984.

Sinclair, A. J. L. and P. H. Roodt. 'Dosent en Student'. *Standpunte* [124] 3rd series, 29.4 (August 1976), 29–35.

Sitwell, Osbert. 'The British Empire Exhibition'. *Vogue* 63.12 (June 1924), 43–5.

Slater, Francis Carey. Preface. *The Centenary Book of South African Verse*. Ed. Francis Carey Slater. London: Longman, Green, 1925, vii–xiv.

—— Preface. *New Centenary Book of South* African *Verse*. Ed. Francis Carey Slater. London: Longmans, Green, 1945. v–xi.

—— *Settler's Heritage*. Alice: Lovedale, 1954.

Slemon, Stephen. 'Unsettling the Empire: Resistance Theory for the Second World'. *World Literature Written in English* 30.2 (Autumn 1990), 30–41.

—— and Helen Tiffin (eds) Introduction. *After Europe: Critical Theory and Post-Colonial Writing*. Sydney: Dangeroo, 1989. ix–xxiii.

Smith, Malvern Van Wyk. *Grounds of* Contest: *A Survey of South African English Literature*. Cape Town: Jutalit, 1990.

South Africa 89.1151 (14 January 1911), 71; 89.1150 (7 January 1911), cover; 89.1152 (21 January 1911), 137.

Soyinka, Wole. 'The Fight for Human Existence'. (Lagos) *Sunday Post* 3 June 1962, 11.

—— 'From a Common Backcloth: A Reassessment of the African Literary Image'. 1963. *Art, Dialogue and Outrage: Essays on Literature and Culture*. 1988. London: Methuen, 1993, 7–14.

Stanley, Liz. *Feminism and Friendship: Two Essays on Olive Schreiner*. Manchester: University of Manchester Department of Sociology, 1985.

—— *Imperialism, Labour and the New Woman: Olive Schreiner's Social Theory*. Durham: Sociologypress, 2002.

Statutes of the Union of South Africa 1927–1928. 2 vols. Cape Town: Government Printer, 1928. Vol. 2, 2–6.

Stead, W. T. 'The Fascination of South Africa'. *The Review of Reviews* 4.19 (July 1891), 36.

—— 'The Book of the Month: The Novel of the Modern Woman'. *The Review of Reviews* 10 (July 1894), 64 -74.

Stern, James. 'Out of Africa'. *New Republic* (22 March 1948), 28–9.

Steward, Alexander. *You Are Wrong, Father Huddleston*. London: Bodley Head, 1956.

Street, Allen. 'Displaced Persons'. *Current Literature* (October 1948), 176.

Stuckert, Klaus. 'The Heart of the Matter'. *The CRNLE Reviews Journal* 2 (1980), 47–50.

Stynen, Ludo. Review of *The Heart of Redness*. *World Literature Today* (April–June 2003), 89.

Sullivan, Alvin (ed). *British Literary Magazines: The Victorian and Edwardian Age, 1837–1913*. Westport, CT: Greenwood, 1984.

—— *British Literary Magazines: The Modern Age, 1914–1984*. New York: Greenwood, 1986.

Sullivan, Richard. 'Fine Novel of a Present-Day Zulu'. *New York Times Book Review* (1 February 1948), Section 7, 6.

Sutherland, John. *Victorian Novelists and Publishers*. London: Athlone, 1976.

Szeman, Imre. *Zones of Instability: Literature, Postcolonialism, and the Nation*. Baltimore and London: Johns Hopkins University Press, 2003.

T. M. O. 'Without Fanfare, A Fine Novel'. (Kansas City) *Star* (23 February 1948). APC, PC1/1/1/2.

Tafelberg, 'Nuwe Digbundels'. Advertisement. *Standpunte* [123] 3rd series, 29.3 (June 1976), inside front cover.

Tate, Dennis. 'Stefan Heym: East German Dissident Author', *Guardian* (17 December 2001), 20.

Temple, Peter. 'City Man's Novel of Violence has Compelling Power'. *Argus* (1 May 1974), 34.

—— 'J. M. Coetzee: Major Talent in S African Literary Scene'. *Argus* (10 June 1974), B3.

Timothy, Catherine. E-mail to Andrew van der Vlies. 30 April 2002.

Tlali, Miriam. 'In Search of Books'. *Star* (30 July 1980). Reprinted in Michael Chapman (ed.) *Soweto Poetry*. Johannesburg: McGraw-Hill, 1982. 44–5.

The Modern Muse: Poems of To-Day, British and American. London: English Association, 1934.

Titlestad, P. J. H. 'Chairman's Report on "Burger's Daughter"', 'In the Publications Appeal Board, Directorate of Publications v. The Committee of Publications'. In Gordimer et al. *What Happened to Burger's Daughter*. Emmarentia: Taurus, 1980. 40–3.

Toerien, Barend J. 'Enkele Aantekeninge'. *Standpunte* [124] 3rd series, 29.4 (August 1976), 58–62.

—— Review of *From the Heart of the Country*. *World Literature Today* 52.3 (summer 1978), 510.

Trilling, Lionel. *The Liberal Imagination: Essays on Literature and Society*. 1950. London: Secker & Warburg, 1951.

Trollope, Anthony. *South Africa*. London: Chapman & Hall, 1876, vol. 1 of 2.

Tuchman, Gaye with Nina E. Fortin. *Edging Women Out: Victorian Novelists, Publishers, and Social Change*. London: Routledge, 1989.

Unwin, V. and James Currey. 'The African Writers' Series Celebrates Thirty Years'. *Southern African Review of Books* (March–April 1993), 3–6.

Van der Vlies, Andrew. 'The Editorial Empire: The Fiction of "Greater Britain", and the Early Readers of Olive Schreiner's *The Story of an African Farm*'. *TEXT: An Interdisciplinary Annual of Textual Studies* 15 (2002), 237–60.

—— 'Alan Paton'. In Jay Parini (ed.) *World Writers in English*. 2 vols. New York: Scribner's, 2003, vol. 2, 495–514.

—— 'Alex La Guma'. In Jay Parini (ed.) *World Writers in English*. 2 vols. New York: Scribner's, 2003, vol. 1, 249–68.

—— 'Olive Schreiner'. In Jay Parini (ed.) *World Writers in English*. 2 vols. New York: Scribner's, 2003, vol. 2, 625–44.

—— '"Your Passage Leaves its Track of ... Change": Textual Variation in Roy Campbell's "Tristan da Cunha", 1926–1945'. *English Studies in Africa* 46.1 (2003), 47–61.

—— Review of Christopher Heywood, *A History of South African Literature* (Cambridge: Cambridge University Press, 2004). *Review of English Studies* [226] 56.4 (2005), 691–93.

—— 'William Plomer'. In Jay Parini (ed.) *British Writers Supplement XI*. New York: Scribner's; Farmington Hills, MI: Thomson Gale, 2005, 213–29.

Van Rooyen, J. C. W. 'Summary and Decision', 'In the Publications Appeal Board, Directorate of Publications v. The Committee of Publications'. In Gordimer et al. *What Happened to* Burger's Daughter. Emmarentia: Taurus, 1980, 36–40.

Vann, J. Don. 'Chapman and Hall'. In Patricia J. Anderson and Jonathan Rose (eds), *British Literary Publishing Houses, 1820–1880*. Detroit, MI: Gale, 1991, 95–109.

Visser, Nicholas. 'Postcoloniality of a Special Type: Theory and Its Appropriations in South Africa'. *Yearbook of English Studies* 27 (1997), 79–94.

Vital, Anthony. 'Situating Ecology in Recent South African Fiction: J. M. Coetzee's *The Lives of Animals* and Zakes Mda's *The Heart of Redness*'. *Journal of South African Studies* 31.2 (June 2005), 297–313.

Voss, Tony. 'Revisions of Early Editions of *The Story of an African Farm*'. Unpublished essay. 1997. TS copy. NELM.

—— 'The First Two Editions of Olive Schreiner's *The Story of an African Farm*: A Schedule of Variations Between the Two Texts'. Unpublished essay. 1997. TS copy. NELM.

Wade, Michael. 'Art and Morality in Alex La Guma's *A Walk in the*

Night'. In Kenneth Parker (ed.) *The South African Novel in English: Essays in Criticism and Society*. London: Macmillan, 1978, 164–91.

Walder, Dennis. *Post-Colonial Literatures in English: History, Language, Theory*. Oxford: Blackwell, 1998.

Walker, Eric A. (ed). *The Cambridge History of the British Empire*. 8 vols. Cambridge: Cambridge University Press, 1963, vol. 8: *South Africa, Rhodesia and the High Commission Territories*.

Watson, Stephen. 'Speaking: J. M. Coetzee'. *Speak* 1.3 (1978), 23–4.

—— 'Cry, the Beloved Country and the Failure of Liberal Vision'. *English in Africa* 9.1 (May 1982), 29–44.

—— 'Colonialism and the Novels of J. M. Coetzee'. In Graham Huggan and Stephen Watson (eds) *Critical Perspectives on J. M. Coetzee*. Houndmills: Macmillan, 1996. 13–36.

Watts(-Dunton), Theodore. 'The Future of American Literature'. *The Fortnightly Review*, n.s. 55.294 (June 1891), 910–26.

Waugh, Arthur. *A Hundred Years of Publishing*. London: Chapman & Hall, 1930.

Waugh, Evelyn. *Ninety-Two Days*. London: Duckworth, 1934.

Weill, Kurt. *Lost in the Stars*. New York: Crawford Music, 1946.

Wiehahn, R. 'Memo on "Burger's Daughter"', 'In the Publications Appeal Board, Directorate of Publications v. The Committee of Publications'. In Gordimer et al. *What Happened to* Burger's Daughter. Emmarentia: Taurus, 1980. 48–9.

Wilde, Oscar. *The Soul of Man Under Socialism*. 1891. London: Journeyman, 1988.

Wilhelm, Peter. 'Vietnam, SA Powerfully Linked' (Review of *Dusklands*). *Star* (24 April 1974), 21.

—— 'The Single-Dreamer'. *Poetry South Africa: Selected Papers from Poetry '74*. Ed. Peter Wilhelm and James A. Polley. Johannesburg: Donker, 1976.

Williams, Orlo. Review of *I Speak of Africa*. *Criterion* (January 1928), 83.

Willis, J. H., Jr. *Leonard and Virginia Woolf as Publishers: The Hogarth Press, 1917–41*. Charlottesville: University Press of Virginia, 1992.

Winfrey, Oprah (OprahNewsletter@oprah.com). Book Club E-mail. 29 October 2003.

Wollman, Maurice (ed). *Modern Poetry, 1922–1934: An Anthology*. London: Macmillan, 1934.

—— *Poems of Twenty Years: An Anthology, 1918–1938*. London: Macmillan, 1938.

Wood, Miss Bessie. 'A Visit to a South African Ostrich Farm'. *The Woman's World* (November 1888), 32–5.

Woolf, Leonard. *Downhill All the Way: An Autobiography of the Years 1919–1939*. London: Hogarth, 1968.

Woolmer, J. Howard. *A Checklist of the Hogarth Press 1917–1946*.

Revere, PA: Woolmer, Brotherson, 1986.

Xuma, A. B. 'Black Spots or White Spots?' *The African Drum* 2.3 (March 1952), 25.

Yeats, W. B. *Letters on Poetry from W. B. Yeats to Dorothy Wellesley*. Ed. Dorothy Wellesley. Oxford: Oxford University Press, 1940.

—— (ed.) *The Oxford Book of Modern Verse 1892–1935*. New York: Oxford University Press, 1936.

Young, Francis Brett. 'South African Literature'. *The London Mercury* 19.113 (March 1929), 507–16.

—— 'Out of Africa Something New'. *Sunday Times* (26 September 1948), 3.

Young, Robert J. C. *Colonial Desire: Hybridity in Theory, Culture and Race*. London: Routledge, 1995.

Zell, Hans M. et al. (eds) *A New Reader's Guide to African Literature*. 2nd edn. London: Heinemann, 1983.

Zimbler, Jarad. 'Under Local Eyes: The South African Publishing Context of J. M. Coetzee's *Foe*'. *English Studies in Africa* 47.1 (2004), 47–59.

Zug, James. '"Far from Dead": The Final Years of the *Guardian*, 1960–1963'. In Les Switzer and Mohamed Adhikari (eds) *South Africa's Resistance Press: Alternative Voices in the Last Generation Under Apartheid*. Africa Series No. 74. Athens, OH: Ohio University Centre for International Studies, 2000, 128–75.

Index

Note: italicised page numbers refer to illustrations; literary works appear at the end of entries for authors' names; 'n.' after a page reference indicates the number of a note on that page.